SIGMUND FREUD

THERAPY AND TECHNIQUE

With an Introduction by the Editor

Philip Rieff

COLLIER BOOKS
NEW YORK, N.Y.

This Collier Books edition is published by arrangement with Basic Books, Inc.

Collier Books is a division of The Crowell-Collier Publishing Company

First Collier Books Edition 1963

Some of the Views Expressed by Freud in This Volume

On hypnosis
"I gave up the suggestive technique, and with it hypnosis, so early in my practice because I despaired of making suggestion powerful and enduring enough to effect permanent cures. In all severe cases I saw the suggestions which had been applied crumble away again; and then the disease or some substitute for it returned. Besides all this I have another reproach against this method, namely, that it conceals from us all insight into the play of mental forces."

On repression
"Sexual need and privation are merely one factor at work in the mechanism of neurosis. . . . The other, no less essential, factor, which is all too readily forgotten, is the neurotic's aversion from sexuality, his incapacity for loving, that feature of mind which I have called 'repression.' "

On the "riddles" in neuroses
"Psychoneuroses are substitutive gratifications of instincts the existence of which one is forced to deny to oneself and others. Their capacity to exist depends on this distortion and disguise. When the riddle they hold is solved and the solution is accepted by the sufferers these diseases will no longer be able to exist. There is hardly anything quite like it in medicine; in fairy-tales you hear of evil spirits whose power is broken when you can tell them their name which they have kept secret."

On the psychoanalyst's couch
"I adhere firmly to the plan of requiring the patient to recline upon a sofa, while one sits behind him out of his sight. This arrangement has an historic meaning; it is the last vestige of the hypnotic method out of which psychoanalysis was evolved; but for many reasons it deserves to be retained. The first is a personal motive, one that others may share with me, however. I cannot bear to be gazed at for eight hours a day."

Volumes in the Collier Books edition of
The Collected Papers of Sigmund Freud

Each volume has an Introduction by the Editor, Philip Rieff.

Contents

Introduction

Freud never wrote a systematic treatise on his therapeutic techniques. The papers collected here represent the best writing he did on the subject. As with almost every other conceivable general category of Freud's thought, remarks on therapy and technique are scattered throughout his writings, and it is quite impossible to claim that this selection is exhaustive. The reader will find that Part IV of *Studies on Hysteria*, the second chapter of *The Interpretation of Dreams*, lectures 27 and 28 of Freud's *Introductory Lectures*, chapter two of *Beyond the Pleasure Principle*, chapter five of *The Question of Lay Analysis*, lecture 34 of the *New Introductory Lectures*, and chapter six of the posthumously published *An Outline of Psychoanalysis* contain further important materials on the theory of therapy.

As in other volumes, so far as other criteria of organization permit, I have arranged this material on therapeutic technique in chronological order.

Freud never examined, in any serious or sustained way, the cultural conditions within which his therapy would have to operate. Yet those conditions may have so altered that the very objects of analytic address—the psychoneuroses—have changed beyond Freudian recognition. Patently, except for cases reported from among the culturally unassimilated, full-blown hysterias are hard to come by nowadays in the psychoanalytic literature. And not only the objects of analytic address but the vehicles of analysis seem to be acquiring a look of obsolescence. It is not at all clear that *repression*, the fundamental mechanism in the entire psychological system, is really so fundamental in American culture today. Because of the importance of assessing the cultural condition within which psychotherapies must organize their effects, in what follows I have attempted an historical overview of, especially, the American culture, with particular reference to psychoanalytic psychotherapy, as a necessary preliminary to a study of effective therapy in our culture.

Four character ideals have competed for dominance over the conduct of life in Western civilization. First, the ideal of *political* man, formed and handed down to us from classical antiquity. Plato was the greatest student of political man, and his most persuasive teacher. From Plato we first learned systematically to divide human nature into higher and lower energies, each level of energy having its appropriate function and assigned a relative value in the proper conduct of life. As it turns out, in Plato, the health and stability of a person is analogous to—and, moreover, dependent upon—the health and stability of the political order: that is, a proper subordination of passions to intellect will follow from the subordination of the uneducated classes to the educated. An ordered inner life depends upon the constituting of the right public order, a correct hierarchy of classes makes for the good private life.

Every society has its own version of a good man. From Plato to the present, the ideal political man has been considered to be the one who participates rationally and responsibly in the processes of public decision. Political man is, in effect, the citizen.

Rooted in the ideals of classical antiquity, the entire political effort of democracy has been to broaden the base of citizenship. But democracy, as it became more popular, developed a powerful alternative to the classical ideal, one in which the citizen could enjoy the privileges of citizenship while avoiding responsibilities. Tocqueville rightly called this type, which he saw flourishing in both the America and France of his time, the "individual." There is a great chapter in the finest and still most informative book on America, and on democracy, ever written: *Democracy in America*. That chapter is called "Of Individualism in Democratic Countries." Tocqueville defines individualism in a psychological rather than a political or economic way; it is a "mature and calm feeling, which disposes each member of the community to sever himself from the mass of his fellows and to draw apart with his family and his friends, so that after he has thus formed a little circle of his own, he willingly leaves society at large to itself." Thus Tocqueville saw individualism sapping the "virtues of public life," until that life is "at length absorbed in downright selfishness." Tocqueville's analysis amounts to a heavy indictment of democratic culture. For he concludes by saying: "Thus not only does democracy make every man forget his ancestors, but it hides his descendants and separates his contemporaries from him; it throws him back forever upon himself alone and threatens in the end to confine him entirely within the solitude of his own heart." In short, himself trained to belief in the classical ideal of political man, Tocqueville saw the highly individualistic American as a defaulted citizen.

Tocqueville was measuring the American character entirely from the character ideal of political man. But in the century before Tocqueville wrote, another character ideal had fully matured: *economic* man, exactly the type Tocqueville called the "individual." Economic man feared and suspected the public life, aiming to stay out of it and cultivate rationally his very own garden, proud in his sense of isolation. In his ideological prime the "individual" met all criticisms that he was a defaulted citizen with the reply that by attending primarily to his own private needs a general satisfaction of the public needs would automatically occur. A moral revolution was the result: what had been lower in the established rank order of responsibilities, the private, was now asserted to be higher.

In the slow accretion of self-images that is the mortar between periods in the history of our civilization, yet a third character ideal persisted, challenging and then adapting first the political ideal and then the economic, but with gradually

weakening effect, until, in our own time, it is being replaced
by a fourth. That fourth character ideal is the main subject of
this essay. The third borrowed the Platonic dichotomy between higher and lower energies, using it for different cultural
purposes. Although originally a naïve and straightforward,
even ecstatic, faith, Christianity could not resist going to the
Greek philosophical schools, as later it could not resist accommodating itself to the desires of economic individualism. As a
result of its historic compromise with classical antiquity, Christianity shaped and handed down to us a *religious* man who
continues to show certain recognizably Greek traits. The
Christian doctrine of human nature grafted faith onto the
place once occupied by the idea of life as a continuing intellectual and moral reeducation for better public service. Both
therapeutic functions merged, and the church became at once
a saving and a pedagogic institution. Certainly, "The Republic," in the Greek conception, is one vast school, complete with
intellectual and vocational programs, for the better training of
more or less capable citizens. In the Gospels, the Church is
set up as a teaching institution superior to the Republic; instead of a universal state, one universal church is to exist for
the better training of the human capacity for faith. Thus,
adapting Greek intellectualism to its own purposes, the main
Christian institution developed a personality type that organized itself around the expectation of achieving faith, asserting it as superior to reason, which could, at best, merely
support and confirm the religious gift of saving grace. Christianity represented a turning inward of the Greek criterion of
well-being which would, later, prove useful to the nominally
Christian economic man, in rationalizing the privacy and self-
centeredness of his way of life.

   The religious man, idealized during the long Christian period, carried with him two alternative strategies for the saving
expression of his character. He could achieve his ideal self
in two opposing ways: either mystic or ascetic. Of these two
alternative procedures, what I have here called the mystic was
first considered the better for achieving perfection in the religious sense, not involving, as did the ascetic way, the exercise of Reason.

These two character ideals persist competitively in our contemporary culture, yet in different degrees of attractiveness. For example, President Kennedy's Inaugural Address aimed at the American "individual" in the Tocquevillean sense of the word, in order to bring him back to an essentially classical ideal of public service. Yet it is possible that economic man, comfortably confined in the solitude of his own heart, will turn out to be a transitional type, with the shortest life-expectancy of all. When, by the turn of the twentieth century, this typical character of the Enlightenment and the great democratic revolutions, American and French, showed a faltering belief in his own superiority to his political and religious predecessors, a successor began to emerge—the *psychological* man of the twentieth century. In what follows, I shall try to present this new motivating idea that Western men, and Americans in particular, have of themselves.

It was at the frayed end of the period at which economic man grew nervous about himself, alone, that Freud first began to see his patients. Because they were unprepared for an ideal of ever-shifting insight as a way of accommodating their lives to a rapidly changing moral environment, Freud's patients of the turn of the century were incredulous and naïve. They demanded some doctrine of right, or a substitute faith. All Freud could give them, in the unyielding honesty of his own insight, was what he himself called the "analytic attitude." Such an attitude, if strictly held, allows for no return to religion, nor to any special doctrine of justice. Freud's concern is entirely with the emotions of the private man, and never with his aims or beliefs except so far as these prove to be mistaken therapies of action, appearing as symptoms rather than cures. Indeed, as I have implied, the earlier therapies of action had failed; Freud offered, instead, the action of therapy. Although it was not always the case, the classical ways of making life worth living, whether religious or political or economic, no longer were adequate to preserve the health of man and give him some measure of self-control and satisfaction. All the received therapies of action were efforts to find an ultimate cure for the difficulties of living where, as experience demonstrated time and again, no cure could possibly exist. All those cures had merely created the conditions for fresh outbursts of the nervous condition from which man suffers when he develops too high a set of aims for himself, and beyond himself.

Thus Freud led an increasingly successful attack on the ancient dichotomizing of human nature into categories of higher and lower, with respect to both ends and means. What is new—indeed revolutionary—about this latest image that Western men have of themselves is that it repudiates the hierarchical master assumption of "higher" and "lower" to which all the predecessors of psychological man have been addicted. Yet, perhaps in part because of this repudiation of both the classical and religious therapies of action, the new character ideal generates its own peculiar nervous tensions. After all, the aims of the individual have not changed. Freud took those aims for granted, as essentially the correct ones. He had the difficult problem of treating a character no longer content to live within the isolation of his own heart but unwilling to give his heart to anything other than himself. Freud could seek only to reconcile Tocqueville's "individual" to his present discontent, and somehow help him continue to live privately within the now rather constricting circle of his family and friends. It is the "individual" that Freud was seeking to defend as best he could, for he saw no alternative way of life.

The anxieties of this isolated individual and defaulting citizen (who, at best, sees the public life as yet another way of helping himself get through his own life) reflect not merely the pressures mounting inside his closed little circles of love and friendship; those anxieties also reflect the lines of personal competition that surround his new-found freedom from public responsibility and theological sovereignty. To meet these double anxieties, Freud taught the analytic attitude; his only alternative would have been to reassert some doctrine curtailing the very individuality that he sought to protect.

Developed for the private needs of private men, shifting with each individual case, the analytic attitude is not easily generalized. Indeed, this doctrinal aspect of psychological manhood is best described, I think, as an anti-doctrine, one

that opposes the therapeutic compulsions of all doctrine as
finally ineffective. Psychological man takes on the attitude of
a scientist, with himself alone as the ultimate object of his science. If the action of the analytic therapy has been effective,
he has learned not to prejudge the options around which the
conduct of his own life might be organized, considering all
options live, and, theoretically, equally legitimate. What matters is not so much the action as the determinants that have
led up to the action. According to the analytic attitude, what
counts is not what we do but why we do it. Thus there may be
a kindness that is neurotic, if it develops out of unconscious
compulsions, and a cruelty that is perfectly normal, if it is
consciously determined upon in a controlled way. Sainthood,
when determined by unconscious and uncontrolled motives,
is neurotic; sinning, when determined by conscious and examined motives, is normal. Of course, the saint may be socially
more valuable than the sinner; he may also be more neurotic.
Freud was honest enough to discover that there was no inherent relation between normality and the norm, such as had
been established in the ages of political and religious man
through the mediating myth that there were natural laws.
Freud could discover no natural harmony of goals worth striving for in life, no value built into conduct and inscribed upon
the universe. With the destruction of natural law, only the analytic attitude could protect the individual from the folly of
being drawn too far outside the protective isolation of his own
self-interest.

To reserve the capacity for neutrality between choices even
while making them, as required by this new science of moral
management, creates a great strain, both intellectually and
emotionally. It demands the capacity to entertain multiple
perspectives upon oneself and even upon beloved others, and
the finesse to shift from one perspective to another, in order
to soften the demands upon oneself in all the major situations
of life—love, parenthood, friendship, work, citizenship. Such
flexibility is not easily acquired. In fact, the attainment of psychological manhood is more difficult than any of the older
versions of maturity precisely because that manhood is no
longer protected by any childish fantasy of having arrived at

some saving place where meanings reside, like gods in their heavens. The best there is to say for oneself in life is that one has lived—"*really* lived," as the American saying goes.

Freud understood the dangers inherent in a situation in which the precious individual was vulnerable to the charge that his life had become meaningless. In answer, he asserted that no fresh access of doctrine could for long decrease that vulnerability. In such cases, the individual merely built his neurosis the more deeply into his character, combining it with some system of belief and action. All such systems of belief and action, with the neurotic factor as the mediating agent, brought more grief than relief to an individual now trying to complete not his task but himself. When the contemplation of self became a vocation, then the old therapies of action based on a saving belief in something other than oneself no longer relieved the individual of the most oppressive of his tensions— those developing in his own private circles of love and friendship. For these therapies were based on now irrelevant attempts to bring the individual too far out of himself, into some relation with a public end that no longer made private sense. What was needed was a therapy the action of which would take place entirely within the circle of the private life; the public life could, perhaps, in time be altered too by the success of the therapeutic effort in the private sphere. Thus, against the clear implication of his analysis of life as devoid of anything more than an endless network of essentially private and individually relevant meanings, Freud offered no large new cosset of a public philosophy—such as those offered by the philosophers, theologians and economists who had preceded him. His is a severe and chill anti-doctrine, for private consumption only, in which the final dichotomy to which Western man is prey—that between an ultimately meaningful and meaningless life—must also be abandoned. Such dichotomies belong to periods of public philosophies and communal theologies. In the era of the individual, each man belongs to an intimate society of his own devising. Civilization has become one vast suburbia, something like Tocqueville's nightmare of the United States and of France, populated by divided communities of two, with perhaps two junior members caught

in the middle of a private and not always civil war: in relation
to these intimate, though divided, communities of two, the
public world is constituted as one vast stranger, who appears
at inconvenient times and makes impossible demands, because he still proclaims one of the old ethics, whether political or religious.

In the time of public philosophies and social religions, all
communities were positive. A positive community is characterized by the fact that it guarantees some kind of salvation
to the private person by virtue of his membership and participation in that community. That sort of community seemed
corrupt to the economic man, with his particular version of
the ascetic ideal as tested mainly by self-reliance and personal
achievement. It appears not so much corrupt as impossible to
the psychological man, with his awareness of both ideology
and rationalization as neurotic factors in social life. As an in-
dividualist, psychological man can only choose to live in
negative communities, barren little islands surrounded by therapeutic activities; but he must live there without any pretense
at a doctrine of salvation. Positive communities were, according to Freud, held together by guilt. They may be attractive
now, in distant retrospect; but the modern individual, faced
with merging his own into the communal effort, would have
found them suffocating. Instead, the individual can use the
community only as the necessary basis for a life-long effort to
complete himself—if not always, or necessarily, to enrich himself. In this way, the therapeutically inclined individual apparently resembles his predecessor, the ascetic.

The resemblance has an historical basis. For, once launched
into some activity, conceiving of himself as an instrument of
God's will, the ascetic type did not stop to ask about the meaning of it all. On the contrary, the more furious his activity the
more the problem of what his activity meant receded from
his mind. In time, the ascetic forgot his originally religious
motives. For a while, perhaps a century, the sheer intensity
of his action proved therapeutic and the atrophy of the original motive passed unnoticed. More precisely, the original motive had collapsed into the pattern of action itself, as Max
Weber noticed in his great, savage peroration to *The Prot-*

estant Ethic and the Spirit of Capitalism. By the time Weber
wrote, however, there were signs of trouble all over this
once ascetic—and now merely businesslike—culture. Questions were being raised, at first by literary men; symptoms
were being raised, by all manner of men. For this reason, the
most fertile soil for the therapeutic type has been in waning
Protestant ascetic cultures, like the American. It is especially
true of Calvinist cultures that they prove receptive to psychotherapeutic substitutes for the original religiously ascetic
motives, in which the emphasis is on retraining for a fuller activity and not on the achievement of some new general
meaning. The permitting conditions for this therapeutic successor to the ascetic type were already present in the assumption of the Protestant activist that the will, or motive, of his
God was unsearchable and his ways quite inexplicable, so that
they could not be understood by any human standard. To
meet the demands of the day was as near as one could come
to doing the pious thing in this—God's—world. To trouble
about meaning was really an impiety—and, of course, friv-
olous, because futile. Thus, for the questions of meaning neither the ascetic nor the therapeutic feels responsible—if his
spiritual discipline has been successful. Such fashionable religious chit-chat as can be heard nowadays about "ultimate
concern" makes sense neither in the ascetic nor in the therapeutic context. To try to relate "ultimate concern" to every-
day behavior would be exhausting and nerve-shattering work
and would effectively block other kinds of work. Neither the
ascetic nor the therapeutic bothers his head about "ultimate
concerns." Such a level of concern is for mystics who cannot
otherwise enjoy their own leisure. In the workaday world,
there are rarely "ultimate concerns," only immediate ones.
Therapy is that respite in everyday life during which the supremacy of the immediate is learned and the importance of
what some religious intellectuals call "ultimate concern" is un-
learned. Such remote areas of experience are brought up as
examples of the neurotic displacement of emotional attention,
thus the better to understand them and put them in their
properly subordinate place as dead events and motives rather
than as the models for events and motives of the present life.

Nietzsche's announcement that the gods were dead seems a little premature, in view of all the difficulty Freud had in rooting the ordinary household god out of every unconscious, where it is deposited by our common childhood experience. Psychoanalysis is thus a form of reeducation toward making Nietzsche's poetic announcement a prosy fact of life.

Therapeutic reeducation is at once a very difficult and yet very modest procedure. It teaches the patient-student how to live with the contradictions that constrict him into a unique personality; this in contrast to the older moral pedagogies, which tried to reorder the contradictions into a hierarchy of superior and inferior, good and evil, capabilities. To become a psychological man is thus to become kinder to the whole self, the private parts as well as the public, the formerly inferior as well as the formerly superior. While older character types were concentrated on the full-time job of trying to order the warring parts of personality into a hierarchy, the Freudian pedagogy, reflecting the changing self-conception of the times, is far more egalitarian: it is the task of psychological man to develop an informed (i.e., healthy) respect for the sovereign and unresolvable basic contradictions that galvanize him into the singularly complicated human being that he is.

Freud's most important ideas finally may have less to do with the "repression" of sexual impulses, which explains neither the past discontents of our civilization nor the present ones, than with "ambivalence." Being a strange new kind of prophet—one who asserted that after the most complete self-searching men must learn to accept themselves as they are— Freud developed fresh hope precisely for that human capacity which is also the mainspring of the human problem: the human capacity to reverse feelings. This hope is grounded in Freud's assumption that human nature is not so much a hierarchy of high-low, good-bad, as his predecessors in the business of prophecy believed, but more a democracy of opposing predispositions, deposited throughout every nature in roughly equal intensities. Where there is love, there is the lurking eventuality of hatred. Where there is ambition, there is the ironic desire for failure. Although he wishes not to know it, a sore loser may be sore mainly because he almost won and is reacting against his wish to lose. Psychoanalysis is full of such mad logic; it is convincing only if the student of his own life accepts Freud's egalitarian revision of the inherited idea of hierarchical human nature.

Yet, although he announced this major revision in the Western self-image, Freud was himself sentimentally attached (as a consequence of his own traditional education) to the old hierarchical assumption. The great healer of the tear in human nature was himself a torn man. (A genuinely analytical biography of Freud has yet to be written.) On the one hand, he analyzed the damage done by this hierarchical structuring of human nature into pejoratively toned "higher" and "lower" categories—indeed, it was precisely this damage that he made it his business to mend. On the other hand, he hoped that somehow, despite the near equality of our warring emotions, Reason, the most aristocratic of them, would, despite its congenital weakness, cleverly manage to reassert itself—not in the high and mighty way preached by Plato and his Christian successors but in a modest, even sly way that would alternately dazzle and lull the more powerful emotions into submission. This way actually demands, I think, the kind of character ideal I have called "psychological" in order to contrast it with the ethically fixed types that preceeded it. In the age of psychological man, clarity about oneself supersedes devotion to an ideal as the standard of good living.

We can now better understand why Freud was an inveterate finder of double meanings, even of some that may not be there; why the latent makes sense only as it contradicts the manifest; why the aggressive movement behind the friendly gesture needs the complement of the friendly gesture behind the aggressive movement. For thus Freud succeeded in challenging every simplicity, including moral simplicity. He encouraged a tolerance of what used to be called, in general, the "low," just as he encouraged a new respect for the young, for the deviant, for the shocking. There was about Freud a calm awaiting of the unexpected that subverts the expectations of a life based on older schemes of an authoritative, set, hierarchical order of conduct. On the institutional level, the Freudian analysis reduces most obviously the hierarchical order of the family, and, moreover, of the "head" of the family. This reduction applies specially to the position of the father. True, in the European context if not in the American, the father appears as the personification of all those heights of repressive command from which, Freud decided, the rules of the moral game could no longer effectively be handed down. Much as he admired the Moses-figures in our culture, Freud considered their techniques of exercising authority obsolete.

A tolerance of ambiguities is the key to what Freud considered the most difficult of all personal accomplishments: a genuinely stable character in an unstable time. Yet just this rare and fine capacity, rejecting as it does the value of ignorance, encourages an equally dangerous attitude when viewed from the perspective of the instability of the times: namely, an attitude of knowing acquiescence.

Being able to recognize the equivocations of which behavior is composed need not, of course, mean their encouragement. Nevertheless, there is a sound basis for what are otherwise hypocritical objections to the immorality of interpretation with which Freudians rip away the façades of moral action. Hypocrisy is a precious thing in any culture. Like reticence, it may help build up those habits of avoidance that swerve us from honest, but head-on, collisions against one another. Nothing about psychoanalytic therapy encourages immoral behavior. The immorality of interpretation aims merely to reveal the bonds of moralized compulsions behind even the most correct and apparently straightforward behavior. But this means that psychoanalysis discourages moral behavior on the old, simple grounds—out of what is now called a *sense* of guilt rather than guilt.

To help us distinguish between guilt and a sense of guilt, between responsibility for an offense committed and fantasy about offenses only intended or merely imagined, seems a moral enough as well as a therapeutic aim. To suffer from scrupulosity is, after all, a well-known perversion of moral ambition, even according to the most elaborate of our established casuistries. But psychoanalysis is more than a mere surgery of handwashing. Freud cuts more deeply than that. His ambition to exhaust the sense of guilt by clinical exposures of it in its every detail may be dangerous, as he himself realized, to the life of a culture that is always necessarily (by his own definition of it) on the defensive. If a self-trained casuist gets along better by resolving his guilt into a sense of guilt, then he is the healthier for that resolution. This is a vulgar and popular misinterpretation of Freud; but there is something about the presuppositions of psychoanalytic therapy that encourages just such misinterpretations. A man can be made healthier without being made better—rather, morally worse. Not the good life but better living is the Freudian standard. It is a popular standard, not difficult to follow, as Americans, despite Freud's wish to make it difficult, were the first to recognize in any significant numbers.

Americans no longer model themselves after the Christian or the Greek. Nor are they such economic men as Europeans believe. The political man of the Greeks, the religious man of the Hebrews and Christians, the enlightened economic man of the eighteenth-century European (the original of that mythical present-day character, the "good European"), has been superseded by a new model for the conduct of life: the psychological man native to the American. This uniquely American type has outgrown his immediate ancestor in one clear sense, for both Socrates and Christ taught economic man to be at least slightly ashamed of himself when he failed to sacrifice lower to higher capacity. Freud is America's great teacher, despite his ardent wish to avoid that fate. For it was precisely the official and parental shams of high ideals that Freud questioned. In their stead, Freud taught lessons which Americans, prepared by their own national experience, learn easily: survive, resign yourself to living within your moral means, suffer no gratuitous failures in a futile search for ethical heights that no longer exist—if ever they did. Freud proclaims the superior wisdom of choosing the second best. He is our Crito, become intellectually more supple than a sick and old Socrates, who might still be foolish enough to justify his own death sentence rather than escape from the prison of his own crippling inhibitions about the sanctity of the State, which he mistakes for his father. Freud appeals so because his wisdom is so tired. Surely he is not to be blamed for living in a time when the inherited aspirations of the Greek, Christian and Humanist past had gone stale, when both Athens and Jerusalem, not to mention Paris, Oxford or the Italian Renaissance cities, have become tourist spots rather than the aim of pilgrims in search of spiritual knowledge. With no place to go for lessons on the conduct of contemporary life, every man must learn, as Freud teaches, to make himself at home in his own grim and gay little Vienna.

The alternatives with which Freud leaves us are grim only if we view them from the perspective of some possibility passed, either as political or religious men. Assuming that these character types are, in his terms, regressive, the grimness is relieved by the gaiety of being free from the historic Western compulsion of seeking large and general meanings for small and highly particular lives. Indeed, the therapy of all therapies, the secret of all secrets, the interpretation of all interpretations, in Freud, is not to attach oneself exclusively or too passionately to any one particular meaning or object. There is discernible in those who practice professionally the analytic attitude, the psychoanalysts themselves, a certain cultivated detachment and calm that is perhaps the finest expression of that individualism to which Tocqueville first referred. In the relation between analyst and patient, one member of that unique community of two must remain an almost total stranger to the other; only if the analyst draws a veil across his own life does he maintain his therapeutic effectiveness. The patient must, in turn, learn how to draw the veil properly around himself. To accomplish this much he needs to develop the full power and liberty of his emotions without paying the price of fixing them too firmly on any object or idea. This he is taught by the experience of ending his relation of intimacy to the analyst himself. Here, again, is the ascetic ideal, shorn of any informing goal or principle; thus divested of the need for compulsive attachments, the ascetic becomes the therapeutic. With Freud, individualism took a great and perhaps final step: the mature and calm feeling that must keep the individual a safe distance from the mass of his fellows can now, in therapy, be so trained that the individual can withdraw an even safer distance from his family and friends. With

Freud, Western man has learned truly the technical possibility of living his inward life alone, at last rid of that crowd of shadows eternally pressing him to pay the price for a past, in his childhood, when he could not have been for himself. This isolation, however, is no longer confining, as Tocqueville, with his classical prejudices favoring political man, thought it must be; rather, in Freud's opinion, it is liberating. At last, in the assurance and control of his consciousness, the Western individual can live alone because he likes it. Left to ourselves, we will use each other; that is, in Freud's mind, the best that can be said about the value of love. All other relations, except those of use, are pretenses with which psychological man, in the sophisticated calm of his detachment, can do without—as he should, for relations that are too close and fixed lead to symptoms that destroy the capacity of an individual to meet the unexpected (e.g., the death of love, or the beloved) in ways of his own choosing.

This does not mean that psychological man is a loner. To live inwardly alone does not imply an absence of company, or even an absence of company manners. On the contrary, psychological man is more circumspect and better behaved than his ascetic forbears: he even has a measured, calculated sense of the therapeutic value of spontaneity. He is no less able to work successfully in organizations than the ascetic. The first organization men of our culture were members of the clergy, dedicated body and soul to their divine institution. Freed from all suspicions of divinity, psychological man can continue to work efficiently in all kinds of institutions, but without permitting his feelings to be dedicated to the service of those institutions. Indeed, this is precisely what Whyte, the author of the famous book on *Organization Man*, asks of him: not that he quit work but that he work without such a naïve and corrupting sense of dedication; that the man use the organization rather than that the organization use the man. David Riesman, too, in his equally famous book, *The Lonely Crowd*, calls for an "autonomous" personality type to succeed the "other-directed" type of the late ascetic period in our business civilization. What both Riesman and Whyte desire, however much they derive in their analysis from Tocqueville, is not a revival of the classical ideal of political man, but far more subtly the creation of a new ideal, the individual free in the sobriety and modesty of his egoism. For this ideal, America already has its theoretician in Sigmund Freud.

Within the elaborate framework of a highly organized society, the ideal of psychological man, filtered through the popularizers of Freud, is gaining in popularity. In a society with so many rules, it is useful to realize, as the psychological man does, that all rules, even therapeutic ones, are made to be broken. The one standard of breakage is that the exception be "self-realizing" and not self-defeating. Freud could not conceive of an action that was not, however disguised and transformed, self-serving; neither could the best minds of the ascetic tradition. It was considered that in serving God one was, properly, serving oneself. Psychological man would phrase the matter somewhat differently: in serving the self one is serving "God." The notion of serving the self through some superior service to another has been in jeopardy throughout the era of economic man. Now that jeopardy has been resolved, the notion destroyed. For, in the era of psychological man, the self is the only reputable and effective god-term.

Perhaps the image of psychological man presented here is the one most appropriate and safe for use in this age. It is the self-image of a traveling man rather than a missionary. Unfortunately for culture and good taste, the salesman always cruelly parodies the preacher—without being able to help doing so, for his cultural history has dictated to the salesman the rhetorical style of the missionary. Freud distrusted that style, even for medical missionaries—or, more precisely, for missionaries of a saving medicine; he never "sold" his doctrine, as now some of his successors have done, to their real profit, with the patent elixir of "self-realization." Freud's own personal style is more suited to the American temper, with its characteristic lack of piety toward "higher" things, a respectful interest in the "lower," and a detachment from both. Like Freud, the American feels most comfortable when he is the man in the middle, neither on one side nor the other. How the American will preserve his sense of individuality finally, I do not know. Perhaps he will give up the struggle and return to some more profoundly social doctrine. It is certain, I think, that Freud has supplied the most subtly powerful technique of self-defense in the history of individualism. There is a guiding genius in Freud that Americans have been quick to recognize, for they, most of all, want to achieve that mature and calm feeling of detachment which prevents religious outburst or political experiment.

Philip Rieff

University of Pennsylvania
1962

Therapy and Technique

I

Hypnotism and Suggestion[1]
(1888)

This book has already received warm commendation from

---

[1] [This work, to which the title has been added by the present translator, is Freud's preface to his translation of Bernheim's *De la suggestion et de ses applications à la thérapeutique* (1886; second ed. 1887). The German original has never been reprinted and was not included in Freud's *Gesammelte Schriften*. In his *Autobiographical Study* (1925a), Freud relates how he spent some months in Paris in 1885-86 studying under Charcot and then returned to Vienna to set up as a specialist in nervous diseases. He goes on to describe his awakening interest in hypnotism and suggestion and how in the summer of 1889 he visited Bernheim at Nancy. "I had many stimulating conversations with him," he writes, "and undertook to translate into German his two works upon suggestion and its therapeutic effects." There is some mistake here, for in fact, as will be seen, his preface to his translation of the first of Bernheim's books is dated a year earlier than this, in August, 1888. The book bore the title *Die Suggestion und ihre Heilwirkung* and was published in Vienna by Deuticke. The date 1888 also appears on the title-page, but the work was evidently issued in parts, for a postscript by the translator apologizing for some delay in the publication of its second half is dated January, 1889. However this may be, the preface belongs to the period during which Freud's interest was passing over from physiology to psychology, and it may perhaps claim to be his earliest published writing in the field of psychology. Translation, reprinted from *Int. J. Psycho-Anal.*, 27 (1946), 59, by James Strachey.]

Professor Forel of Zurich, and it is to be hoped that its readers
will discover in it all the qualities which have led the translator to present it in German. They will find that the work of
Dr. Bernheim of Nancy provides an admirable introduction to
the study of hypnotism (a subject which can no longer be
neglected by physicians), that it is in many respects stimulating
and indeed enlightening, and that it is well calculated to destroy the belief that the problem of hypnosis is still surrounded, as Meynert asserts, by a halo of absurdity.

The achievement of Bernheim (and of his colleagues at
Nancy who are working along the same lines) consists precisely in having stripped the manifestations of hypnotism of
their strangeness by linking them up with familiar phenomena
of normal psychological life and of sleep. The principal value
of this book seems to me to lie in the evidence it gives of the
relations between hypnotic phenomena and the ordinary processes of waking and sleeping, and in its bringing to light the
psychological laws that apply to both classes of events. In this
way the problem of hypnosis is carried over completely into
the sphere of psychology, and "suggestion" is established as
the nucleus of hypnotism and the key to its understanding.
Moreover in the last chapters the importance of suggestion
is traced in fields other than that of hypnosis. In the second
part of the book evidence is offered that the use of hypnotic
suggestion provides the physician with a powerful therapeutic
method, which seems indeed to be the most suitable for combating certain nervous disorders and the most appropriate to
their mechanism. This lends the volume a quite unusual practical importance. And its insistence upon the fact that both
hypnosis and hypnotic suggestion can be applied, not only to
hysterical and to seriously neuropathic patients, but also to
the majority of healthy persons, is calculated to extend the
interest of physicians in this therapeutic method beyond the
narrow circle of neuropathologists.

The subject of hypnotism has had a most unfavourable reception among the leaders of the German medical profession
(apart from such few exceptions as Krafft-Ebing, Forel, etc.).
Yet, in spite of this, one may venture to express a wish that
German physicians may turn their attention to this problem

and to this therapeutic procedure, since it remains true that in scientific matters it is always experience, and never authority without experience, that gives the final verdict, whether in favour or against. Indeed, the objections which we have hitherto heard in Germany against the study and use of hypnosis deserve attention only on account of the names of their authors, and Professor Forel has had little trouble in refuting a whole crowd of those objections in a short essay.

Some ten years ago the prevalent view in Germany was still one which doubted the reality of hypnotic phenomena and sought to explain the accounts given of them as due to a combination of credulity on the part of the observers and of simulation on the part of the subjects of the experiments. This position is to-day no longer tenable, thanks to the works of Heidenhain and Charcot, to name only the greatest of those who have testified to their belief in the reality of hypnotism. Even the most violent opponents of hypnotism have become aware of this, and consequently their writings, though they still betray a clear inclination to deny the reality of hypnosis, also include attempts at explaining it and thus in fact recognize the existence of these phenomena.

Another line of argument hostile to hypnosis rejects it as being dangerous to the mental health of the subject and labels it as "an experimentally produced psychosis." Evidence that hypnosis leads to injurious results in a few cases would be no more decisive against its general usefulness than, for instance, the occurrence of isolated instances of death under chloroform narcosis forbids the use of chloroform for the purposes of surgical anaesthesia. It is a very remarkable fact, however, that this analogy cannot be carried any further. The largest number of accidents in chloroform narcosis are experienced by the surgeons who carry out the largest number of operations. But the majority of reports of the injurious effects of hypnosis are derived from observers who have worked very little with hypnosis or not at all, whereas all those research workers who have had a large amount of hypnotic experience are united in their belief in the harmlessness of the procedure. In order, therefore, to avoid any injurious effects in hypnosis, all that is probably necessary is to carry out the procedure with care, with a sufficiently sure touch and upon correctly selected cases. It must be added that there is little to be gained by calling suggestions "compulsive ideas" and hypnosis "an experimental psychosis." It seems likely, indeed, that more light will be thrown on compulsive ideas by comparing them with suggestions than the other way round. And anyone who is scared by the abusive term "psychosis" may well ask himself whether our natural sleep has any less claim to that description—if, indeed, there is anything at all to be gained from transporting technical names out of their proper spheres. No, hypnotism is in no danger from this quarter. And as soon as a large enough number of doctors are in a position to report observations of the kind that are to be found in the second part of Bernheim's book, it will become an established fact that hypnosis is a harmless condition and that to induce it is a procedure "worthy" of a physician.

This book also discusses another question, which at the present time divides the supporters of hypnotism into two opposing camps. One party, whose opinions are voiced by Dr. Bernheim in these pages, maintains that all the phenomena of hypnotism have the same origin: they arise, that is, from a suggestion, a conscious idea, which has been introduced into the brain of the hypnotized person by an external influence and has been accepted by him as though it had arisen spontaneously. On this view all hypnotic manifestations would be mental phenomena, effects of suggestions. The other party, on the contrary, insist that some at least of the manifestations of hypnotism are based upon physiological changes, that is, upon displacements of excitability in the nervous system, occurring without those parts of the brain being involved whose activity produces consciousness; they speak, therefore, of the physical or physiological phenomena of hypnosis.

The principal subject of this dispute is "major hypnotism" ["*grande hypnotisme*"]—the phenomena described by Charcot in the case of hypnotized hysterics. Unlike normal hypnotized persons, hysterics are said to exhibit three stages of hypnosis, each of which is distinguished by special physical signs of a most remarkable kind (such as enormous neuro-muscular hy-

perexcitability, somnambulistic contractures, etc.). It will easily be understood that the conflict of opinion that has just
been touched upon must have an important bearing in connection with this region of facts. If the supporters of the suggestion theory are right, all the observations made at the
Salpêtrière are worthless; indeed, they become errors in observation. The hypnosis of hysterics would have no characteristics of its own; but every physician would be free to produce
any symptomatology that he liked in the patients he hypnotized. We should not learn from the study of major hypnotism what alterations in excitability succeed one another in
the nervous system of hysterics in response to certain stimuli;
we should merely learn what intentions Charcot suggested (in
a manner of which he himself was unconscious) to the subjects of his experiments—a thing entirely irrelevant to our
understanding alike of hypnosis and of hysteria.

It is easy to see the further implications of this view and
what a convenient explanation it promises of the symptomatology of hysteria in general. If suggestion by the physician
has falsified the phenomena of hysterical hypnosis, it is quite
possible that it may also have interfered with the observation
of the rest of hysterical symptomatology: it may have laid
down laws governing hysterical attacks, paralyses, contractures, etc., which are only related to the neurosis by suggestion
and which consequently lose their validity as soon as another
physician in another place makes an examination of hysterical
patients. These inferences follow quite logically, and they have
in fact already been drawn. Hückel (1888) expresses his conviction that the first *"transfert"* (the transferring of sensibility from a part of the body to the corresponding part on the
other side) made by a hysteric was suggested to her on some
particular historical occasion and that since then physicians
have continued constantly producing this professedly physiological symptom afresh by suggestion.

I am convinced that this view will be most welcome to those
who feel an inclination—and it is still the predominant one in
Germany to-day—to overlook the fact that hysterical phenomena are governed by laws. Here we should have a splendid
example of how neglect of the mental factor of suggestion

has misled a great observer into the artificial and false creation of a clinical type as a result of the capriciousness and
easy malleability of a neurosis.

Nevertheless there is no difficulty in proving piece by piece
the objectivity of the symptomatology of hysteria. Bernheim's
criticisms may be fully justified in regard to investigations
such as those of Binet and Féré; and in any case those criticisms will give evidence of their importance in the fact that in
every future investigation of hysteria and hypnotism the need
for excluding the element of suggestion will be more consciously kept in view. But the principal points of the symptomatology of hysteria are safe from the suspicion of having
originated from suggestion by a physician. Reports coming
from past times and from distant lands, which have been collected by Charcot and his pupils, leave no room for doubt
that the peculiarities of hysterical attacks, of hysterogenic
zones, of anaesthesias, paralyses and contractures, have been
manifested at every time and place just as they were at the
Salpêtrière when Charcot carried out his memorable investigation of that major neurosis. "*Transfert*" in particular, which
seems to lend itself especially well to proving the suggestive
origin of hysterical symptoms, is indubitably a genuine process. It comes under observation in uninfluenced cases of hysteria: one frequently comes across patients in whom what is
in other respects a typical hemi-anaesthesia stops short at one
organ or extremity, and in whom this particular part of the
body retains its sensibility on the insensible side whereas the
corresponding part on the other side has become anaesthetic.
Moreover, "*transfert*" is a phenomenon which is physiolog-
ically intelligible. As has been shown by investigations in Germany and France, it is merely an exaggeration of a relation
which is normally present between symmetrical parts of the
body: thus, it can be produced in a rudimentary form in
healthy persons. Many other hysterical symptoms of sensibility also have their root in normal physiological relations, as
has been beautifully demonstrated by the investigations of
Urbantschitsch. This is not the proper occasion for carrying
out a detailed justification of the symptomatology of hysteria;
but we may accept the statement that in essentials it is of a

real, objective nature and not falsified by suggestion on the part of the observer. This does not imply any denial that the mechanism of hysterical manifestations is a mental one: but it is not the mechanism of suggestion on the part of the physician.

Once the existence of objective, physiological phenomena in hysteria has been demonstrated, there is no longer any need to abandon the possibility that hysterical "major" hypnotism may present phenomena which are not derived from suggestion on the part of the investigator. Whether these do in fact occur must be left to a further enquiry with this end in view. Thus it lies with the Salpêtrière school to prove that the three stages of hysterical hypnosis can be unmistakably demonstrated upon a newly arrived experimental subject even when the most scrupulous behaviour is maintained by the investigator; and no doubt such proof will not be long in coming. For already the description of major hypnotism offers symptoms which tend most definitely against their being regarded as mental. I refer to the increase in neuro-muscular excitability during the lethargic stage. Anyone who has seen how, during lethargy, light pressure upon a muscle (even if it is a facial muscle or one of the three external muscles of the ear which are never contracted during life) will throw the whole fasciculus concerned into tonic contraction, or how pressure upon a superficial nerve will reveal its terminal distribution—anyone who has seen this will inevitably assume that the effect must be attributed to physiological reasons or to deliberate training and will without hesitation exclude unintentional suggestion as a possible cause. For suggestion cannot produce anything which is not contained in consciousness or introduced into it. But our consciousness knows only of the end-result of a movement; it knows nothing of the operation and arrangement of the individual muscles and nothing of the anatomical distribution of the nerves in relation to them. I shall show in detail in a work which is shortly to appear[2] that the characteristics

[2] [In fact not published till five years later, in 1893: "Some Points in a Comparative Study of Organic and Hysterical Paralyses," *Early Psychoanalytic Writings,* Collier Books edition BS 188V.]

of hysterical paralyses are bound up with this fact and that this is why hysteria shows no paralyses of individual muscles, no peripheral paralyses and no facial paralyses of a central nature. Dr. Bernheim should not have neglected to produce the phenomenon of neuro-muscular hyperexcitability by means of suggestion; the omission constitutes a serious gap in his argument against the three stages.

Thus physiological phenomena do occur at all events in hysterical major hypnotism. But in normal, minor hypnotism, which, as Bernheim justly insists, is of greater importance for our understanding of the problem, every manifestation—so it is maintained—comes about by means of suggestion, by mental means. Even hypnotic sleep, it seems, is itself a result of suggestion: sleep sets in owing to normal human suggestibility, because Bernheim arouses an expectation of sleep. But there are other occasions, on which the mechanism of hypnotic sleep seems nevertheless to be a different one. Anyone who has hypnotized much will sometimes have come upon subjects who can only be put to sleep with difficulty by talking, while, on the contrary, it can be done quite easily if they are made to stare at something for a little. Indeed, who has not had the experience of a patient falling into a hypnotic sleep whom he has had no intention of hypnotizing and who certainly had no previous conception of hypnosis? A female patient takes her place for the purpose of having her eyes or throat examined; there is no expectation of sleep either on the part of the physician or of the patient; but no sooner does the beam of light fall on her eyes than she goes to sleep and, perhaps for the first time in her life, she is hypnotized. Here, surely, any conscious mental connecting link could be excluded. Our natural sleep, which Bernheim compares so happily with hypnosis, behaves in a similar fashion. As a rule we bring on sleep by suggestion, by mental preparedness and expectation of it; but occasionally it comes upon us without any effort on our part as a result of the physiological condition of fatigue. So too when children are rocked to sleep or animals hypnotized by being held in a fixed position it can hardly be a question of mental causation. Thus we have reached the position adopted by Preyer and Binswanger in Eulenburg's *Real-*

encyclopädie: there are both mental and physiological phenomena in hypnotism, and hypnosis itself can be brought about in the one manner or the other. Indeed, in Bernheim's own description of his hypnoses there is unmistakably one objective factor independent of suggestion. If this were not so, then, as Jendrássik (*Archives de Neurologie*, XI, 1886) logically insists, hypnosis would bear a different appearance according to the individuality of each experimenter: it would be impossible to understand why increase of suggestibility should follow a regular sequence, why the musculature should invariably be influenced only in the direction of catalepsy, and so on.

We must agree with Bernheim, however, that the partitioning of hypnotic phenomena under the two headings of physiological and mental leaves us with a most unsatisfied feeling: a connecting link between the two classes is urgently needed. Hypnosis, whether it is produced in the one way or in the other, is always the same and shows the same appearances. The symptomatology of hysteria[3] hints in many respects at a psychological mechanism, though this need not be the mechanism of suggestion. And, finally, suggestion is at an advantage over the physiological conditions, since its mode of operation is incontestable and relatively clear, while we have no further knowledge of the mutual influences of the nervous excitability to which the physiological phenomena must go back. In the remarks which follow, I hope to be able to give some indication of the connecting link between the mental and physiological phenomena of hypnosis of which we are in search.

[3] The relations between hysteria and hypnotism are no doubt very intimate, but they are not so close as to justify one in representing an ordinary hysterical attack as a hypnotic state with several stages, as Meynert has done before the Vienna Society of Medicine (reported in *Wiener medic. Blätter*, No. 23, 1888). In this paper, indeed, a general confusion seems to have been made of our knowledge about these two conditions. For Charcot is spoken of as distinguishing *four* stages of hypnosis, whereas in fact he only distinguishes *three*, and the fourth stage, the so-called "somniant" stage, is nowhere mentioned except by Meynert. On the other hand, Charcot does ascribe *four* stages to the hysterical attack.

In my opinion the shifting and ambiguous use of the word "suggestion" lends to the antithesis a deceptive sharpness which it does not in reality possess. It is worth while considering what it is which we can legitimately call a "suggestion." No doubt some kind of mental influence is implied by the term; and I should like to put forward the view that what distinguishes a suggestion from other kinds of mental influence, such as a command or the giving of a piece of information or instruction, is that in the case of a suggestion an idea is aroused in another person's brain which is not examined in regard to its origin but is accepted just as though it had arisen spontaneously in that brain. A classical example of a suggestion of this kind occurs when a physician says to a hypnotized subject: "Your arm must stay where I put it" and the phenomenon of catalepsy thereupon sets in; or again when the physician raises the subject's arm time after time after it has dropped, until the subject guesses that the physician wants it to be held up. But on other occasions we speak of suggestion where the mechanism of origin is evidently a different one. For instance, in the case of many hypnotized subjects catalepsy sets in without any injunction being given: the arm that has been raised remains raised of its own accord, or the subject maintains the posture in which he went to sleep unaltered unless there is some interference. Bernheim calls this result too a suggestion, saying that the posture itself suggests its maintenance. But in this case the part played by external stimulus is evidently smaller and the part played by the physiological condition of the subject, which disallows any impulse for altering his posture, is greater than in the former cases. The distinction between a directly mental and an indirect (physiological) suggestion may perhaps be seen more clearly in the following example. If I say to a hypnotized subject: "Your right arm is paralysed; you can't move it," I am making a directly mental suggestion. Instead of this, Charcot gives the subject a light blow on his arm; [the subject finds he is unable to move it]. Or Charcot says to him: "Look at that hideous face! Hit out at it!"; the subject hits out and his arm drops down paralysed. In these two last cases an external stimulus has, to begin with, produced a feeling of painful exhaustion in the arm; and this in turn, spontaneously and independently of any intervention on the part of the physician, has suggested paralysis—if such an expression is still applicable here. In other words, it is a question in these cases not so much of suggestions as of stimulation to *autosuggestions*. And these, as anyone can see, contain an objective factor, independent of the physician's will, and they reveal a connection between various conditions of innervation or excitation in the nervous system. It is autosuggestions such as these that lead to the production of spontaneous hysterical paralyses and it is an inclination to such autosuggestions rather than suggestibility which, from the point of view of the physician, characterizes hysteria; nor do the two seem by any means to run parallel.

I need not insist on the fact that Bernheim too works to a very large extent with indirect suggestions of this sort—that is, with stimulations to autosuggestion. His procedure for bringing about sleep, as described in the opening pages of the present volume, is essentially a mixed one: suggestion pushes open the doors which are in fact slowly opening of themselves by autosuggestion.

Indirect suggestions, in which a series of intermediate links arising from the subject's own activity are inserted between the external stimulus and the result, are none the less mental processes; but they are no longer exposed to the full light of consciousness which falls upon direct suggestions. For we are far more accustomed to bring our attention to bear upon external perceptions than upon internal processes. Indirect suggestions or autosuggestions can accordingly be described equally as physiological or as mental phenomena, and the term "suggestion" has the same meaning as the reciprocal provocation of mental states according to the laws of association. Shutting the eyes leads to sleep because it is linked to the concept of sleep through being one of its most regular accompaniments: one portion of the manifestations of sleep suggests the other manifestations which go to make up the phenomenon as a whole. This linking-up lies in the nature of the nervous system and not in any arbitrary decision by the physician; it cannot occur unless it is based upon alterations in the excitability of the relevant portions of the brain, in the innervation of the vasomotor centres, etc., and it thus presents alike a psychological and a physiological aspect. As is the case wherever states of the nervous system are linked together, it may run its course in either direction. The idea of sleep may lead to feelings of fatigue in the eyes and muscles and to a corresponding condition of the vasomotor nerve centres; or on the other hand the condition of the musculature or a stimulus acting on the vasomotor nerves may in itself cause the sleeper to wake, and so on. All that can be said is that it would be just as one-sided to consider only the psychological side of the process as to attribute the whole responsibility for the phenomena of hypnosis to the vascular innervation.

How does this affect the antithesis between the mental and the physiological phenomena of hypnosis? There was a meaning in it so long as by suggestion was understood a directly mental influence exercised by the physician which forced any symptomatology he liked upon the hypnotized subject. But this meaning disappears as soon as it is realized that even suggestion only releases sets of manifestations which are based upon the functional peculiarities of the subject's nervous system, and that in hypnosis characteristics of the nervous system other than suggestibility make themselves felt. The question might still be asked whether all the phenomena of hypnosis must *at some point* pass through the mental sphere; in other words—for the question can have no other sense—whether the changes in excitability which occur in hypnosis invariably affect only the region of the cerebral cortex. By thus putting the question in this other form we seem to have decided the answer to it. There is no justification for making such a contrast as is here made between the cerebral cortex and the rest of the nervous system: it is improbable that so profound a functional modification of the cerebral cortex could occur unaccompanied by significant alterations in the excitability of the other parts of the brain. We possess no criterion which enables us to distinguish exactly between a mental process and a physiological one, between an act occurring in the cerebral cortex and one occurring in the subcortical substance; for "consciousness," whatever that may be, is not attached to every activity of the cerebral cortex, nor is it always attached in an equal degree to any particular one of its activities; it is not a thing which is bound up with any locality in the nervous system.[4] It therefore seems to me that the question whether hypnosis exhibits mental or physiological phenomena cannot be accepted in this general form and that the decision in the case of each individual phenomenon must be made dependent upon a special investigation.

To this extent I feel justified in saying that, whereas on the one hand Bernheim's work goes outside the field of hypnosis, on the other hand it leaves a portion of its subject-matter out of account. But it is to be hoped that German readers of Bernheim will now have the opportunity of recognizing what an instructive and valuable contribution he has made in thus describing hypnotism from the standpoint of suggestion.

Vienna, *August*, 1888

[4] [In this connection, it is relevant to quote a footnote added by Freud by way of criticism to a passage in his translation of Bernheim's book (p. 116): "It appears to me unjustifiable, and unnecessary, to assume that an executive act changes its localization in the nervous system if it is begun consciously and continued later unconsciously. It is, on the contrary, probable that the portion of the brain concerned can operate with a varying amount of attention (or consciousness)."]

II

A Case of Successful Treatment by Hypnotism

WITH SOME REMARKS ON THE ORIGIN OF HYSTERICAL SYMPTOMS THROUGH "COUNTER-WILL"[1]
(1893)

I propose in the following pages to publish an isolated case of a successful treatment by hypnotic suggestion because, owing to a number of attendant circumstances, it was more convincing and more lucid than the majority of our successful treatments.

I have been acquainted for many years with the woman whom I was thus able to assist at an important moment of her existence, and she remained under my observation for several years afterwards. The disorder from which she was relieved by hypnotic suggestion had made its first appearance some time earlier. She had struggled against it in vain and

---

[1] ["Ein Fall von hypnotischer Heilung." First published *Z. Hypnotismus, Suggestionstherapie, Suggestionslehre und verwandte psycholog. Forsch.*, 1 (1892-3); reprinted *Ges. Schr.*, 1, 258, and *Ges. W.*, 1. Translation by James Strachey.]

been driven by it to an act of renunciation which, with my help, she was spared on a second occasion. A year later the same disorder appeared yet again, and was once more overcome in the same manner. The therapeutic success was of value to the patient and persisted as long as she desired to carry out the function affected by the disorder. Finally, it was possible in this case to trace the simple psychical mechanism of the disorder and to bring it into relation with similar processes in the field of neuropathology.

It was a case, if I may now cease talking in riddles, of a mother who was unable to feed her new-born child till hypnotic suggestion intervened, and whose experiences with an earlier and a later child provided controls of the therapeutic success such as are seldom obtainable.

The subject of the following case history is a young woman between twenty and thirty years of age with whom I happen to have been acquainted from her childhood. Her capability, her quiet common sense and her naturalness made it impossible for anyone, including her family doctor, to regard her as neurotic. Taking the circumstances that I am about to narrate into account, I must describe her, in Charcot's happy phrase, as an *hystérique d'occasion*. This category, as we know, does not exclude the most admirable of qualities and otherwise uninterrupted nervous health. As regards her family, I am acquainted with her mother, who is not in any way neurotic, and a younger sister who is similarly healthy. A brother suffered from a typical neurasthenia of early manhood, and this ruined his career. I am familiar with the aetiology and course of this form of illness, which I come across repeatedly every year in my medical practice. Starting originally with a good constitution, the patient is haunted by the usual sexual difficulties at puberty; there follow years of overwork as a student, preparation for examinations, and an attack of gonorrhea, followed by a sudden onset of dyspepsia accompanied by obstinate and inexplicable constipation. After some months the constipation is replaced by pressure in the head, depression and incapacity for work. Thenceforward the patient grows increasingly self-centred and his character more and more restricted, till he becomes a torment to his family. I am not certain whether it is not possible to *acquire* this form of neurasthenia with all its elements and therefore, especially as I am not acquainted with my patient's other relatives, I leave it an open question whether we are to assume the presence in her family of a hereditary predisposition to neurosis.

When the time approached for the birth of the first child of her marriage (which was a happy one) the patient intended to feed the infant herself. The delivery was not more difficult than is usual with a primiparous mother who is no longer very youthful; it was terminated with the forceps. Nevertheless, though her bodily build seemed favourable, she did not succeed in feeding the infant satisfactorily. There was a poor flow of milk, pains were brought on when the baby was put to the breast, the mother lost appetite and showed an alarming unwillingness to take nourishment, her nights were agitated and sleepless. At last, after a fortnight, in order to avoid any further risk to the mother and infant, the attempt was abandoned as a failure and the child was transferred to a wet-nurse. Thereupon all the mother's troubles immediately cleared up. I must add that I am not able to give a medical or eye-witness account of this first attempt at lactation.

Three years later a second baby was born; and on this occasion external circumstances added to the desirability of avoiding a wet-nurse. But the mother's attempts at feeding the child herself seemed even less successful and to provoke even more painful symptoms than the first time. She vomited all her food, became agitated when it was brought to her bedside and was completely unable to sleep. She became so much depressed at her incapacity that her two family doctors—physicians of such wide repute in Vienna as Dr. Breuer and Dr. Lott—would not hear of any prolonged attempt being made on this occasion. They recommended that one more effort should be made—with the help of hypnotic suggestion—and, on the evening of the fourth day, arranged for me to be brought in professionally, since I was already personally acquainted with the patient.

I found her lying in bed with flushed cheeks and furious at her inability to feed the baby—an inability which increased at every attempt but against which she struggled with all her strength. In order to avoid the vomiting, she had taken no nourishment the whole day. Her epigastrium was distended and sensitive to pressure; manual palpation showed morbid peristalsis of the stomach; there was odourless eructation from time to time and the patient complained of having a constant bad taste in her mouth. The area of gastric resonance was considerably increased. Far from being welcomed as a saviour in the hour of need, it was obvious that I was being received with a bad grace and that I could not count on the patient having much confidence in me.

I at once attempted to induce hypnosis by ocular fixation, at the same time making constant suggestions of the symptoms of sleep. After three minutes the patient was lying back with the peaceful expression of a person in profound sleep. I cannot recollect whether I made any tests for catalepsy and other symptoms of pliancy. I made use of suggestion to contradict all her fears and the feelings on which those fears were based: "Do not be afraid. You will make an excellent nurse and the baby will thrive. Your stomach is perfectly quiet, your appetite is excellent, you are looking forward to your next meal, etc." The patient went on sleeping while I left her for a few minutes, and when I had woken her up showed amnesia for what had occurred. Before I left the house I was also under the necessity of contradicting a worried remark by the patient's husband to the effect that his wife's nerves might be ruined by hypnosis.

Next evening I was told something which seemed to me a guarantee of success but which, oddly enough, had made no impression on the patient or her relations. She had had a meal the evening before without any ill effects, had slept peacefully and in the morning had taken nourishment herself and fed the baby irreproachably. The rather abundant midday meal, however, had been too much for her. No sooner had it been brought in than her former disinclination returned; vomiting set in even before she had touched it. It was impossible to put the child to her breast and all the objective signs were the same as they had been when I had arrived the previous evening. I produced no effect by my argument that, since she was now convinced that her disorder *could* disappear and in fact *had* disappeared for half a day, the battle was already won. I now brought on the second hypnosis, which led to a state of somnambulism as quickly as the first, and I acted with greater energy and confidence. I told the patient that five minutes after my departure she would break out against her family with some acrimony: what had happened to her dinner? did they mean to let her starve? how could she feed the baby if she had nothing to eat herself? and so on.

When I returned on the third evening the patient refused to have any further treatment. There was nothing more wrong with her, she said: she had an excellent appetite and plenty of milk for the baby, there was not the slightest difficulty when it was put to her breast, and so on. Her husband thought it rather queer, however, that after my departure the evening before she had clamoured violently for food and had remonstrated with her mother in a way quite unlike herself. But since then, he added, everything had gone all right.

There was nothing more for me to do. The mother fed her child for eight months; and I had many opportunities of satisfying myself in a friendly way that they were both doing well. I found it hard to understand, however, as well as annoying, that no reference was ever made to my remarkable achievement.

But my time came a year later, when a third child made the same demands on the mother and she was as unable to meet them as on the previous occasions. I found the patient in the same condition as the year before and positively embittered against herself because her will could do nothing against her disinclination for food and her other symptoms; and the first evening's hypnosis only had the result of making her feel more hopeless. Once again after the second hypnosis the symptoms were so completely cut short that a third was not required. This child too, which is now eighteen months old, was fed without any trouble and has enjoyed uninterrupted good health.

In face of this renewed success the patient and her husband unbent and admitted the motive that had governed their behaviour towards me. "I felt ashamed," the woman said to me, "that a thing like hypnosis should be successful where I myself, with all my will-power, was helpless." Nevertheless, I do not think either she or her husband have overcome their dislike of hypnosis.

I shall now pass on to consider what may have been the psychical mechanism of this disorder of my patient's which was thus removed by suggestion. I have not, as in certain other cases which I shall discuss elsewhere [Breuer and Freud, 1893], direct information on the subject; and I am thrown back upon the alternative of deducing it.

There are certain ideas which have an affect of expectancy attached to them. They are of two kinds: ideas of my doing this or that—what we call *intentions*—and ideas of this or that happening to me—*expectations* proper. The affect attached to them is dependent on two factors, first on the degree of importance which the outcome has for me, and secondly on the degree of uncertainty inherent in the expectation of that outcome. The subjective uncertainty, the counter-expectation, is itself represented by a collection of ideas to which I shall give the name of "distressing antithetic ideas" ["*peinliche Kontrastvorstellungen*"]. In the case of an intention, these antithetic ideas will run: "I shall not succeed in carrying out my intentions because this or that is too difficult for me and I am unfit to do it; I know, too, that certain other people have also failed in a similar situation." The other case, that of an expectation, needs no comment: the antithetic idea consists in enumerating all the things that could possibly happen to me other than the one I desire. Further along this line we should reach the *phobias*, which play so great a part in the symptomatology of the neuroses. But let us return to the first category, the intentions. How does a person with a healthy ideational life deal with antithetic ideas against an intention? With the powerful self-confidence of health, he suppresses and inhibits them so far as possible, and excludes them from his associations. This often succeeds to such an extent that the antithetic ideas against an intention are as a rule not manifestly visible; their existence only becomes probable when neuroses are taken into account. On the other hand, where a neurosis is present—and I am explicitly referring not to hysteria alone but to the *status nervosus* in general—we have to assume that there exists a *primary* tendency to depression and to a lowering of self-confidence, such as we find very highly developed and in isolation in melancholia. In neuroses, then, great attention is paid to antithetic ideas against intentions, perhaps because the subject-matter of such ideas fits in with the mood of the neurosis, or perhaps because antithetic ideas, which would otherwise have been absent, flourish in the soil of a neurosis.

When this intensification of antithetic ideas relates to *expectations*, if the case is one of a simple *status nervosus*, the effect is shown in a generally pessimistic frame of mind; in case of neurasthenia, associations from the most accidental sensations occasion the numerous phobias of neurasthenics. If the intensification attaches to *intentions*, it gives rise to the disturbances which are summed up under the description of *folie du doute*, and which have as their subject-matter distrust of the subject's own capacity. Precisely at this point the two major neuroses, neurasthenia and hysteria, each behave in a characteristic manner. In neurasthenia the pathologically intensified antithetic idea becomes attached, along with the volitional idea, to a *single* act of consciousness; it detracts from the volitional idea and brings about the weakness of will which is so striking in neurasthenics and of which they themselves are aware. The process in hysteria differs from this in two respects, or possibly only in one. [Firstly,] in accordance with the tendency to a dissociation of consciousness in hysteria, the distressing antithetic idea, which has the appearance of being inhibited, is removed from association with the intention and continues to exist as a disconnected idea, often unconsciously to the patient himself. [Secondly,] it is supremely characteristic of hysteria that, if it should come to the carrying out of the intention, the inhibited antithetic idea can put itself into effect through the agency of the somatic innervations just as easily as does a volitional idea in normal circumstances. The antithetic idea establishes itself, so to speak, as a *"counter-will,"* while the patient is aware with astonishment of having a will which is resolute but powerless. Perhaps, as I have said, these two factors are at bottom one and the same: it may be that the antithetic idea is only able to put itself into effect because it is not inhibited by its connection with the intention in the same way as it itself inhibits the intention.[2]

If in our present case the mother who was prevented by neurotic difficulties from feeding her child had been a neurasthenic, her behaviour would have been different. She would have felt conscious dread of the task before her, she would have been greatly concerned with the various possible accidents and dangers and, after much temporizing with anxieties and doubts, would after all have carried out the feeding without any difficulty; or, if the antithetic idea had gained the upper hand, she would have abandoned the task because she felt afraid of it. But the hysteric behaves quite otherwise. She may not be conscious of her fear, she is quite determined to carry her intention through and sets about it without hesitating. Then, however, she behaves as though it was her will not to feed the child on any account. Moreover, this will evokes in her all the subjective symptoms which a malingerer would put forward as an excuse for not feeding her child: loss of appetite, aversion to food, pains when the child is put to her breast. And, since the counter-will exercises greater control over the body than does conscious simulation, it also produces a number of objective signs in the digestive tract which malingering would be unable to bring about. Here, in contrast to the *weakness* of will shown in neurasthenia, we have a *perversion* of will; and, in contrast to the resigned irresoluteness shown in the former case, here we have astonishment and embitterment at a disunity which is incomprehensible to the patient.

I therefore consider that I am justified in describing my patient as an *hystérique d'occasion*, since she was able, as a result of a fortuitous cause, to produce a complex of symptoms with a mechanism so supremely characteristic of hyste-

[2] In the interval between writing this and correcting the proofs, I have come across a work by H. Kaan (1893) containing similar arguments.

ria. It may be assumed that in this instance the fortuitous cause was the patient's excited state before the first confinement or her exhaustion after it. A first confinement is, after all, the greatest shock to which the female organism is subject, and as a result of it a woman will as a rule produce any neurotic symptoms that may be latent in her disposition.

It seems probable that the case of this patient is a typical one and throws light upon a large number of other cases in which breast-feeding or some similar function is prevented by neurotic influences. Since, however, in the case I have reported I have only arrived at the psychical mechanism by inference, I hasten to add an assurance that I have frequently been able to establish the operation of a similar psychical mechanism in hysterical symptoms *directly*, by investigating the patient under hypnosis.[3]

Here I will mention only one of the most striking instances.[4] Some years ago I treated an hysterical lady who showed great strength of will in those of her dealings which were unaffected by her illness; but in those which *were* so affected she showed no less clearly the weight of the burden imposed on her by her numerous and oppressive hysterical impediments and incapacities. One of her striking characteristics was a peculiar noise which intruded, like a *tic*, into her conversation. I can best describe it as a singular clicking of the tongue accompanied by a sudden spasmodic closing of the lips. After observing it for some weeks, I once asked her when and how it had first originated. "I don't know when it was," she replied, "oh! a long time ago." This led me to regard it as a genuine *tic*, till it occurred to me one day to ask the patient the same question in deep hypnosis. This patient had access in hypnosis (without there being any necessity to

---

[3] See the preliminary statement by J. Breuer and S. Freud on "The Psychical Mechanism of Hysterical Phenomena," which is appearing at the same time as the present paper in Mendel's *Zentralblatt*, Nos. 1 and 2, 1893. [*Early Psychoanalytic Writings*, Collier Books edition, BS 188V.]

[4] [This patient was subsequently made the subject of the second case history in Breuer and Freud's *Studies in Hysteria* (1895).]

suggest the idea to her) to the whole store of her memories—
or, as I should prefer to put it, to the whole extent of her
consciousness, which was restricted in her waking life. She
promptly answered: "It was when my younger girl was so ill
and had been having convulsions all day but had fallen asleep
at last in the evening. I was sitting beside her bed and thought
to myself: 'Now you must be absolutely quiet, so as not to
wake her.' It was then that the clicking came on for the first
time. Afterwards it passed off. But once, some years later,
when we were driving through the forest near ——, a violent
thunderstorm came on and a tree beside the road just ahead
of us was struck by lightning, so that the coachman had to
rein in the horses suddenly, and I thought to myself: 'Now,
whatever you do, you mustn't scream, or the horses will bolt.'
And at that moment it came on again, and has persisted ever
since." I was able to convince myself that the noise she made
was not a genuine *tic*, since, from the moment it was in this
way traced back to its origin, it disappeared and never returned during all the years I remained in contact with the
patient. This however was the first occasion on which I was
able to observe the origin of hysterical symptoms through
the putting into effect of a distressing antithetic idea, that is,
through counter-will. The mother, worn out by anxieties and
her duties as a nurse, made a decision not to let a sound pass
her lips for fear of disturbing her child's sleep, which had
been so long in coming. But in her exhausted state the
attendant antithetic idea that she nevertheless *would* do it
proved to be the stronger; it made its way to the innervation
of the tongue, which her decision to remain silent may perhaps
have forgotten to inhibit, broke through her closed lips and
produced a noise which thenceforward remained fixated for
many years, especially after the same procedure had been
gone through on a second occasion.

There is one objection that must be met before we can
fully understand this process. It may be asked how it comes
about that it is the *antithetic* idea that gains the upper hand
as a result of general exhaustion (which is what constitutes
the predisposing situation for the event). I should reply by

putting forward the theory that the exhaustion is in fact only a *partial* one. What are exhausted are those elements of the nervous system which form the material foundation of the ideas associated with *primary* consciousness; the ideas that are excluded from that chain of associations—that is, from the normal ego—the inhibited and suppressed ideas, are *not* exhausted, and they consequently predominate at the moment when the disposition to hysteria emerges.

Anyone who is well acquainted with hysteria will observe that the psychical mechanism which I have been describing offers an explanation not merely of isolated hysterical occurrences but of major portions of the symptomatology of hysteria as well as of one of its most striking characteristics. Let us keep firmly in mind the fact that it is the distressing antithetic ideas (inhibited and rejected by normal consciousness) which press forward at the moment of the emergence of the disposition to hysteria and find their way to the somatic innervation, and we shall then hold the key to an understanding of the peculiarity of the deliria of hysterical attacks as well. It is owing to no chance coincidence that the hysterical deliria of nuns during the epidemics of the Middle Ages took the form of violent blasphemies and unbridled erotic language or that (as Charcot remarked in the first volume of his *Leçons du Mardi*) it is precisely well-brought-up and well-behaved boys who suffer from hysterical attacks in which they give free play to every kind of rowdiness, every kind of wild escapade and bad conduct. It is the suppressed—the laboriously suppressed—groups of ideas that are brought into action in these cases, by the operation of a sort of counter-will, when the subject has fallen a victim to hysterical exhaustion. Perhaps, indeed, the connection may be a more intimate one, for the hysterical condition may perhaps be *produced* by the laborious suppression; but in the present paper I have not been considering the psychological features of that condition. Here I am merely concerned with explaining why—assuming the presence of the disposition to hysteria—the symptoms take the particular form in which we in fact observe them.

This emergence of a counter-will is chiefly responsible for

the characteristic which often gives to hysterics the appearance almost of being possessed by an evil spirit—the characteristic, that is, of not being able to do something precisely at the moment when they want to most passionately, of doing the exact opposite of what they have been asked to do, and of being obliged to cover what they most value with abuse and contempt. The perversity of character shown by hysterics, their itch to do the wrong thing, to appear to be ill just when they most want to be well—compulsions such as these (as anyone will know who has had to do with these patients) may often affect the most irreproachable characters when for a time they become the helpless victims of their antithetic ideas.

The question of what becomes of inhibited intentions seems to be meaningless in regard to normal ideational life. We might be tempted to reply that they simply do not occur. The study of hysteria shows that nevertheless they *do* occur, that is to say that the physical modification corresponding to them is retained, and that they are stored up and enjoy an unsuspected existence in a sort of shadow kingdom, till they emerge like bad spirits and take control of the body, which is as a rule under the orders of the predominant ego-consciousness.

I have already said that this mechanism is supremely characteristic of hysteria; but I must add that it does not occur only in hysteria. It is present in striking fashion in *tic convulsif*, a neurosis which has so much symptomatic similarity with hysteria that its whole picture may occur as a part-manifestation of hysteria. So it is that Charcot, if I have not completely misunderstood his teachings on the subject, after keeping the two separate for some time, could only find one distinguishing mark between them—that hysterical *tic* disappears sooner or later, while genuine *tic* persists. The picture of a severe *tic convulsif* is, as we know, made up of involuntary movements (frequently, according to Charcot and Guinon, in the nature of grimaces or of performances which have at one time had a meaning), of coprolalia, of echolalia and of obsessive ideas belonging to the range covered by *folie du doute*. Now it is surprising to learn that Guinon, who had no notion whatever of going into the psychical mechanism of these symptoms, tells us that some of his patients arrived at their spasms and grimaces because an antithetic idea had put itself into effect. These patients reported that on some particular occasion they had seen a similar *tic*, or a comedian intentionally making a similar grimace, and felt afraid that they might be obliged to imitate the ugly movement. Thenceforward they had actually begun imitating it. No doubt only a small proportion of the involuntary movements occurring in *tics* originate in this way. On the other hand, it would be tempting to attribute this mechanism to the origin of coprolalia, a term used to describe the involuntary, or rather, the unwilling ejaculation of the foulest words which occurs in *tics*. If so, the root of coprolalia would be the patient's perception that he cannot prevent himself from producing some particular sound, probably an "ahem." He would then become afraid of losing control over other sounds as well, especially over words such as any well-brought-up man avoids using, and this fear would lead to what he feared coming true. No anamnesis confirming this suspicion is quoted by Guinon, and I myself have never had occasion to question a patient suffering from coprolalia. On the other hand I have found in the same writer's work a report upon another case of *tic* in which the word that was involuntarily spoken did not, exceptionally enough, belong to the coprolalic vocabulary. This was the case of an adult man who was afflicted with the necessity of calling out "Maria!" When he was a schoolboy he had had a sentimental attachment to a girl of that name; he had been completely absorbed in her, and this, it may be supposed, predisposed him to a neurosis. He began at that time to call out his idol's name in the middle of his school classes, and the name persisted with him, as a *tic*, half a lifetime after he had got over his love-affair. I think the explanation must be that his most determined endeavour to keep the name secret was reversed, at a moment of special excitement, into the counter-will and that thereafter the *tic* persisted as it did in the case of my second patient. If my explanation of this instance is correct, it would be tempting to derive coprolalic *tic* proper from the

same mechanism, since obscene words are secrets that we all
know and the knowledge of which we try to conceal from one
another.[5]

[5] I will merely add a suggestion that it would be repaying to study
elsewhere than in hysteria and [illegible] the way in which the [illegible]
[illegible] [illegible] [illegible] [illegible] frequently assure within
the limits of the normal.

III

Freud's Psychoanalytic Method[1]
(1904)

The particular method of psychotherapy which Freud practises and terms psychoanalysis is an outgrowth of the so-called cathartic treatment discussed by him in collaboration with J. Breuer in the *Studien über Hysterie*, published in 1895. This cathartic therapy was Breuer's invention and was first employed by him when treating an hysterical patient about ten years before; in so doing he had obtained an insight into the pathogenesis of her symptoms. At the personal suggestion of Breuer, Freud revived this method and tried it with a large number of patients.

The cathartic mode of treatment presupposed that the patient could be hypnotised and was based on the widening of consciousness which occurs in hypnosis. Its goal was to remove the morbid symptoms, and it attained this end by making the patient revert to the psychic state in which the symptom had appeared for the first time. In this state there

1 From Löwenfeld: *Psychische Zwangserscheinungen*, 1904. [This chapter was written at Dr. Löwenfeld's request as a part of the section on psychotherapy in the latter's book.—Translated by J. Bernays.]

came up in the hypnotised patient's mind memories, thoughts and impulses which had previously dropped out of consciousness, and, as soon as he had related these to the physician, accompanying this expression with intense emotion, the symptom was overcome and its return done away with. This experience, which could regularly be made, was taken by the authors in their joint paper to signify that the symptom represents suppressed processes which had not reached consciousness, that is, that it represents a transformation ("conversion") of these processes. They explained the therapeutic effectiveness of their treatment by the discharge of the previously "strangulated" affect attaching to the suppressed mental acts ("abreaction"). But in practice the simple outline of the therapeutic operation was almost always complicated by the circumstance that it was not a single ("traumatic") impression, but in most cases a series of impressions—to be viewed in its entirety only with difficulty—which had participated in the creation of the symptom.

The main characteristic of the cathartic method, in contrast to all other methods used in psychotherapy, consists in the fact that its therapeutic efficacy does not lie in the suggestive prohibitive command of the physician. The expectation is rather that the symptoms will disappear automatically as soon as the operation, based on certain hypotheses concerning the psychic mechanism, succeeds in diverting the course of mental processes from the direction which previously had found an outlet in the formation of the symptom.

The changes which Freud introduced in Breuer's cathartic method of treatment were at first changes in technique; these, however, brought about new results and have finally necessitated a different though not contradictory conception of the therapeutic task.

The cathartic method had already renounced suggestion; Freud went one step further and gave up hypnosis as well. At the present time he treats his patients as follows: without exerting any other kind of influence he invites them to recline in a comfortable position on a couch, while he himself is seated on a chair behind them outside their field of vision. He does not ask them to close their eyes and avoids touching them as well as any other form of procedure which might remind them of hypnosis. The consultation thus proceeds like a conversation between two equally wakeful persons, one of whom is spared every muscular exertion and every distracting sensory impression which might draw his attention from his own mental activity.

Since it depends upon the will of the patient whether he is to be hypnotised or not, no matter what the skill of the physician may be, and since a large number of neurotic patients cannot be hypnotised by any means whatever, it followed that with the abandonment of hypnosis the applicability of the treatment was assured to an unlimited number of patients. On the other hand, the widening of consciousness, which had supplied the physician with just that psychic material of memories and images by the help of which the transformation of the symptoms and the liberation of the affects was accomplished, was now missing. Unless a substitute could be found for this missing element all therapeutic effect was out of the question.

Freud now found an entirely adequate substitute in the "associations" of the patients; that is, in the involuntary thoughts most frequently regarded as disturbing elements and therefore ordinarily pushed aside whenever they cross an intention of following a definite train of thought.

In order to secure these ideas and associations he asks the patient to "let himself go" in what he says, "as you would do in a conversation which leads you 'from cabbages to kings.' " Before he asks them for a detailed account of their case-history he admonishes them to relate everything that passes through their minds, even if they think it unimportant or irrelevant or nonsensical; he lays special stress on their not omitting any thought or idea from their story because to relate it might be embarrassing or painful to them. In the task of collecting this material of otherwise neglected ideas Freud made the observations which became the determining factors of his entire theory. There were gaps in the patient's memory even in narrating his case: actual occurrences were forgotten, the chronological order was confused, or causal connections of events were broken, yielding unintelligible effects. No neurotic case-history is without amnesia of some kind or other. If the patient is urged to fill these gaps in his memory by serious application of his attention it is noticed that all the ideas which occur to him are pushed back by him with all critical means available, until at last he feels actual discomfort when the memory has really returned. From this experience Freud concludes that the amnesias are the result of a process which he calls *repression* and the motivation of which he finds in feelings of "pain" (*Unlust*). The psychical forces which have brought about this repression are traceable, according to him, to the *resistance* which operates against the reintegration of these memories.

The factor of resistance has become one of the cornerstones of his theory. The ideas otherwise pushed aside with all kinds of excuses—as those mentioned above—he regards as derivatives of the repressed psychical manifestations (thoughts and impulses), as distortions of these because of the resistance which is exerted against their reproduction.

The greater the resistance, the greater is the distortion. The value for the therapeutic technique of these unintentional thoughts lies in their relation to the repressed psychical material. If one possesses a procedure which makes it possible to arrive at the repressed from the associations, at the distorted material from the distortions, then what was formerly unconscious in mental life may be made accessible to consciousness even without hypnosis.

Freud has developed on this basis an art of interpretation which takes on the task of freeing, as it were, the pure metal of the repressed thoughts from the ore of the unintentional ideas. The objects of this work of interpretation are not only the patient's ideas but also his dreams, which open up the straightest road to the knowledge of the unconscious, his unintentional as well as his purposeless actions (symptomatic acts) and the blunders he makes in every-day life (slips of the tongue, erroneous acts, and the like). The details of this technique of interpretation or translation have not yet been published by Freud. According to the hints he has given they comprise a number of rules, reached empirically, of how the unconscious material may be reconstructed from the associations, directions how to interpret the fact when the patient's ideas cease to flow, and experience concerning the most important typical resistances that arise in the course of such a treatment. A bulky volume called *Die Traumdeutung*, published by Freud in 1900, may be regarded as the forerunner of an initiation into his technique.

From these remarks concerning the technique of the psychoanalytic method the conclusion could be drawn that its inventor has given himself needless trouble and has made a mistake in abandoning the less complicated hypnotic mode of procedure. However, in the first place, the technique of psychoanalysis is much easier in practice once one has learnt it than any description of it would indicate, and secondly, there is no other way which leads to the desired goal, so the hard road is still the shortest one to travel. The objection to hypnosis is that it conceals the resistance and for this reason has obstructed the physician's insight into the play of psychic forces. Hypnosis does not do away with the resistance but only avoids it and therefore yields only incomplete information and transitory therapeutic success.

The task which the psychoanalytic method tries to perform may be formulated in different ways, which are, however, in their essence equivalent. It may, for instance, be stated thus: the task of the cure is to remove the amnesias. When all gaps in memory have been filled in, all the enigmatic products of mental life elucidated, the continuance and even the renewal of the morbid condition is impossible. Or the formula may be expressed in this fashion: all repressions are to be undone; the mental condition is then the same as if all amnesias are removed. Another formulation reaches further; the problem consists in making the unconscious accessible to consciousness, which is done by overcoming the resistances. But it must be remembered that such an ideal condition is not present even in the normal and further that it is only rarely possible to carry the treatment to a point approaching this condition. Just as health and sickness are not qualitatively different from each other but are only gradually separated in an empirically determined way, so the aim of the treatment will never be anything else but the practical recovery of the patient, the restoration of his ability and capacity for enjoyment and an active life. In a cure which is incomplete or in which success is not perfect, one at any rate achieves a considerable improvement in the general mental condition, while the symptoms (though now of smaller importance to the patient) may continue to exist without stamping him as an invalid.

The therapeutic process remains the same, apart from insignificant modifications, for all the symptom-formations of the varied manifestations of hysteria, and all forms of the obsessional neurosis. This does not imply, however, that there can be an unlimited application of this method. The nature of the psychoanalytic method involves indications and contraindications with respect to the person to be treated as well as with respect to the clinical picture. Chronic cases of psychoneuroses with few violent or dangerous symptoms are the most favourable ones for psychoanalysis; so in the first place all forms of the obsessional neurosis, obsessive thinking and acting, and cases of hysteria in which phobias and aboulias play the most important part; further, all somatic expressions of hysteria whenever they do not, as in anorexia, require the physician to attend promptly to the speedy removal of symptoms. In acute cases of hysteria it will be necessary to await a calmer stage; in all cases where nervous exhaustion dominates the clinical picture a treatment which in itself demands effort, brings only slow improvement, and for a time cannot consider the persistence of the symptoms is to be avoided.

Various qualifications are demanded in the person if he is to be beneficially affected by psychoanalysis. To begin with, he must be capable of a psychically normal condition; during periods of confusion or melancholic depression nothing can be accomplished even in cases of hysteria. Furthermore, a certain measure of natural intelligence and ethical development may be required of him; with worthless persons the physician soon loses the interest which makes it possible for him to enter profoundly into the mental life of the patient. Deep-rooted malformations of character, traits of an actually degenerative constitution show themselves during treatment as sources of a resistance that can scarcely be overcome. In this respect the constitution of the patient does in fact set a limit to the curative effect of psychotherapy. If the patient's age is near or above the fifties the conditions for psychoanalysis become unfavorable. The mass of psychical material can then no longer be thoroughly inspected; the time required for recovery is too long; and the ability to undo psychic processes begins to grow weaker.

In spite of all limitations, the number of persons suitable for psychoanalytic treatment is extraordinarily large and the extension which has come to our therapeutic knowledge from this method is, according to Freud, very considerable. Freud requires long periods, six months to three years, for an effective treatment; yet he informs us that up to the present, from various circumstances which may easily be divined, he has for the most part been in a position to try his treatment only on very severe cases; patients have come to him after many years of illness, completely incapacitated for life, and after being disappointed by all kinds of treatments, have had recourse to his new and much-suspected method as to a last resort. In cases of less severe illness the duration of the treatment might well be much shorter, and momentous advantage in the way of prevention for the future might be gained.

IV

On Psychotherapy[1]
(1904)

About eight years have passed since I had the opportunity, on the invitation of your lamented chairman, Professor von Reder, of speaking here on the subject of hysteria. Shortly before that occasion I had published, in 1895, in collaboration with Dr. Joseph Breuer, the *Studien über Hysterie* in which, on the basis of the new knowledge which we owe to this investigator, an attempt was made to introduce a novel therapy for the neuroses. Fortunately, I may say, the efforts of our "Studies" have been successful; the ideas expressed in them concerning the action of psychical traumas through retention of affect, as well as the conception of hysterical symptoms which explains them as the result of an emotion transposed from the realm of the mental to the physical—ideas for which we created the terms "abreaction" and "conversion"—are to-day generally known and understood. There is, at least in German-speaking countries, no presentation of hysteria to-

[1] First published in the *Wiener Medizinische Presse*, 1905, No. 1. Lecture delivered before the College of Physicians, in Vienna, December 12, 1904. [Translated by J. Bernays.]

day that does not to some extent take them into account, and
we have no colleagues who do not follow at least for a short
distance the road pointed out by us. And yet, while they
were still new, these propositions and the terms for them must
have sounded not a little strange!

I cannot say the same of the therapeutic method which
was introduced to our colleagues at the same time as our
theory; it is still struggling for recognition. There may be special reasons for this. At that time the technique of the
process was as yet undeveloped; it was impossible for me to
give medical readers of the book the directions necessary to
enable them to carry through this method of treatment completely. But causes of a general nature have certainly also
played a part. To many physicians, even to-day, psychotherapy seems to be the offspring of modern mysticism and,
compared with our physico-chemical specifics which are applied on the basis of physiological knowledge, appears quite
unscientific and unworthy of the attention of a serious investigator. Allow me, therefore, to defend the cause of psychotherapy before you, and to point out to you what may be
described as unjust or mistaken in this condemnation of it.

In the first place, let me remind you that psychotherapy is
in no way a modern method of healing. On the contrary, it
is the most ancient form of therapy in medicine. In Löwenfeld's instructive work (*Lehrbuch der gesamten Psychother-
apie*) many of the methods of primitive and ancient medical
science are described. The majority of them must be classed
under the head of psychotherapy; in order to effect a cure a
condition of "expectant faith" was induced in sick persons,
the same condition which answers a similar purpose for us
to-day. Ever since physicians have come upon other therapeutic agents, psychotherapeutic endeavours of one kind or another have never completely disappeared from medicine.

Secondly, let me draw your attention to the fact that we
physicians cannot discard psychotherapy altogether, simply
because the other person so intimately concerned in the process of recovery—the patient—has no intention of giving it up.
You will know of the increase in knowledge on this subject
that we owe to the Nancy school, to Liébeault and Bernheim.

An element dependent on the psychical disposition of the patient enters as an accompanying factor, without any such intention on our part, into the effect of every therapeutic process initiated by a physician; most frequently it is favourable to recovery, but often it acts as an inhibition. We have learned to use the word "suggestion" for this phenomenon, and Möbius has taught us that the unreliability which we deplore in so many of our therapeutic measures may be traced back actually to the disturbing influence of this very powerful factor. All physicians, therefore, yourselves included, are continually practising psychotherapy, even when you have no intention of doing so and are not aware of it; it is disadvantageous, however, to leave entirely in the hands of the patient what the mental factor in your treatment of him shall be. In this way it is uncontrollable; it can neither be measured nor intensified. Is it not then a justifiable endeavour on the part of a physician to seek to control this factor, to use it with a purpose, and to direct and strengthen it? This and nothing else is what scientific psychotherapy proposes.

And, in the third place, I would remind you of the well-known experience that certain diseases, in particular the psychoneuroses, are far more readily accessible to mental influences than to any other form of medication. It is not a modern dictum but an old saying of physicians that these diseases are not cured by the drug but by the physician, that is by the personality of the physician, inasmuch as through it he exerts a mental influence. I am well aware that you favour the view which Vischer, the professor of aesthetics, expressed so well in his parody of Faust:

"Ich weiss, das Physikalische
Wirkt öfters aufs Moralische"[2]

But is it not more reasonable and more likely to happen that moral, that is, mental means can influence the moral side of a human being?

There are many ways and means of practising psychother-

[2] [I know that the physical/Often influences the moral.]

apy. All that lead to recovery are good. Our usual word of comfort, which we dispense very liberally to our patients— "Never fear, you will soon be all right again"—corresponds to one of these psychotherapeutic methods; only, now that deeper insight has been won into the neuroses, we are no longer forced to confine ourselves to the word of comfort. We have developed the technique of hypnotic suggestion, and psychotherapy by diversion of attention, by exercise, and by eliciting suitable affects. I despise none of these methods and would use them all under proper conditions. If I have actually come to confine myself to one form of treatment, to the method that Breuer called *cathartic*, which I myself prefer to call "analytic," it is because I have allowed myself to be influenced by purely subjective motives. Because of the part I have played in founding this therapy, I feel a personal obligation to devote myself to closer investigation of it and to the development of its technique. And I may say that the analytic method of psychotherapy is the one that penetrates most deeply, and carries farthest, the one by means of which the most extensive transformations can be wrought in patients. Putting aside for a moment the therapeutic point of view, I may also say of it that it is the most interesting method, the only one which informs us at all about the origin and interrelation of morbid manifestations. Owing to the insight which we gain into mental illness by this method, it alone should be capable of leading us beyond its own limits and of pointing out the way to other forms of therapeutic influence.

Permit me now to correct several mistakes that have been made in regard to this cathartic or analytic method of psychotherapy, and give a few explanations on the subject.

(*a*) I have observed that this method is very often confounded with hypnotic treatment by suggestion; I have noticed this because it happens comparatively often that colleagues who do not ordinarily confide their cases to me send me patients—refractory patients, of course—with a request that I should hypnotise them. Now I have not used hypnosis for therapeutic purposes for the last eight years (except for a few special experiments) so that I habitually send back these cases with the recommendation that anyone who relies upon hypnosis may perform it himself. There is, actually, the greatest possible antithesis between suggestive and analytic technique—the same antithesis that in regard to the fine arts the great Leonardo da Vinci summed up in the formulas: *Per via di porre* and *per via di levare*. Painting, says Leonardo, works *per via di porre*, for it applies a substance—particles of colour—where there was nothing before, on the colourless canvas; sculpture, however, proceeds *per via di levare*, since it takes away from the rough stone all that hides the surface of the statue contained in it. The technique of suggestion aims in a similar way at proceeding *per via di porre*; it is not concerned with the origin, strength and meaning of the morbid symptoms, but instead, it superimposes something—a suggestion—and expects this to be strong enough to restrain the pathogenic idea from coming to expression. Analytic therapy, on the other hand, does not seek to add or to introduce anything new, but to take away something, to bring out something; and to this end concerns itself with the genesis of the morbid symptoms and the psychical context of the pathogenic idea which it seeks to remove. It is by the use of this mode of investigation that analytic therapy has increased our knowledge so notably. I gave up the suggestive technique, and with it hypnosis, so early in my practice because I despaired of making suggestion powerful and enduring enough to effect permanent cures. In all severe cases I saw the suggestions which had been applied crumble away again; and then the disease or some substitute for it returned. Besides all this I have another reproach against this method, namely, that it conceals from us all insight into the play of mental forces; it does not permit us, for example, to recognize the *resistance* with which the patient clings to his disease and thus even fights against his own recovery; yet it is this phenomenon of resistance which alone makes it possible to comprehend his behaviour in daily life.

(b) It seems to me that among my colleagues there is a widespread and erroneous impression that this technique of searching for the origins of the symptoms and removing the manifestations by means of this investigation is an easy one which can be practised off-hand, as it were. I conclude this from the fact that not one of all those who show an interest in my therapy and pass definite judgements upon it has ever asked me how I actually go about it. There can be but one reason for this, namely, that they think there is nothing to enquire about, that the thing is perfectly obvious. Again, I am now and then astonished to hear that in this or that ward of a hospital a young assistant has received an order from his chief to undertake a "psychoanalysis" of an hysterical patient. I am sure he would not be allowed to examine an extirpated tumour until he had convinced his chiefs that he was conversant with histological technique. Similarly, a report reaches my ears that this or that colleague has arranged appointments with a patient in order to undertake a mental treatment of the case, though I am certain that he knows nothing of the technique of any such therapy. His expectation must be therefore that the patient will offer him his secrets as a present, as it were, or perhaps he looks for salvation in some sort of confession or confidence. I should not be surprised if an invalid were injured rather than benefited by being treated in such a fashion. For it is not so easy to play upon the instrument of the soul. I am reminded at this point of a world-famed neurotic, although certainly he was never treated by a physician but existed only in a poet's imagination: I mean Hamlet, Prince of Denmark. The King appointed the two courtiers, Rosenkranz and Guildenstern, to follow him, to question him and drag from him the secret of his depression. He wards them off; then flutes are brought on the stage and Hamlet, taking one of them, begs one of his torturers to play upon it, telling him that it is as easy as lying. The courtier excuses himself for he knows no touch of the instrument, and when he cannot be persuaded to try it, Hamlet finally breaks out with these words: "Why, look you now, how unworthy a thing you make of me, you would play upon me.—You would pluck out the heart of my mystery; you would sound me from my lowest note to the top of my compass; and there is much music, excellent voice, in this little organ; yet you cannot make it speak. *'Sblood, do you think I am easier to be played on than a pipe? Call me what instrument you will, though you can fret me you cannot play upon me.*" (Act III, scene 2.)

(c) From certain of my remarks you will have gathered that there are many characteristics in the analytic method which prevent it from being an ideal form of therapy. *Tuto, cito, jucunde*: investigation and probing do not indicate speedy results, and the resistance already mentioned would prepare you to expect unpleasantness in various ways. Psychoanalytic treatment certainly makes great demands upon the patient as well as upon the physician. From the patient it requires perfect sincerity—a sacrifice in itself; it absorbs time and is therefore also costly; for the physician it is no less time-absorbing, and the technique which he must study and practise is fairly laborious. I consider it quite justifiable to resort to more convenient methods of healing as long as there is any prospect of attaining anything by their means. That, after all, is the only point at issue. If the more difficult and lengthy method accomplishes considerably more than the short and easy one, then, in spite of everything, the use of the former has its justification. Just consider how much more inconvenient and costly is the Finsen therapy of lupus than the method of cauterizing and scraping previously employed; and yet the use of the former signifies a considerable advance, for it performs a radical cure. Although I do not wish to carry this comparison to all lengths, the psychoanalytic method may claim a similar privilege. Actually, I have been able to elaborate and to test my therapeutic method only on severe, nay, the severest cases; at first my material consisted entirely of patients who had tried everything else without success, and had spent long years in sanatoria. I have scarcely been able to bring together sufficient material to enable me to say how my method would work with those cases of lighter, episodically appearing invalidism which we see recover under all kinds of influences and even spontaneously. Psychoanalytic therapy was created through and for the treatment of patients permanently unfitted for life, and its great triumph has been that by its measures a satisfactorily large number of these have been rendered permanently fit for existence. In the face of such an achievement all the effort expended seems trivial. We cannot conceal from ourselves what, as physicians, we are in the habit of denying to our patients, namely, that a severe neurosis is no less serious for the sufferer than any cachexia, any of the dreaded major diseases.

(*d*) The conditions under which this method is indicated, or contra-indicated, can scarcely be definitely laid down as yet, because of the many limitations to which the scope of my activities have been subjected in practice. Nevertheless, I will attempt to discuss a few of them here:

1. It is important that the morbid condition of the patient should not be allowed to blind one in making an estimate of his whole personality; those patients who do not possess a reasonable degree of education and a fairly reliable character should be refused. It must not be forgotten that there are healthy persons as well as unhealthy ones who are good for nothing in life, and that there is much too prompt an inclination to ascribe to their malady everything which makes such people unfit, if they show the slightest symptoms of a neurosis. In my opinion a neurosis is by no means a stamp of degeneracy, though it may often enough be found in one person in conjunction with the manifestations of degeneration. Now analytic psychotherapy is not a process suited to the treatment of neuropathic degeneration; on the contrary, degeneracy acts as a hindrance to its effectiveness. Nor is the method applicable to any who are not urged to seek a cure by their own sufferings, but who undergo treatment only because they are forced into it by the authority of relatives. The qualification which is the determining factor of fitness for psychoanalytic treatment—that is, whether the patient is educable—must be discussed from yet another standpoint.

2. To be quite safe, one should limit one's choice of patients to those who possess a normal mental condition, since in the psychoanalytic method this is used as a foothold from which to obtain control of the morbid manifestations. Psychoses, states of confusion and deeply-rooted (I might say toxic) depression are therefore not suitable for psychoanalysis; at least not for the method as it has been practised up to the present. I do not regard it as by any means impossible

that by suitable changes in the method we may succeed in advancing beyond these hindrances—and so be able to initiate a psychotherapy of the psychoses.

3. The age of patients has this importance in determining their fitness for psychoanalytic treatment, that, on the one hand, near or above the fifties the elasticity of the mental processes, on which the treatment depends, is as a rule lacking—old people are no longer educable—and, on the other hand, the mass of material to be dealt with would prolong the duration of the treatment indefinitely. In the other direction the age limit can be determined only individually; youthful persons, even under the age of adolescence, are often exceedingly amenable to influence.

4. Psychoanalysis should not be attempted when the speedy removal of dangerous symptoms is required, as for example, in a case of hysterical anorexia.

By this time you will have received the impression that the field of analytic psychotherapy is a very narrow one, since you have really heard nothing from me except the indications which point against it. There remain, however, cases and types of disease enough on which this therapy may be tested, as for instance, all chronic forms of hysteria with residual manifestations, the broad field of obsessive conditions, aboulias, and the like.

It is gratifying that precisely the most valuable and most highly developed persons are best suited for these curative measures; and one may also safely claim that in cases where analytic psychotherapy can achieve but little, any other therapy would certainly not have been able to effect anything.

(e) You will no doubt wish to enquire about the possibility of doing harm by undertaking a psychoanalysis. In reply to this I may say that if you are willing to judge impartially, if you will consider this procedure in the same spirit of critical fairness that you show to our other therapeutic methods, you will have to agree with me that no injury to the patient is to be feared when the treatment is conducted with real comprehension. Anyone who is accustomed, like the lay public, to blame the treatment for whatever happens during an illness will doubtless judge differently. It is not so very long ago since the same prejudice was directed against our hydropathic establishments. Many a patient who was advised to go into an establishment of the kind hesitated because he had known someone who had entered the place as a nervous invalid and had become insane there. As you will imagine, these were cases of early general paralysis that could still in the first stage be sent to a hydropathic establishment; once there, they had run their inevitable course until manifest mental derangement supervened: but the public blamed the water as the originator of this disastrous change. When it is a matter of new kinds of therapeutic influence even physicians are not always free from such errors of judgement. I recall once making an attempt at psychotherapy with a woman who had passed the greater part of her life in a state alternating between mania and melancholia. I took on the case at the close of a period of melancholia and for two weeks things seemed to go smoothly; in the third week we were already at the beginning of the next attack of mania. This was undoubtedly a spontaneous transformation of the symptoms, since in two weeks analytic psychotherapy cannot accomplish anything. And yet the eminent physician (now deceased) who saw the case with me could not refrain from the remark that psychotherapy was probably to blame for this "relapse." I am quite convinced that he would have shown himself possessed of more critical judgement in other circumstances.

(f) Finally, I must confess that it is hardly fair to take up your attention for so long on the subject of psychoanalytic therapy without telling you in what this treatment consists and on what it is based. Still, as I am forced to be brief, I can only hint at this. This therapy, then, is based on the recognition that unconscious ideas—or better, the unconsciousness of certain mental processes—constitutes the direct cause of the morbid symptoms. We hold this opinion in common with the French school (Janet) which, by the way, owing to too crude a schematization, refers the cause of hysterical symptoms to an unconscious *idée fixe*. Now please do not be afraid that this is going to land us in the depths of philosophical obscurities. Our unconscious is not quite the same thing as that of philosophers and, moreover, the majority of philosophers decline all knowledge of "unconscious mentality." If, however, you will look at the matter from our point of view, you will understand that the transformation of this unconscious material in the mind of the patient into conscious material must have the result of correcting his deviation from normality and of lifting the compulsion to which his mind has been subjected. For conscious will-power governs only the conscious mental processes, and every mental compulsion is rooted in the unconscious. Nor need you ever fear that the patient will be harmed by the shock accompanying the introduction of the unconscious into consciousness, for you can convince yourselves theoretically that the somatic and emotional effect of an impulse that has become conscious can never be so powerful as that of an unconscious one. It is only by the application of our highest mental energies, which are bound up with consciousness, that we can command all our impulses.

There is, however, another point of view which you may take up in order to understand the psychoanalytic method. The discovery of the unconscious and the introduction of it into consciousness is performed in the face of a continuous *resistance* on the part of the patient. The process of bringing this unconscious material to light is associated with "pain" (*Unlust*), and because of this pain the patient again and again rejects it. It is for you then to interpose in this conflict in the patient's mental life. If you succeed in persuading him to accept, by virtue of a better understanding, something that up to now, in consequence of this automatic regulation by pain, he has rejected (repressed), you will then have accomplished something towards his education. For it is an education even to induce a person who dislikes leaving his bed early in the morning to do so all the same. Psychoanalytic treatment may in general be conceived of as such a *re-education in overcoming internal resistances*. Re-education of this kind is, however, in no respect more necessary to nervous patients than in regard to the mental element in their sexual life. For nowhere else have civilization and education done so much harm as in this field, and this is the point, as experience will show you, at which to look for those aetiologies of the neuroses that are amenable to influence; since the other aetiological factor, the constitutional component, consists of something fixed and unalterable. And from this it comes that one important qualification is required of the physician in this work: not only must his own character be irreproachable— "As to morals, that goes without saying," as the hero of Vischer's novel *Auch Einer* was wont to say—but he must also have overcome in his own mind that mixture of lewdness and prudery with which, unfortunately, so many people habitually consider sexual problems.

At this juncture another remark is perhaps not out of place. I know that the emphasis which I lay upon the part played by sexuality in creating the psychoneuroses has become generally known. But I know, likewise, that qualifications and exact particularization are of little use to the general public; there is very little room in the memory of the multitude; it really only retains an undigested kernel of any proposition and fabricates an extreme version which is easy to remember. It may be that this has happened with many physicians, too, so that they vaguely apprehend the content of my doctrine to be that I regard sexual privation as the ultimate cause of the neuroses. In the conditions of life in modern society there is certainly no lack of sexual privation. This being so, would it not be simpler to aim directly at recovery by recommending the satisfaction of sexual needs as a therapeutic measure, instead of undertaking the circuitous path of mental treatment? I know of nothing which could impel me to suppress such an inference if it were justified. The real state of things, however, is otherwise. Sexual need and privation are merely one factor at work in the mechanism of neurosis; if there were no others the result would be dissipation, not disease. The other, no less essential, factor, which is all too readily forgotten, is the neurotic's aversion from sexuality, his incapacity for loving, that feature of the mind which I have called "repression." Not until there is a conflict between the two tendencies does nervous illness break out, and therefore to counsel the active gratification of sexual needs in the psychoneuroses can only very rarely be described as good advice.

Let me conclude with the following defensive remark. We

will hope that, when freed from every prejudice, your interest in psychotherapy may lend us support in this way—that you also will then achieve success even with severe cases of psychoneurosis.

V

The Future Prospects of Psychoanalytic Therapy[1] (1910)

AN ADDRESS DELIVERED BEFORE THE SECOND INTERNATIONAL PSYCHOANALYTICAL CONGRESS AT NUREMBERG IN 1910

Since the objects for which we are assembled here to-day are mainly practical, I shall choose a practical theme for my introductory address and appeal to your interest in medical, not in scientific, matters. I can imagine what your opinion about the success of our therapy probably is, and I assume that most of you have already passed through the two stages which all beginners go through, that of enthusiasm at the unexpected increase in our therapeutic achievements, and that of depression at the magnitude of the difficulties which stand in the way of our efforts. Whichever of these stages in development, however, each of you may happen to be going through

[1] First published in *Zentralblatt*, Bd. I., 1910; reprinted in *Sammlung*, Dritte Folge. [Translated by Joan Riviere.]

at the moment, my intention to-day is to show you that we have by no means come to the end of our resources for combating the neuroses, and that we may expect a substantial improvement in our therapeutic prospects before very long.

This improvement will come, I think, from three sources:

1. From internal progress.
2. From increased prestige.
3. From the general effect of our work.

1. Under "internal progress" I understand advances (a) in our analytical knowledge, (b) in our technique.

(a) Advances in our knowledge. We are, of course, still a long way from knowing all that is required for an understanding of the unconscious minds of our patients. Now it is clear that every advance in our knowledge means an increase in the power of our therapy. As long as we understood nothing, we accomplished nothing; the more we understand the more we shall achieve. At its beginning psychoanalytic treatment was inexorable and exhaustive. The patient had to say everything himself, and the physician's part consisted of urging him on incessantly. To-day things have a more friendly air. The treatment is made up of two parts, out of what the physician infers and tells the patient, and out of the patient's work of assimilation, of "working through," what he hears. The mechanism of our curative method is indeed quite easy to understand; we give the patient the conscious idea of what he may expect to find (bewusste Erwartungsvorstellung), and the similarity of this with the repressed unconscious one leads him to come upon the latter himself. This is the intellectual help which makes it easier for him to overcome the resistances between conscious and unconscious. Incidentally, I may remark that it is not the only mechanism made use of by the analytic method; you all know that far more powerful one which lies in the use of the "transference." I intend soon to undertake an exposition of these various factors, which are so important for an understanding of the cure, in a Practice of Psychoanalysis. And, further, in speaking to you I need not rebut the objection that the way in which we practise the method to-day obscures its testimony to the correctness of our hypotheses; you will not forget that this evidence is to be found elsewhere, and that a therapeutic procedure cannot be performed in the same way as a theoretical investigation.

Now let me refer briefly to various fields in which we both have much to learn that is new and do actually make new discoveries daily. First of all, there is the matter of symbolism in dreams and in the unconscious—a fiercely contested subject, as you know! It is no small credit to our colleague, W. Stekel, that, indifferent to all the objections of our opponents, he has undertaken a study of dream-symbols. In this there is indeed much still to learn; my *Traumdeutung*, which was written in 1899, awaits important amplification from researches into symbolism.

I will say a few words about one of the symbols that has lately been recognized. Not long ago it came to my knowledge that a psychologist whose views are not too distant from ours had remarked to one of us that we undoubtedly overestimate the hidden sexual significance of dreams; his most frequent dream was of going upstairs, and there could certainly be nothing sexual about that. Our attention being thus drawn to it, we began to study the incidence of stairs, steps and ladders in dreams, and soon could establish the fact that stairs and such things are certainly a symbol of coitus. The underlying element which the two things have in common is not difficult to discover; one climbs an acclivity in rhythmic movements, accompanied by increasing breathlessness, and in a few rapid leaps can be down below again. Thus the rhythm of coitus reappears in climbing steps. We will not forget to adduce the usages of speech in this connection. It shows us that "mounting" is used quite simply as a symbol for the sexual act. In German one says "the man is a *Steiger, nachsteigen.*" In French the steps of a stair are called "*marches*"; "*un vieux marcheur,*" *ein alter Steiger* both mean an old profligate. The dream-material from which these newly recognized symbols are derived will in due time be put before you by the committee we are about to form for collecting and studying symbols. An account of another interesting symbol, of the idea of "rescue" and its changes in significance, will appear in the second volume of our *Jahrbuch*. However, I must break off here or I shall not reach my other points.

Every one of you will know from his own experience the total change in one's attitude to a new case when once one has thoroughly mastered the structure of some typical cases of illness. Assuming now that we had narrowly defined the regular elements in the composition of the various forms of neurosis, just as we have already succeeded in doing for hysterical symptom-formation, how much more assured we should be in our prognoses! Just as an obstetrician knows by examining the placenta whether it has been completely expelled or whether noxious fragments of it still remain, so we should be able, independently of the success of the cure and the patient's present condition, to say whether the work had been completely carried to an end or whether we had to expect relapses and fresh onsets of illness.

(b) I will hasten on to the innovations in the field of technique, where indeed nearly everything still awaits definitive settlement, and much is only now beginning to come clear. There are now two aims in psychoanalytic technique: to save the physician effort and to open up for the patient the freest access to his unconscious. You know that our technique has been transformed in important respects. At the time of the cathartic treatment we set ourselves the aim of elucidating the symptoms, then we turned away from the symptoms to discovering the "complexes," to use Jung's indispensable word; now, however, our work is aimed directly at finding out and overcoming the "resistances," and we can with justification rely on the complexes coming to light as soon as the resistances have been recognized and removed. Some of you have since shown a desire to formulate and classify these resistances. Now I beg you to examine your material and see whether you can confirm the following statement: In male patients the most important resistances to the treatment seem to be derived from the father-complex and to express themselves in fear of the father, and in defiance and incredulity towards him.

Other innovations in technique relate to the physician himself. We have begun to consider the "counter-transference," which arises in the physician as a result of the patient's influence on his unconscious feelings, and have nearly come to the point of requiring the physician to recognize and over-come this counter-transference in himself. Now that a larger number of people have come to practise psychoanalysis and mutually exchange their experiences, we have noticed that every analyst's achievement is limited by what his own complexes and resistances permit, and consequently we require that he should begin his practice with a self-analysis and should extend and deepen this constantly while making his observations on his patients. Anyone who cannot succeed in this self-analysis may without more ado regard himself as unable to treat neurotics by analysis.

We are also now coming to the opinion that the analytic technique must undergo certain modifications according to the nature of the disease and the dominating instinctual trends in the patient. Our therapy was, in fact, first designed for conversion-hysteria; in anxiety-hysteria (phobias) we must alter our procedure to some extent. The fact is that these patients cannot bring out the material necessary for resolving the phobia so long as they feel protected by retaining their phobic condition. One cannot, of course, induce them to give up their protective measures and work under the influence of anxiety from the beginning of the treatment. One must therefore help them by interpreting their unconscious to them until they can make up their minds to do without the protection of their phobia and expose themselves to a now comparatively moderate degree of anxiety. Only when they have done so does the material necessary for achieving solution of the phobia become accessible. Other modifications of technique which seem to me not yet ready for discussion will be required in the treatment of obsessional neurosis. In this connection very important questions arise, which are not yet elucidated: how far the instincts involved in the conflict in the patient are to be allowed some gratification during the treatment, and what difference it then makes whether these impulses are active (sadistic) or passive (masochistic) in nature.

I hope you have received the impression that, when all that can at present be merely glimpsed is known and when we have established all the improvements in technique to which deeper experience with our patients must lead us, then our medical practice will reach a degree of precision and certainty of success which is not to be had in all medical specialties.

2. I said that we had much to expect from the increase in prestige which must accrue to us as time goes on. I need hardly say much to you about the importance of authority. Only very few civilized persons are capable of existing without reliance on others or are even capable of coming to an independent opinion. You cannot exaggerate the intensity of man's inner irresolution and craving for authority. The extraordinary increase in the neuroses since the power of religion has waned may give you some indication of it. The impoverishment of the ego due to the tremendous effort in repression demanded of every individual by culture may be one of the principal causes of this state of things.

Hitherto the weight of authority with its enormous "suggestive" force has been against us. All our therapeutic successes have been achieved in spite of this suggestion; it is surprising that any success was to be had at all in the circumstances. I will not let myself go to the extent of describing to you the agreeable things that happened during the time when I alone represented psychoanalysis. I know that when I assured my patients that I knew how to relieve them permanently of their sufferings they looked round my modest abode, thought of my want of fame and honours, and regarded me like a man who possesses an infallible system in a gambling-place, of whom people say that if he could do what he professes he would look very different. Nor was it really at all pleasant to operate on people's minds while colleagues whose duty it was to assist took a pleasure in spitting into the field of operation, and while at the first signs of blood or restlessness in him the patient's relatives threatened one. An operation may surely cause reactions; in surgery we became used to that long ago. Nobody believed in me, in fact, just as even to-day very few believe in us; under such conditions many an attempt was bound to fail. To estimate the increase in our therapeutic capacities that will ensue when general recognition is accorded us, you should think of the different positions of gynaecologists in Turkey and in the West. All that a woman's physician may do there is to feel the pulse of an arm which is stretched out to him through a hole in the wall. And his curative results are in proportion to the inaccessibility of their object; our opponents in the West wish to restrict our access over our patients' minds to something very similar. But now that the force of public opinion drives sick women to the gynaecologist, he has become their helper and saviour. Now do not say that, even if the weight of public opinion comes to our aid and so much increases our successes, that will in no way prove the validity of our hypotheses. Suggestion is supposed to be able to do anything, and our successes would then be results of suggestion and not of psychoanalysis. Public opinion is at present suggesting hydropathic cures, diet cures, electricity cures for nervous persons, but that does not enable these measures to remove the neuroses. It will be seen whether psychoanalytic treatment can accomplish more than they.

But now, to be sure, I must damp the ardour of your expectations. The community will not hasten to grant authority to us. It is bound to offer resistance to us, for we adopt a critical attitude towards it; we accuse it of playing a great part itself in causing the neuroses. Just as we make any single person our enemy by discovering what is repressed in him, so the community cannot respond with sympathy to a relentless exposure of its injurious effects and deficiencies; because we destroy illusions we are accused of endangering ideals. It seems, therefore, that the state of things from which I expect such great advantages for our therapeutic results will never arrive. And yet the situation is not so hopeless as one might think at the present time. Powerful though the feelings and the self-interest of men may be, yet intellect is a power too. It has not, perhaps, the power that makes itself felt immediately, but one that is all the more certain in the end. The most mordant verities are heard at last, after the interests they injure and the emotions they rouse have exhausted their frenzy. It has always been so, and the unwelcome truths which we psychoanalysts have to tell the world will undergo the same fate. Only it will not come very quickly; we must be able to wait.

3. Finally, I have to explain to you what I mean by the "general effect" of our work, and how I come to set my hopes

on it. This consists in a very remarkable therapeutic constellation which could perhaps not be repeated anywhere else and which will appear strange to you too at first, until you recognize in it something you have long been familiar with. You know, of course, that the psychoneuroses are substitutive gratifications of instincts the existence of which one is forced to deny to oneself and others. Their capacity to exist depends on this distortion and disguise. When the riddle they hold is solved and the solution accepted by the sufferers these diseases will no longer be able to exist. There is hardly anything quite like it in medicine; in fairy-tales you hear of evil spirits whose power is broken when you can tell them their name which they have kept secret.

Now in place of a single sick person put the whole community of persons liable to neuroses, persons ill and persons well; in place of the acceptance of the solution in the first put a general recognition in the second; and a little reflection will show you that this substitution cannot alter the result at all. The success which the therapy has with individuals must appear in the many too. Diseased people cannot let their various neuroses become known—their apprehensive overanxiousness which is to conceal their hatred, their agoraphobia which betrays disappointed ambition, their obsessive actions which represent self-reproaches for evil intentions and precautions against them—when all their relatives and every stranger from whom they wish to conceal their thoughts and feelings know the general meaning of these symptoms, and when they know themselves that the manifestations of their disease produce nothing which others cannot instantly understand. The effect, however, will not be merely that they will conceal their symptoms—a design, by the way, which would be impossible to execute; for this concealment will destroy the purpose of the illness. Disclosure of the secret will have attacked, at its most sensitive point, the "aetiological equation" from which the neuroses descend, will have made the "advantage through illness" illusory, and consequently in the end nothing can come of the changed situation brought about by the indiscretions of physicians but an end of producing these illnesses.

If this hope seems utopian to you, you may remember that certain neurotic phenomena have already been dispelled by this means, although only in quite isolated instances. Think how common hallucinations of the Virgin Mary were in peasant-girls in former times. So long as such a phenomenon brought a flock of believers and resulted perhaps in a chapel being built on the sacred spot, the visionary state of these maidens was inaccessible to influence. To-day even the priesthood has changed its attitude to such things; it allows police and medical men to visit the seer, and since then the Virgin appears very seldom. Or allow me to study the same processes, that I have been describing as taking place in the future, in an analogous situation which is on a smaller scale and consequently more easily appreciated. Suppose that a number of ladies and gentlemen in good society had planned a picnic at an inn in the forest one day. The ladies make up their minds that if one of them wants to relieve a natural need she will say aloud that she is going to pick flowers; but a wicked fellow hears of this secret and has printed on the programme which is sent round to the whole party—"If the ladies wish to retire they are requested to say that they are going to pick flowers." Of course after this no lady will think of availing herself of this flowery pretext, and other freshly devised formulas of the same kind will be seriously compromised by it. What will be the result? The ladies will own up to their natural needs without shame and none of the men will take exception to it. Let us return to the serious aspect of our problem. A number of people who find life's conflicts too difficult to solve have taken flight into neurosis and in this way won an unmistakable, although in the end too costly, advantage through illness. What would these people have to do if their flight into illness were barred by the indiscreet revelations of psychoanalysis? They would have to be honest, own up to the instincts that are at work in them, face the conflict, fight for what they want or go without, and the tolerance from the community which is bound to ensue as a result of psychoanalytical knowledge would help them in their task.

Let us remember, however, that it is not for us to advance upon life as fanatical hygienists or therapeutists. We must admit that this ideal prevention of all neurotic illness would not be advantageous to every individual. A good number of those who now take flight into illness would not support the conflict under the conditions we have assumed, but would rapidly succumb or would commit some outrage which would be worse than if they themselves fell ill of a neurosis. The neuroses have in fact their biological function as defensive measures and their social justification; the "advantage through illness" that they provide is not always a purely subjective one. Is there one of you who has not at some time caught a glimpse behind the scenes in the causation of a neurosis and had to allow that it was the least of the evils possible in the circumstances? And should one really require such sacrifices in order to exterminate the neuroses, while the world is all the same full of other inextinguishable miseries?

Should we therefore abandon our efforts to explain the hidden meaning of neurotic manifestations, regarding it as dangerous to the individual and harmful to the interests of society; should we give up drawing the practical conclusion from a piece of scientific insight? No; I think that nevertheless our duty lies in the other direction. The "advantage through illness" provided by the neuroses is indeed on the whole and in the end detrimental to the individual as well as to society. The distress that our work of revelation may cause will but affect a few. The change to a more honest and honourable attitude in the world in general will not be bought too dearly by these sacrifices. But above all, all the energies which are to-day consumed in the production of neurotic symptoms, to serve the purposes of a world of phantasy out of touch with reality, will, even if they cannot at once be put to uses in life, help to strengthen the outcry for those changes in our civilization from which alone we can hope for better things for our descendants.

I will let you go, therefore, with the assurance that you do your duty in more than one sense by treating your patients psychoanalytically. You are not merely working in the service of science, by using the only and irreplaceable opportunity for discovering the secrets of the neuroses; you are not only giving your patients the most efficacious remedy for their sufferings available at the present time; but you are contributing your share to that enlightenment of the many from which we expect to gain the authority of the community in general and thus to achieve the most far-reaching prophylaxis against neurotic disorders.

VI

Observations on "Wild" Psychoanalysis[1]
(1910)

A few days ago an elderly lady, under the protection of a
female friend, called upon me for a consultation, complaining
of anxiety-states. She was in the second half of the forties, fairly well preserved, and had obviously not yet finished with her
womanhood. A divorce from her last husband had been the
occasion exciting the anxiety-states; but the anxiety had become greatly intensified, according to her account, since she
had consulted a young physician in the suburb she lived in,
for he had informed her that her sexual desires were the cause
of her anxiety. He said that she could not tolerate the loss of
intercourse with her husband, and so there were only three
ways by which she could recover her health—she must either
return to her husband, or take a lover, or satisfy herself. Since
then she had been convinced that she was incurable, for she
would not return to her husband, and the other two alterna-

[1] First published in *Zentralblatt*, Bd. I., 1910; reprinted in *Sammlung*, Dritte Folge. [Translated by Joan Riviere.]

tives were repugnant to her moral and religious feelings. She had come to me, however, because the doctor had said that I was responsible for this new opinion, and that she had only to come and ask me to confirm what he said, and I should tell her that this and nothing else was the truth. The friend who was with her, a still older, pinched and unhealthy-looking woman, then implored me to assure the patient that the doctor was mistaken. It could not possibly be true, for she herself had been a widow for many years, and had remained respectable without suffering from anxiety.

I will not dwell on the awkward predicament in which I was placed by this visit, but instead will consider the conduct of the practitioner who sent this lady to me. First, however, it will be as well to adopt a cautious attitude, which may possibly not be superfluous—indeed we will hope so. Long experience has taught me—as it may others—not to accept straight away as true what patients, especially nervous patients, relate about their physician. A neurologist not only easily becomes the object of many of the patient's hostile feelings, whatever method of treatment he employs; he must also sometimes resign himself to accepting responsibility, by a kind of projection, for the buried repressed wishes of his nervous patients. That such accusations then nowhere find more credence than among other physicians is a melancholy but a significant circumstance.

I have some grounds, therefore, for hoping that this lady gave me a tendenciously distorted account of what her physician had said, and that I do a man who is unknown to me an injustice by connecting my remarks about "wild" psychoanalysis with this incident. But all the same, by doing so I may perhaps prevent others from acting wrongly towards their patients.

Let us suppose, therefore, that her medical practitioner spoke to the patient exactly as she reported of him. Everyone will at once vouchsafe the criticism that if a physician holds it necessary to discuss the question of sexuality with a woman he must do so with tact and consideration. Compliance with this demand, however, coincides with carrying out certain of the *technical* regulations of psychoanalysis; moreover, the physician in question was ignorant of a number of the *scientific* principles of psychoanalysis or had misapprehended them, and thus showed how little understanding of its nature and purposes he had in fact acquired.

We will begin with the second of these, with his scientific errors. His advice to the lady shows clearly in what sense he understands the expression "sexual life"—in the popular sense, namely, in which by sexual needs nothing is meant but the need for coitus or analogous acts producing orgasm and emission of sexual secretions. The physician cannot have been unaware, however, that psychoanalysis is commonly reproached with having extended the connotation of the term "sexual" far beyond its usual range. The fact is undisputed; whether it may justly be used as a reproach shall not be discussed here. In psychoanalysis the term "sexuality" comprises far more; it goes lower and also higher than the popular sense of the word. This extension is justified genetically; we reckon as belonging to "sexual life" all expressions of tender feeling, which spring from the source of primitive sexual feelings, even when those feelings have become inhibited in regard to their original sexual aim or have exchanged this aim for another which is no longer sexual. For this reason we prefer to speak of *psychosexuality*, thus laying stress on the point that the mental factor should not be overlooked or underestimated. We use the word sexuality in the same comprehensive sense as that in which the German language uses the word *lieben* (to love). And we have long known that a mental lack of satisfaction with all its consequences can exist where there is no lack of normal sexual intercourse; as therapeutists, too, we have constantly to remember that the unsatisfied sexual trends (the substitutive satisfactions of which in the form of nervous symptoms we have to combat) can often find only very inadequate outlet in coitus or other sexual acts.

Anyone not sharing this psychoanalytical point of view has no right to call to his aid psychoanalytical theories concerned with the aetiological significance of sexuality. By emphasizing exclusively the somatic factor in sexuality he certainly simplifies the problem greatly, but he alone must bear the responsibility for what he does.

A second and equally gross misunderstanding is discernible behind the physician's advice.

It is true that psychoanalysis puts forward lack of sexual satisfaction as the cause of nervous disorders. But does it not also go much further than this? Is its teaching to be ignored as too complicated when it declares that nervous symptoms arise from a conflict between two forces—on the one hand, the libido (which is for the most part excessive), and on the other, a too severe aversion from sexuality or a repression? No one who remembers this second factor, which is by no means secondary in importance, can ever believe that sexual satisfaction in itself constitutes a remedy of general reliability for the sufferings of neurotics. A good number of nervous persons are, indeed, either in the actual circumstances or altogether incapable of satisfaction. If they were capable of it, if they were without their inner resistances, the strength of the instinct itself would point the way to satisfaction for them even though no physician recommended it. What is the good, therefore, of advice such as that supposed to have been given to this lady by her physician?

Even if it could be justified scientifically, it is not advice that she can carry out. If she had had no inner resistances against onanism or against a liaison she would of course have adopted one of these measures long before. Or does the physician think that a woman of over forty has never heard of such a thing as taking a lover, or does he overestimate his influence so much as to think that she could never decide upon such a step without medical recommendation?

All this seems very simple, and yet it must be admitted that there is one factor which often complicates the issue in forming a judgement. Some nervous states which we call the *actual* neuroses, such as typical neurasthenia and pure forms of anxiety-neurosis, obviously depend on the physical factor in sexual life, and we have no certain knowledge of the part played in them by the mental factor and by repression. In such cases it is natural that the physician should first consider some "actual" therapy, some alteration in the physical sexual way of life, and he does so with perfect justification if his diagnosis is correct. The lady who consulted the young physician complained chiefly of anxiety-states, and so he probably assumed that she was suffering from an *anxiety-neurosis*, and felt justified in recommending an actual therapy to her. Again a convenient misapprehension! A person suffering from anxiety is not for that reason necessarily suffering from anxiety-neurosis; a diagnosis of it cannot be based on its name; one has to know what manifestations are comprised in an anxiety-neurosis, and be able to distinguish it from other pathological states in which anxiety appears. My impression was that the lady in question was suffering from anxiety-hysteria, and the whole value of such nosographical distinctions, one which quite justifies them, lies in the fact that they indicate a different aetiology and a different therapy. No one who took into consideration the possibility of anxiety-hysteria in this case would have fallen into the error of neglecting the mental factors, as this physician did with his three alternatives.

Oddly enough, the three therapeutic alternatives of this would-be psychoanalyst leave no room for—psychoanalysis! This woman can only be cured of her anxiety by returning to her husband, or by satisfying her needs by onanism or with a lover. And where does analytic treatment come in, the treatment which we regard as the first remedy in anxiety-states?

This brings us to the *technical* errors to be remarked in the way that, according to our assumption, this physician proceeded. The idea that a neurotic is suffering from a sort of ignorance, and that if one removes this ignorance by telling him facts (about the causal connection of his illness with his life, about his experiences in childhood, and so on) he must recover, is an idea that has long been superseded, and one derived from superficial appearances. The pathological factor is not his ignorance in itself, but the root of this ignorance in his *inner resistances*; it was they that first called this ignorance into being, and they still maintain it now. In combating these resistances lies the task of the therapy. Telling the patient what he does not know because he has repressed it, is only one of the necessary preliminaries in the therapy. If knowledge about his unconscious were as important for the patient as the inexperienced in psychoanalysis imagine, it would be sufficient to cure him for him to go to lectures or read books.

Such measures, however, have as little effect on the symptoms of nervous disease as distributing menu-cards in time of famine has on people's hunger. The analogy goes even further than its obvious application, too; for describing his unconscious to the patient is regularly followed by intensification of the conflict in him and exacerbation of his symptoms.

Since, however, psychoanalysis cannot dispense with making this disclosure to patients, it prescribes that two conditions are to be fulfilled before it is done. First, by preparatory work, the repressed material must have come very near to the patient's thoughts, and secondly, he must be sufficiently firmly attached by an affective relationship to the physician (transference) to make it impossible for him to take fresh flight again.

Only when these two conditions are fulfilled is it possible to recognize and to overcome the resistances which have led to the repression and the ignorance. Psychoanalytic measures, therefore, cannot possibly dispense with a fairly long period of contact with the patient, and attempts to bully the patient during his first consultation by brusquely telling him the hidden things one infers behind his story are technically reprehensible; they mostly lead to their own doom, too, by inspiring a hearty dislike for the physician in the patient and putting an end to any further influence.

Besides all this, one may sometimes make a false inference, and one is never in a position to discover the whole truth. In psychoanalysis these exact technical precautions take the place of a vague demand, implying a peculiar talent, for "medical tact."

It is not enough, therefore, for a physician to know a little of what psychoanalysis has discovered; he must also have familiarized himself with its technique if he wishes his medical practice to be guided by a psychoanalytic point of view. This technique is even to-day not to be learnt from books, and it is certainly not to be discovered independently without great sacrifices of time, labour and success. It is to be learnt, like other medical measures, from those who are already proficient in it. In forming a judgement on the incident that I took as a starting-point for these remarks, therefore, it is a matter of some significance that I do not know the physician who is said to have given the lady such advice and have never before heard his name.

Neither for myself nor for my friends and co-workers is it pleasant to claim in this way a monopoly in the use of psychoanalytic technique. But in face of the danger to patients and to the cause of psychoanalysis which one foresees in this "wild" psychoanalysis, we have no other choice. In the spring of 1910 we founded an International Psychoanalytical Association, in which the members admit their participation by allowing publication of their names, in order to be able to repudiate responsibility for what is done by those who do not belong to us and yet call their methods "psychoanalysis." For as a matter of fact "wild" analysts of this kind do more harm to the cause of psychoanalysis than to individual patients. I have often found that a clumsy feat of a similar kind led to good results in the end, although it first produced an exacerbation of the patient's condition. Not always, but still often. When he has abused the physician enough and feels impervious enough to any further influence of the kind, his symptoms give way, or he decides to take some step leading to recovery. The final improvement then "comes of itself," or is ascribed to some entirely harmless treatment by another physician to whom the patient turned afterwards. In the case of the lady whose complaint against her doctor we have heard, I should say that, in spite of all, the wild psychoanalyst did more for her than some highly respected authority who might have told her she was suffering from a "vasomotor neurosis." He did force her attention to the real cause of her trouble, or in that direction, and in spite of all her struggles that cannot be without some favourable results. But he has done himself harm and helped to intensify the prejudices which patients feel, owing to their natural resistances, against the ways of psychoanalysts. And this can be avoided.

VII

The Employment of Dream-Interpretation in Psychoanalysis[1]
(1912)

The *Zentralblatt für Psychoanalyse* was not designed solely to keep its readers informed of the advances made in psychoanalytical knowledge, and itself to publish lesser contributions to the subject; but it aims also at presenting to the student a clear outline of what is already known, so that by means of suitable directions the beginner in analytical practice should be saved waste of time and effort. Henceforward, therefore, articles of a didactic nature and a technical content, not necessarily containing new matter, will appear in this Journal.

The question with which I now intend to deal is not that of the technique of dream-interpretation; neither the methods by which dreams may be interpreted nor the use of such in-

---

[1] First published in the *Zentralblatt*, Bd. II., 1912; reprinted in *Sammlung*, Vierte Folge. [Translated by Joan Riviere.]

[The following six papers (omitting No. X.) originally formed a Series of Papers on Technique, and are reprinted together in the *Sammlung*.]

terpretations when made will be considered, but merely the
way in which the analyst should employ the art of dream-interpretation in the psychoanalytic treatment of patients. There
are undoubtedly different ways of going to work in the matter, but then the answer to questions of technique in analysis
is never a matter of course. Although there may perhaps be
more than one good road to follow, still there are very many
bad ones, and a comparison of the various methods can only
be illuminating, even if it should not lead to a decision in
favour of any particular one.

Anyone coming from the study of dream-interpretation to
analytic practice will retain his interest in the content of
dreams, and his inclination will be to interpret as fully as possible every dream related by the patient. But he will soon remark that he is now working under very different conditions,
and that in attempting to carry out such an intention he will
come into conflict with the most immediate aims of the treatment. Even if a patient's first dream proves to be admirably
suited for the introduction of the first explanations to be given,
other dreams will straightway appear, so long and so obscure
that the full meaning cannot be extracted from them in the
limited hour of one day's work. If the physician pursues the
work of interpretation throughout the next few days, fresh
dreams which have been produced in the meantime will have
to be put aside until he can regard the first dream as finally
resolved. The supply of dreams is at times so copious, and
the patient's progress towards comprehension of them so slow,
that a suspicion will force itself upon the analyst that the appearance of the material in this form may be simply a
manifestation of the patient's resistance perceiving a taking
advantage of the inability of the method to master adequately
what is so presented. Moreover, the treatment will meanwhile
have fallen some way behind the present and quite lost touch
with actuality. In opposition to this method stands the rule
that it is of the greatest importance for the cure that the analyst should always be aware of what is chiefly occupying the
surface of the patient's mind at the moment, that he should
know just what complexes and resistances are active and what
conscious reaction to them will govern the patient's behaviour.

It is seldom if ever advisable to sacrifice this therapeutic aim to an interest in dream-interpretation.

Then if we take account of this rule how are we to proceed with interpreting dreams in analysis? More or less as follows: The interpretation which can be obtained in an hour should be taken as sufficient and it is not to be counted a loss if the content of a dream is not fully revealed. On the following day, the thread of the dream is not to be taken up again as a matter of course, unless it is first evident that nothing has happened meanwhile to come more into the foreground of the patient's thoughts. Therefore no exception in favour of uninterrupted dream-interpretation is to be made to the rule that what first comes to the patient's mind is first to be dealt with. If fresh dreams occur before the others are disposed of, they must be attended to, and no uneasiness need be felt about neglecting the others. If the dreams become altogether too diffuse and voluminous, all hope of completely unravelling them should tacitly be given up at the start. One must generally guard against displaying special interest in the meaning of dreams, or arousing the idea that the work would come to a standstill if no dreams were forthcoming; otherwise there is a danger of resistance being directed against the production of dreams and a risk of bringing about a cessation of them. The patient must be brought to believe, on the contrary, that material is always at hand for analysis, regardless of whether or not he has dreams to report or what measure of attention is bestowed upon them.

It will now be asked: If dreams are in practice only to be interpreted in this restricted way, will not too much valuable material which might throw light on the unconscious be lost? The answer to this is as follows: The loss is by no means so great as might appear from a superficial view of the matter. To begin with, the analyst should recognize that in cases of severe neurosis any elaborate dream-productions are to be regarded as, theoretically and in the nature of the case, incapable of complete solution. A dream of this kind is often based on the entire pathogenic material of the case, as yet unknown to both analyst and patient (so-called descriptive and biographical dreams, etc.), and is sometimes equivalent to a translation into dream-language of the whole content of the neurosis. In the attempt to find the meaning of such a dream all the latent, as yet untouched resistances will be roused to activity and soon make it impossible to penetrate very far. The full interpretation of such a dream will coincide with the completion of the whole analysis; if a note is made of it at the beginning, it may be possible to understand it at the end, after many months. In the same way as with the elucidation of a single symptom (the main symptom, perhaps), the explanation will depend upon the whole analysis, during which one must endeavour to lay hold of first this, then that, fragment of its meaning, one after another, until one can finally piece them all together. Similarly, no more can be expected of a dream in the early stages of the analysis; one must be content with bringing a single pathogenic wish-motive to light in the attempt at interpretation.

Thus nothing that could have been attained is abandoned by relinquishing the idea of a perfect dream-interpretation; neither is anything lost, as a rule, by breaking off from one dream to another more recent one. We have found from fine examples of fully analysed dreams that the several successive scenes of one dream may contain the same idea running through them all, perhaps with gathering distinctness, and likewise we have learnt that several dreams occurring on the same night are generally nothing more than attempts, expressed in various forms, to represent one meaning. In general, we can rest assured that every wish-impulse which creates a dream to-day will re-appear in other dreams as long as it has not been understood and withdrawn from the control of the unconscious. It often happens, therefore, that the best way to complete the interpretation of a dream is to dismiss it and to devote attention to a new dream, which may contain the same material in perhaps a more accessible form. I know that it is making a great demand, not only on the patient but also on the physician, to expect them both to put aside all thought of the conscious aim of the treatment, and to abandon themselves to promptings which, in spite of all, still seem to us so accidental. But I can answer for it that one is rewarded every time that one resolves to have faith in one's theoretical principles, and prevails upon oneself not to compete with the guidance of the unconscious towards the establishment of the connection.

I submit, therefore, that dream-interpretation should not be pursued in analytic treatment as an art for its own sake, but that its use should be subject to those technical rules that govern the conduct of the analysis throughout. Naturally, one can at times adopt the other course and give way a little to theoretical interest; but one should always be well aware of what one is doing. Another situation to be considered is that which has arisen since we have acquired more confidence in our understanding of dream-symbolism, and in this way know ourselves to be more independent of the patient's associations. An unusually skilful interpreter will sometimes be able to see through every dream a patient brings without requiring him to go through the tedious and time-absorbing process of dissection. Such an analyst does not experience these conflicts between the demands of the cure and those of dream-interpretation. And then he will be tempted to make full use every time of his interpretations, by telling the patient all that he has seen in the dream. In so doing, however, he will be conducting the analysis in a way which departs considerably from the established method, as I shall point out in another connection. Beginners in analytic practice, at any rate, are urged against taking this exceptional case as a model.

Every analyst will be in the position of this supposed expert of ours in regard to the first dreams that his patients bring on beginning the treatment, before they have learnt anything of the process of dream-interpretation. These initial dreams are, so to speak, naïve; they betray a great deal to the auditor, like the dreams of so-called healthy people. The question then arises whether the analyst is promptly to translate and communicate to the patient all that he himself sees in them. However, this question will not be answered here, for it obviously forms part of the wider question: at what stage in the treatment and how rapidly should the analyst guide him to the knowledge of that which lies veiled in the patient's mind? The more the patient has learnt of the method of dream-interpretation the more obscure do his later dreams become, as a rule. All the acquired knowledge about dreams serves also as a warning to the dream-work.

In the "scientific" works about dreams, which in spite of their repudiation of dream-interpretation have received a new stimulus from psychoanalysis, one repeatedly finds a very superfluous care exercised about the accurate preservation of the text of the dream. This is thought necessary in order to guard it against the distortions and accretions supervening in the hours immediately after waking. Even many psychoanalysts, in giving the patient instructions to write down the dream immediately upon waking, seem not to rely consistently enough upon their knowledge of the conditions of dream-making. This direction is superfluous in the treatment; and the patients are glad enough to make use of it to disturb their slumbers and to display eager obedience where it cannot serve any useful purpose. Even if the substance of a dream is in this way laboriously rescued from oblivion, it is easy enough to convince oneself that nothing has thereby been achieved for the patient. The associations will not come to the text, and the result is the same as if the dream had not been preserved. The physician certainly has acquired some knowledge which he would not have done otherwise. But it is by no means the same thing whether the analyst knows something or the patient knows it; later on the importance of this distinction in the technique of psychoanalysis will be more fully considered.

In conclusion, I will mention a particular type of dream which, in the nature of the case, occurs only in the course of psychoanalytic treatment, and may bewilder or deceive beginners in practice. These are the corroborating dreams which follow, as one may say, like "hangers-on"; they are easily translated, and contain merely what has been arrived at by analysis of the previous few days' material. It looks as though the patient had had the amiability to reproduce for us in dream-form exactly what we had been "suggesting" to him immediately beforehand in the treatment. The more experienced analyst will certainly have some difficulty in attributing any such graciousness to the patient; he accepts such dreams as hoped-for confirmations, and recognizes that they are only to be observed under certain conditions brought about under the influence of the treatment. The great majority of the dreams forge ahead of the analysis, so that, after subtraction of all that in them which is already known and understood, there still remains a more or less clear indication of something hitherto deeply hidden.

VIII

The Dynamics of the Transference[1]
(1912)

The almost inexhaustible subject of "transference" has recently been dealt with in this Journal by W. Stekel in a descriptive manner.[2] I wish to add a few remarks in order to make clear how it happens that the transference inevitably arises during the analysis and comes to play its well-known part in the treatment.

Let us bear clearly in mind that every human being has acquired, by the combined operation of inherent disposition and of external influences in childhood, a special individuality in the exercise of his capacity to love—that is, in the conditions which he sets up for loving, in the impulses he gratifies by it, and in the aims he sets out to achieve in it.[3] This forms

---

1 First published in the *Zentralblatt*, Bd. II., 1912; reprinted in *Sammlung*, Vierte Folge. [Translated by Joan Riviere.]

2 *Zentralblatt*, Bd. II., Nr. II. S. 26.

3 We will here provide against misconceptions and reproaches to the effect that we have denied the importance of the inborn (constitutional) factor because we have emphasized the importance of infantile impressions. Such an accusation arises out of the narrowness with which mankind looks for causes, inasmuch as one single causal

a *cliché* or stereotype in him, so to speak (or even several), which perpetually repeats and reproduces itself as life goes on, in so far as external circumstances and the nature of the accessible love-objects permit, and is indeed itself to some extent modifiable by later impressions. Now our experience has shown that of these feelings which determine the capacity to love only a part has undergone full psychical development; this part is directed towards reality, and can be made use of by the conscious personality, of which it forms part. The other part of these libidinal impulses has been held up in development, withheld from the conscious personality and from reality, and may either expend itself only in phantasy, or may remain completely buried in the unconscious so that the conscious personality is unaware of its existence. Expectant libidinal impulses will inevitably be roused, in anyone whose need for love is not being satisfactorily gratified in reality, by each new person coming upon the scene, and it is more than probable that both parts of the libido, the conscious and the unconscious, will participate in this attitude.

It is therefore entirely normal and comprehensible that the libido-cathexes, expectant and in readiness as they are in

factor satisfies him, in spite of the many commonly underlying the face of reality. Psychoanalysis has said much about the "accidental" component in aetiology and little about the constitutional, but only because it could throw new light upon the former, whereas of the latter it knows no more so far than is already known. We deprecate the assumption of an essential opposition between the two series of aetiological factors; we presume rather a perpetual interchange of both in producing the results observed. *Daimon kai tyche* determine the fate of man; seldom, perhaps never, one of these powers alone. The relative aetiological effectiveness of each is only to be measured individually and in single instances. In a series comprising varying degrees of both factors extreme cases will certainly also be found. According to the knowledge we possess we shall estimate the parts played by the forces of heredity and of environment differently in each case, and retain the right to modify our opinion in consequence of new knowledge. Further, we may venture to regard the constitution itself as a residue from the effects of accidental influences upon the endless procession of our forefathers.

those who have not adequate gratification, should be turned also towards the person of the physician. As we should expect, this accumulation of libido will be attached to prototypes, bound up with one of the *clichés* already established in the mind of the person concerned, or, to put it in another way, the patient will weave the figure of the physician into one of the "series" already constructed in his mind. If the physician should be specially connected in this way with the father-imago (as Jung has happily named[4] it) it is quite in accordance with his actual relationship to the patient; but the transference is not bound to this prototype; it can also proceed from the mother- or brother-imago and so on. The peculiarity of the transference to the physician lies in its excess, in both character and degree, over what is rational and justifiable—a peculiarity which becomes comprehensible when we consider that in this situation the transference is effected not merely by the conscious ideas and expectations of the patient, but also by those that are under suppression, or unconscious.

Nothing more would need to be said or would perplex us concerning this characteristic of the transference, if it were not that two points which are of particular interest to psychoanalysts still remain unexplained by it. First, it is not clear why neurotic subjects under analysis develop the transference so much more intensely than those who are not being analysed; and secondly, it remains a mystery why in analysis the transference provides the *strongest resistance* to the cure, whereas in other forms of treatment we recognize it as the vehicle of the healing process, the necessary condition for success. Experience shows, and a test will always confirm it, that when the patient's free associations fail[5] the obstacle can be removed every time by an assurance that he is now possessed by a thought which concerns the person of the physician or something relating to him. No sooner is this explanation given

---

[4] *Symbole und Wandlungen der Libido.*
[5] I mean here, when really nothing comes to his mind, and not when he keeps silence on account of some slight disagreeable feeling.

than the obstacle is removed, or at least the absence of thoughts has been transformed into a refusal to speak.

It appears at the first glance to be an enormous disadvantage in psychoanalysis as compared with other methods that in it the transference, elsewhere such a powerful instrument for success, should become here the most formidable ally of the resistance. On closer consideration, however, the first of these difficulties at least will disappear. It is not the fact that the transference in psychoanalysis develops more intensely and immoderately than outside it. Institutions and homes for the treatment of nervous patients by methods other than analysis provide instances of transference in its most excessive and unworthy forms, extending even to complete subjection, which also show its erotic character unmistakably. A sensitive observer, Gabriele Reuter, depicted these facts at a time when psychoanalysis hardly existed, in a remarkable book[6] which altogether reveals great insight into the nature and causes of the neuroses. This peculiarity of the transference is not, therefore, to be placed to the account of psychoanalysis but is to be ascribed to the neurosis itself. The second problem still remains unexplained.

This problem must now be tackled at close quarters: Why does the transference in analysis confront us as resistance? Let us call to mind the psychological situation in the treatment. One of the invariable and indispensable preliminary conditions in *every* case of psychoneurosis is the process which Jung has aptly named *introversion* of the libido.[7] This means that the quantity of libido which is capable of becoming conscious, and is directed towards reality, has become diminished, while the part which is unconscious and turned away from reality (and, although it may still nourish phantasies in the person concerned, belongs to the unconscious) is by so much increased. The libido (entirely or in part) has found its way back into regression and has re-animated the infantile

[6] *Aus guter Familie,* 1895.

[7] Although many of Jung's utterances give the impression that he sees introversion as something characteristic of dementia praecox and not observable to the same extent in the other neuroses.

imagos[8]; and thither we pursue it in the analytic treatment, aiming always at unearthing it, making it accessible to consciousness and at last serviceable to reality. Wherever in our analytic delving we come upon one of the hiding-places of the withdrawn libido, there ensues a battle; all the forces which have brought about the regression of the libido will rise up as "resistances" against our efforts in order to maintain the new condition. For if the introversion or regression of the libido had not been justified by some relation to the outer world (in the broadest terms, by a frustration of some desired gratification) and at the time been even expedient, it would never have taken place at all. Yet the resistances which have this origin are not the only ones, nor even the most powerful. The libido at the disposal of the personality had always been exposed to the attraction of unconscious complexes (strictly speaking, of that part of those complexes which belongs to the unconscious), and underwent regression because the attraction of reality had weakened. In order to free it, this attraction of the unconscious must now be overcome; that is, the repression of the unconscious impulses and their derivatives, which has subsequently developed in the mind of the person concerned, must be lifted. Here arises by far the greater part of the resistances, which so often succeed in upholding the illness, even though the original grounds for the recoil from reality have now disappeared. From both these sources come the resistances with which the analysis has to struggle. Every step of the treatment is accompanied by resistance; every single thought, every mental act of the patient's, must

[8] It would be easy to say: the libido has re-invested the infantile "complexes." But this would be erroneous; it would be correct only if expressed thus: "the unconscious part of these complexes." The exceptional intricacy of the theme dealt with in this essay tempts one to discuss further a number of adjunct problems, which require elucidation before one can speak definitely enough about the psychical processes here described. Such problems are: The definition of the boundary between introversion and regression; the incorporation of the complex-doctrine into the libido-theory; the relationship of phantasy-creation to the conscious, the unconscious, and to reality; etc. I need not apologize for having resisted these temptations here.

pay toll to the resistance, and represents a compromise between the forces urging towards the cure and those gathered to oppose it.

Now as we follow a pathogenic complex from its representative in consciousness (whether this be a conspicuous symptom or something apparently quite harmless) back to its root in the unconscious, we soon come to a place where the resistance makes itself felt so strongly that it affects the next association, which has to appear as a compromise between the demands of this resistance and those of the work of exploration. Experience shows that this is where the transference enters on the scene. When there is anything in the complex-material (the content of the complex) which can at all suitably be transferred on to the person of the physician such a transference will be effected, and from it will arise the next association; it will then manifest itself by the signs of resistance— for instance, a cessation in the flow of associations. We conclude from such experiences that this transferred idea is able to force itself through to consciousness in preference to all other possible associations, just *because* it also satisfies resistance. This type of incident is repeated innumerable times during an analysis. Over and over again, when one draws near to a pathogenic complex, that part of it which is first thrust forward into consciousness will be some aspect of it which can be transferred; having been so, it will then be defended with the utmost obstinacy by the patient.[9]

Once this point is won, the elements of that complex which are still unresolved cause little further difficulty. The longer the analysis lasts, and the more clearly the patient has recognized that distortions of the pathogenic material in themselves offer no protection against disclosure, the more consistently he makes use of that variety of distortion which

[9] From which, however, one need not infer in general any very particular pathogenic importance in the point selected for resistance by transference. In warfare, when a bitter fight is raging over the possession of some little chapel or a single farmhouse, we do not necessarily assume that the church is a national monument, or that the barns contain the military funds. Their value may be merely tactical; in the next onslaught they will very likely be of no importance.

obviously brings him the greatest advantage, the distortion by transference. These incidents all converge towards a situation in which eventually all the conflicts must be fought out on the field of transference.

Transference in analysis thus always seems at first to be only the strongest weapon of the resistance, and we are entitled to draw the inference that the intensity and duration of the transference are an effect and expression of the resistance. The mechanism of transference is indeed explained by the state of readiness in which the libido that has remained accumulated about the infantile imagos exists, but the part played by it in the process of cure is only intelligible in the light of its relation to the resistance.

How does it come about that the transference is so pre-eminently suitable as a weapon of resistance? One might think that this could easily be answered. It is surely clear enough that it must become peculiarly difficult to own up to any particular reprehended wish when the confession must be made to the very person with whom that feeling is most concerned. To proceed at all in such situations as this necessity produces would appear hardly possible in real life. This impossibility is precisely what the patient is aiming at when he merges the physician with the object of his emotions. Yet on closer consideration we see that this apparent gain cannot supply the answer to the riddle, for, on the contrary, an attitude of affectionate and devoted attachment can surmount any difficulty in confession; in analogous situations in real life we say: "I don't feel ashamed with you; I can tell you everything." The transference to the physician might quite as well relieve the difficulties of confession, and we still do not understand why it aggravates them.

The answer to this reiterated problem will not be found by pondering it any further, but must be sought in the experience gained by examination of individual instances of transference-resistance occurring in the course of an analysis. From these one perceives eventually that the use of the transference for resistance cannot be understood so long as one thinks simply of "transference." One is forced to distinguish "positive" transference from "negative" transference, the transference of affectionate feeling from that of hostile feeling, and to deal separately with the two varieties of the transference to the physician. Positive transference can then be divided further into such friendly or affectionate feelings as are capable of becoming conscious and the extensions of these in the unconscious. Of these last, analysis shows that they invariably rest ultimately on an erotic basis; so that we have to conclude that all the feelings of sympathy, friendship, trust and so forth which we expend in life are genetically connected with sexuality and have developed out of purely sexual desires by an enfeebling of their sexual aim, however pure and non-sensual they may appear in the forms they take on to our conscious self-perception. To begin with we knew none but sexual objects; psychoanalysis shows us that those persons whom in real life we merely respect or are fond of may be sexual objects to us in our unconscious minds still.

So the answer to the riddle is this, that the transference to the physician is only suited for resistance in so far as it consists in *negative* feeling or in the repressed *erotic* elements of positive feeling. As we "raise" the transference by making it conscious we detach only these two components of the emotional relationship from the person of the physician; the conscious and unobjectionable component of it remains, and brings about the successful result in psychoanalysis as in all other remedial methods. In so far we readily admit that the results of psychoanalysis rest upon a basis of suggestion; only by suggestion we must be understood to mean that which we, with Ferenczi,[10] find that it consists of—influence on a person through and by means of the transference-manifestations of which he is capable. The eventual independence of the patient is our ultimate object when we use suggestion to bring him to carry out a mental operation that will necessarily result in a lasting improvement in his mental condition.

The next question is, Why do these manifestations of transference-resistance appear only in psychoanalysis and not in other forms of treatment, in institutions, for example? The

[10] Ferenczi, *Introjection and Transference.*

answer is that they do appear there also, but they need to be recognized for what they are. The outbreak of negative transference is a very common occurrence in institutions; as soon as he is seized by it the patient leaves, uncured or worse. The erotic transference has not such an inhibitory effect in institutions, since there, as otherwise in life, it is decorously glossed over, instead of being exposed; nevertheless, it betrays itself unequivocally as resistance to the cure, not, indeed, by driving the patient out of the place—on the contrary, it binds him to the spot—but just as certainly by keeping him away from real life. Actually it is quite unimportant for his cure whether or not the patient can overcome this or that anxiety or inhibition in the institution; what is of importance, on the contrary, is whether or not he will be free from them in real life.

The negative transference requires a more thorough elucidation than is possible within the limits of this paper. It is found in the curable forms of the psychoneuroses alongside the affectionate transference, often both directed on to the same person at the same time, a condition for which Bleuler has coined the useful term ambivalence.[11] This ambivalence of the feelings appears to be normal up to a point, but a high degree of it is certainly a special peculiarity of neurotics. In the obsessional neurosis an early "splitting of the pairs of opposites" seems to characterize the instinctual life and to form one of the constitutional conditions of this disease. The ability of neurotics to make the transference a form of resistance is most easily accounted for by ambivalence in the flow of feelings. Where the capacity to transfer feeling has come to be of an essentially negative order, as with paranoids, the possibility of influence or cure ceases.

After all this investigation we have so far considered one

[11] E. Bleuler, *Dementia Praecox oder Gruppe der Schizophrenien,* in Aschaffenburg's *Handbuch der Psychiatrie,* 1911; also a Lecture on Ambivalence in Berne, 1910, abstracted in *Zentralblatt für Psychoanalyse,* Bd. I., S. 266. W. Stekel had previously suggested the term *bipolarity* for the same phenomenon.

aspect only of transference-phenomena; some attention must be given to another side of this question. Those who have formed a true impression of the effect of an extreme transference-resistance on the patient, of the way in which as soon as he comes under its influence he is hurled out of all reality in his relation to the physician—how he then arrogates to himself freedom to ignore the psychoanalytic rule (to communicate without reserve whatever goes through his mind), how all the resolutions with which he entered upon the analysis then become obliterated, and how the logical connections and conclusions which just before had impressed him deeply then become matters of indifference to him—will need some further explanation than that supplied by the factors mentioned above to account for this effect, and these other factors are, indeed, not far to seek; they lie again in the psychological situation in which the analysis has placed the patient.

In following up the libido that is withdrawn from consciousness we penetrate into the region of the unconscious, and this provokes reactions which bring with them to light many of the characteristics of unconscious processes as we have learnt to know them from the study of dreams. The unconscious feelings strive to avoid the recognition which the cure demands; they seek instead for reproduction, with all the power of hallucination and the inappreciation of time characteristic of the unconscious. The patient ascribes, just as in dreams, currency and reality to what results from the awakening of his unconscious feelings; he seeks to discharge his emotions, regardless of the reality of the situation. The physician requires of him that he shall fit these emotions into their place in the treatment and in his life-history, subject them to rational consideration, and appraise them at their true psychical value. This struggle between physician and patient, between intellect and the forces of instinct, between recognition and the striving for discharge, is fought out almost entirely over the transference-manifestations. This is the ground on which the victory must be won, the final expression of which is lasting recovery from the neurosis. It is undeniable that the subjugation of the transference-manifestations provides the greatest difficulties for the psychoanalyst; but it must not be forgotten that they, and they only, render the invaluable service of making the patient's buried and forgotten love-emotions actual and manifest; for in the last resort no one can be slain *in absentia* or *in effigie.*

IX

Recommendations for Physicians on the Psychoanalytic Method of Treatment[1] (1912)

The technical rules which I bring forward here have been evolved out of my own experience in the course of many years, after I had renounced other methods which had cost me dear. It will easily be seen that they may be summed up, or at least many of them, in one single injunction. My hope is that compliance with them will spare physicians practising analysis much unavailing effort and warn them of various possibilities which they might otherwise overlook. I must, however, expressly state that this technique has proved to be the only method suited to my individuality; I do not venture to deny that a physician quite differently constituted might feel impelled to adopt a different attitude to his patients and to the task before him.

(a) To the analyst who is treating more than one patient in the day, the first necessity with which he is faced will seem the hardest. It is, of course, that of keeping in mind all the in-

[1] First published in *Zentralblatt*, Bd. II., 1912; reprinted in *Sammlung*, Vierte Folge. [Translated by Joan Riviere.]

numerable names, dates, detailed reminiscences, associations, and effects of the disease which each patient communicates during the treatment in the course of months or years, and not confounding them with similar material proceeding from other patients treated simultaneously or previously. When one is required to analyse six, eight, or even more patients daily, the effort of memory necessary to achieve this evokes incredulity, astonishment, or even pity in the uninformed. Curiosity is inevitably aroused about the technique which makes it possible to deal with such abundance of material, and the expectation is that some special means are required for the purpose.

The technique, however, is a very simple one. It disclaims the use of any special aids, even of note-taking, as we shall see, and simply consists in making no effort to concentrate the attention on anything in particular, and in maintaining in regard to all that one hears the same measure of calm, quiet attentiveness—of "evenly-hovering attention," as I once before described it. In this way a strain which could not be kept up for several hours daily and a danger inseparable from deliberate attentiveness are avoided. For as soon as attention is deliberately concentrated in a certain degree, one begins to select from the material before one; one point will be fixed in the mind with particular clearness and some other consequently disregarded, and in this selection one's expectations or one's inclinations will be followed. This is just what must not be done, however; if one's expectations are followed in this selection there is the danger of never finding anything but what is already known, and if one follows one's inclinations anything which is to be perceived will most certainly be falsified. It must not be forgotten that the meaning of the things one hears is, at all events for the most part, only recognizable later on.

It will be seen, therefore, that the principle of evenly-distributed attention is the necessary corollary to the demand on the patient to communicate everything that occurs to him without criticism or selection. If the physician behaves otherwise he is throwing aside most of the advantage to be gained by the patient's obedience to the "fundamental rule of psychoanalysis." For the physician the rule may be expressed thus: All conscious exertion is to be withheld from the capacity for attention, and one's "unconscious memory" is to be given full play; or to express it in terms of technique, pure and simple: One has simply to listen and not to trouble to keep in mind anything in particular.

What one achieves in this way will be sufficient for all requirements during the treatment. Those elements of the material which have a connection with one another will be at the conscious disposal of the physician; the rest, as yet unconnected, chaotic and indistinguishable, seems at first to disappear, but rises readily into recollection as soon as the patient brings something further to which it is related, and by which it can be developed. The undeserved compliment of a "remarkably good memory" which the patient pays when one reproduces some detail after a year and a day is then accepted with a smile, whereas a conscious effort to retain a recollection of the point would probably have resulted in nothing.

Mistakes in recollection occur only at times and in places where some personal consideration has intervened (see below); that is, where there is a notable failure to reach the ideal set up for the analyst. Confusion with the communications of other patients arises very rarely. In a disagreement with the patient whether he said some particular thing, or how he said it, the physician is usually right.[2]

(b) I do not recommend that during the sitting, in the patient's presence, full notes should be made or a shorthand record kept, and so on. Apart from the unfavourable impression which this makes on many patients, the same considerations as have been advanced in regard to attention also apply here. A prejudicial selection will of necessity be made in taking down notes or shorthand, and part of one's own mental activity is occupied in this way which would be better employed in interpreting what one hears. Exceptions may be

[2] The patient often asserts that he has previously mentioned some particular thing, while one can assure him with calm authority that he has now mentioned it for the first time. It then turns out that the patient had previously had the intention to mention it, but had been hindered in so doing by a resistance which had not yet been overcome. The memory of his intention is indistinguishable in his mind from the memory of the act itself.

made to this rule without reproach in the case of dates, the text of dreams, or single incidents of a noteworthy kind which can easily be detached from their context to serve an independent purpose as examples. I am not in the habit of doing this either, however. I write down examples from memory in the evening after work is over; the text of a dream in which I find something useful I ask the patient to write down for me after he has related it.

(c) Note-taking during the sitting with the patient might be supported on the ground of an intention to publish a scientific study of the case. In theory this can hardly be denied. But in practice it must not be forgotten that exact reports of an analytic history of a case are less valuable than might be expected. Strictly speaking, they only convey that appearance of exactness which "modern" psychiatry presents in many conspicuous instances. They are wearisome to the reader as a rule, and yet they do not go far enough as a substitute for actual presence at the analysis. Altogether, experience shows that a reader who is willing to believe an analyst at all will give him credit for the touch of revision to which he has subjected his material; but if the reader is unwilling to take analysis or the analyst seriously, the most faithful shorthand reports of the treatment of cases will not influence him. This does not seem to be the way to make up for the deficiency in evidence found in psychoanalytical descriptions of cases.

(d) It is indeed one of the distinctions of psychoanalysis that research and treatment proceed hand in hand, but still the technique required for the one begins at a certain point to diverge from that of the other. It is not a good thing to formulate a case scientifically while treatment is proceeding, to reconstruct its development, anticipate its progress, and take notes from time to time of the condition at the moment, as scientific interests would require. Cases which are thus destined at the start to scientific purposes and treated accordingly suffer in consequence; while the most successful cases are those in which one proceeds, as it were, aimlessly, and allows oneself to be overtaken by any surprises, always presenting to them an open mind, free from any expectations. To swing over as required from one mental attitude to another, to avoid speculation or brooding over cases while the analysis proceeds, and to submit the material gained to the synthetic process only after the analysis is concluded, is the right course for the analyst. The distinction here drawn between the two different attitudes would have no significance if we already possessed all the knowledge (or even the essential knowledge) about the unconscious and the structure of the neuroses which is obtained by means of the analytic work. At the present time we are still far from this goal and must not cut ourselves off from the means by which we can test what we already know and learn more.

(e) I cannot recommend my colleagues emphatically enough to take as a model in psychoanalytic treatment the surgeon who puts aside all his own feelings, including that of human sympathy, and concentrates his mind on one single purpose, that of performing the operation as skilfully as possible. Under present conditions the affective impulse of greatest danger to the psychoanalyst will be the therapeutic ambition to achieve by this novel and disputed method something which will impress and convince others. This will not only cause a state of mind unfavourable for the work in him personally, but he will find himself in consequence helpless against certain of the patient's resistances, upon the struggle with which the cure primarily depends. The justification for this coldness in feeling in the analyst is that it is the condition which brings the greatest advantage to both persons involved, ensuring a needful protection for the physician's emotional life and the greatest measure of aid for the patient that is possible at the present time. An old surgeon once took for his motto the words: *Je le pansai, Dieu le guérit*. The analyst should content himself with a similar thought.

(f) All these rules which I have brought forward coincide at one point which is easily discernible. They all aim at creating for the physician a complement to the "fundamental rule of psychoanalysis" for the patient. Just as the patient must relate all that self-observation can detect, and must restrain all the logical and affective objections which would urge him to select, so the physician must put himself in a position to use all that is told him for the purposes of interpretation and recognition of what is hidden in the unconscious, without substituting a censorship of his own for the selection which the patient forgoes. Expressed in a formula, he must bend his own unconscious like a receptive organ towards the emerging unconscious of the patient, be as the receiver of the telephone to the disc. As the receiver transmutes the electric vibrations induced by the sound-waves back again into sound-waves, so is the physician's unconscious mind able to reconstruct the patient's unconscious, which has directed his associations, from the communications derived from it.

But if the physician is to be able to use his own unconscious in this way as an instrument in the analysis, he must himself fulfil one psychological condition in a high degree. He may tolerate no resistances in himself which withhold from his consciousness what is perceived by his unconscious, otherwise he would introduce into the analysis a new form of selection and distortion which would be far more injurious than that resulting from the concentration of conscious attention. It does not suffice for this that the physician should be of approximate normality himself; it is a justifiable requisition that he should further submit himself to a psychoanalytic purification and become aware of those complexes in himself which would be apt to affect his comprehension of the patient's disclosures. There can be no reasonable doubt about the disqualifying effect of such personal defects; every unresolved repression in the physician constitutes what W. Stekel has well named a "blind spot" in his capacity for analytic perception.

Years ago I replied to the question how one becomes an analyst with the answer: By the analysis of one's own dreams. This training certainly suffices for many people, but not for all those who wish to learn to analyse. Moreover, not everyone is able to interpret his own dreams without the help of another. I count it one of the valuable services of the Zürich school of analysis that they have emphasized this necessity and laid it down as a requisition that anyone who wishes to practise analysis of others should first submit to be analysed himself by a competent person. Anyone taking up the work seriously should choose this course, which offers more than one advantage; the sacrifice involved in laying oneself bare to a stranger without the necessity incurred by illness is amply rewarded. Not only is the purpose of learning to know what is hidden in one's own mind far more quickly attained and with less expense of affect, but impressions and convictions are received in one's own person which may be sought in vain by studying books and attending lectures. In addition, the gain resulting from the lasting personal relationship which usually springs up between the learner and his guide is not to be estimated lightly.

Such analysis of a person who is for all practical purposes healthy will naturally remain uncompleted. Whoever knows how to appreciate the high value of the self-knowledge and increase in self-control so acquired will afterwards continue the analytic examination of his own personality by a self-analysis, and willingly recognize that, in himself as in others, he must always expect to find something new. That analyst, however, who has despised the provision of analysis for himself will be penalized, not merely by an incapacity to learn more than a certain amount from his patient, but by risking a more serious danger, one which may become a danger for others. He will easily yield to the temptation of projecting as a scientific theory of general applicability some of the peculiarities of his own personality which he has dimly perceived; he will bring the psychoanalytic method into discredit, and lead the inexperienced astray.

(g) I will now add a few other rules which will make a transition from the attitude of the physician to the treatment of the patient.

The young and eager psychoanalyst will certainly be tempted to bring his own individuality freely into the discussion, in order to draw out the patient and help him over the confines of his narrow personality. One would expect it to be entirely permissible, and even desirable, for the overcoming of the patient's resistances, that the physician should afford him a glimpse into his own mental defects and conflicts and lead him to form comparisons by making intimate disclosures from his own life. One confidence repays another, and anyone demanding intimate revelations from another must be prepared to make them himself.

But the psychoanalytic relationship is a thing apart; much of it takes a different course from that which the psychology of consciousness would lead us to expect. Experience does not bear witness to the excellence of an affective technique of this kind. Further, it is not difficult to see that it involves a departure from psychoanalytic principles and verges upon treatment by suggestion. It will induce the patient to bring forward sooner and with less difficulty what he already knows and would otherwise have kept back for a time on account of conventional objections. But this technique achieves nothing towards the discovery of the patient's unconscious; it makes him less able than ever to overcome the deeper resistances, and in the more severe cases it invariably fails on account of the insatiability it rouses in the patient, who then tries to reverse the situation, finding the analysis of the physician more interesting than his own. The loosening of the transference, too—one of the main tasks of the cure—is made more difficult by too intimate an attitude on the part of the doctor, so that a doubtful gain in the beginning is more than cancelled in the end. Therefore I do not hesitate to condemn this kind of technique as incorrect. The physician should be impenetrable to the patient, and, like a mirror, reflect nothing but what is shown to him. In practice, it is true, one cannot object to a psychotherapeutist combining a certain amount of analysis with some suggestive treatment in order to achieve a perceptible result in a shorter time—as is necessary, for instance, in institutions; but one may demand that he himself should be in no doubt about what he is doing and should know that his method is not that of true psychoanalysis.

(*h*) Another temptation arises out of the educative function which in a psychoanalytic treatment falls to the physician without any special intention on his part. As the inhibitions in development are undone it inevitably happens that the physician finds himself in a position to point out new aims for the impulses which have been set free. It is but a natural ambition for him then to endeavour to make something specially excellent out of the person whose neurosis has cost so much labour, and to set up high aims for these impulses. But here again the physician should restrain himself and take the patient's capacities rather than his own wishes as his standard. Talent for a high degree of sublimation is not found in all neurotics; of many of them one can believe that they would never have fallen ill had they possessed the art of sublimating their impulses. In pressing them unduly towards sublimation, and cutting them off from the easier and simpler gratifications, life may often be made even harder for them than they feel it otherwise. A physician must always be tolerant of a patient's weakness, and must be content to win back a part of the capacity for work and enjoyment even for a person of but moderate worth. Ambitiousness in the educative direction is as undesirable as in the therapeutic. Moreover, it must not be forgotten that many people succumb to illness in the very effort towards sublimation beyond the limit of their capacity, and that in those who are capable of it the process usually takes place from within as soon as their inhibitions have been removed by the analysis. In my opinion, therefore, efforts to bring about sublimations of the impulses in the course of psychoanalytic treatment are no doubt always praiseworthy but most certainly not in all cases advisable.

(*i*) To what extent should the intellectual co-operation of the patient be called for in the treatment? It is difficult to say anything of general applicability on this point; the personality of the patient is here the principal deciding factor. In any case caution and self-restraint are to be observed in this matter. It is incorrect to set the patient tasks, such as collecting his memories, thinking over a certain period of his life, and so on. On the contrary, the patient has above all to learn, what never comes easily to anyone, that such mental activities as thinking over a matter, or concentrating the will and attention, avail nothing in solving the riddles of the neurosis; but that this can only be done by patiently adhering to the psychoanalytic rule demanding the exclusion of all criticism of the unconscious or of its derivatives. One must especially insist upon the following of the rule most rigidly with those patients whose habitual manoeuvre it is to shirk analysis by sheering off into the intellectual, and who speculate much and often with great wisdom over their condition, thereby sparing themselves from taking steps to overcome it. For this reason I dislike resorting to analytical writings as an aid to patients; I require them to learn by personal experience, and I assure them that in this way they will acquire wider and more valuable knowledge than the whole literature of psychoanalysis could afford them. I recognize, however, that under the conditions of institution treatment it may be very advantageous to employ reading as a preparation for patients in analysis and as a means of creating an atmosphere favourable to influence.

The most urgent warning I have to express is against any attempt to engage the confidence or support of parents or relatives by giving them psychoanalytical books to read—either of an introductory or of an advanced kind. This well-meant step usually has the effect of evoking prematurely the natural and inevitable opposition of the relatives to the treatment, which in consequence is never even begun.

I will here express the hope that advances in the experience of psychoanalysts will soon lead to agreement upon the most expedient technique for the treatment of neurotic persons. As for treatment of the "relatives," I must confess myself utterly at a loss, and I have altogether little faith in any individual treatment of them.

X

Fausse Reconnaissance ("Déjà Raconté") in Psychoanalytic Treatment[1] (1913)

It not infrequently happens in the course of an analytic treatment that the patient, after reporting some fact that he has remembered, will go on to say: *"But I've told you that already"*—while the analyst himself feels sure that this is the first time he has heard the story. If the patient is contradicted upon the point, he will often protest with energy that he is perfectly certain he is right, that he is ready to swear to it, and so on; while the analyst's own conviction that what he has heard is new to him will become correspondingly stronger. To try to decide the dispute by shouting the patient down or by outvying him in protestations would be a most unpsychological proceeding. It is familiar ground that a sense of conviction of the accuracy of one's memory has no objective value; and, since one of the two persons concerned must necessarily be in the wrong, it may just as well be the physician as the patient who has fallen a victim to a paramnesia. The

[1] First published in *Zeitschrift,* Bd. I., 1913; reprinted in *Sammlung,* Vierte Folge. [Translated by James Strachey.]

analyst will admit as much to the patient, will break off the argument, and will postpone a settlement of the point until some later occasion.

In a minority of cases the analyst himself will then recollect that he has already heard the piece of information under dispute, and will at the same time discover the subjective, and often far-fetched, reason which led to this temporary forgetfulness. But in the great majority of cases it is the patient who turns out to have been mistaken; and he can be brought to recognize the fact. The explanation of this frequent occurrence appears to be that the patient really did on some previous occasion have the intention of giving this information, that once or even several times he actually made some remark leading up to it, but that he was then prevented by resistance from carrying out his purpose, and afterwards confounded a recollection of his intention with a recollection of its performance.

Leaving on one side any cases in which there may still be some element of doubt, I will now bring forward a few others which are of special theoretical interest. With certain people it happens, and may even happen repeatedly, that they cling with particular obstinacy to the assertion that they have already told the analyst this or that, when the nature of the circumstances and of the information in question makes it quite impossible that they can be right. For what they claim to have told already once before and what they claim to recognize as something old, which must also be familiar to the physician, turn out to be memories of the greatest importance to the analysis—confirmatory facts for which the analyst has long been waiting, or solutions which wind up a whole section of the work and which he would certainly have made the basis of an exhaustive discussion. In the face of these considerations the patient himself soon admits that his recollection must have deceived him, though he is unable to account for its definite character.

The phenomenon presented by the patient in cases like this deserves to be called a "*fausse reconnaissance*," and is completely analogous to what occurs in certain other cases and has been described as a "*déjà vu.*" In these other cases the subject has a spontaneous feeling such as "I've been in this situation before," or "I've been through all this already," without ever being in a position to confirm his conviction by discovering an actual recollection of the previous occasion. This latter phenomenon, as is well known, has provoked a large number of attempts at explanation, which can be divided roughly into two groups.[2] One class of explanation looks upon the feeling which constitutes the phenomenon as deserving of credence, and assumes that something really has been remembered—the only question being what. The second and far larger class of explanation includes those which maintain, on the contrary, that what we have to deal with is an illusory memory, and that the problem is to discover how this paramnestic error can have arisen. This latter group comprises many widely different hypotheses. There is, for instance, the ancient view, ascribed to Pythagoras, that the phenomenon of the *déjà vu* is evidence of the individual having had a former life; again, there is the hypothesis based upon anatomy (put forward by Wigan in 1860) to the effect that the phenomenon is based upon an absence of simultaneity in the functioning of the two cerebral hemispheres; and finally there are the purely psychological theories, supported by the majority of more recent authorities, which regard the *déjà vu* as an indication of an apperceptive weakness, and assign the responsibility for its occurrence to such causes as fatigue, exhaustion and distraction.

In 1904 Grasset[3] put forward an explanation of the *déjà vu* which must be reckoned as one of the group which "believes" in the phenomenon. He was of opinion that the phenomenon indicates that at some earlier time there has been an *unconscious* perception, which only now makes its way into consciousness under the influence of a new and similar impression. Several other authorities have agreed with this view, and have maintained that the basis of the phenomenon is the recollection of something that has been dreamed and then

---

[2] One of the most recent bibliographies of the subject is to be found in Havelock Ellis, *The World of Dreams*, 1911.

[3] *La sensation du déjà vu.*

forgotten. In both cases it would be a question of the activation of an unconscious impression.

In 1907, in the second edition of my *Psychopathologie des Alltagslebens*, I proposed an exactly similar explanation for this form of apparent paramnesia without mentioning Grasset's paper or knowing of its existence. By way of excuse I may remark that I arrived at my conclusion as the result of a psychoanalytic investigation which I was able to make of an example of *déjà vu* in a female patient; it was extremely clear, though it had occurred twenty-eight years earlier. I shall not reproduce the little analysis in this place. It showed that the situation in which the *déjà vu* occurred was really calculated to revive the memory of an earlier experience of the patient's. The patient, who was at that time a twelve-year-old child, was visiting a family in which there was a brother who was seriously ill and at the point of death, while her own brother had been in a similarly dangerous condition a few months earlier. But with the earlier of these two similar events there had been associated a phantasy that was incapable of entering consciousness—namely, a wish that her brother should die. Consequently, the analogy between the two cases could not become conscious. And the perception of it was replaced by the phenomenon of "having been through it all before," the identity being displaced from the really common element on to the locality.

The name "*déjà vu*" is, as we know, applied to a whole class of analogous phenomena, such as the "*déjà entendu*," the "*déjà éprouvé*" and the "*déjà senti*." The case which I am now about to report, as a single instance out of many similar ones, consists of a "*déjà raconté*"; and it could be traced back to an unconscious resolution which was never carried out.

A patient[4] said to me in the course of his associations: "When I was playing in the garden with a knife (that was when I was five years old) and cut through my little finger—

---

[4] [A detailed analysis of this patient's case will be found in "From the History of an Infantile Neurosis," *Three Case Histories*, essay III, Collier Books edition BS 191V.]

oh, I only *thought* it was cut through—but I've told you about that already."

I assured him that I had no recollection of anything of the kind. He insisted with increasing conviction that it was impossible he could be mistaken. I finally put an end to the argument in the manner I have described above and asked him in any case to repeat the story. Then we should see where we were.

"When I was five years old, I was playing in the garden near my nurse, and was carving with my pocket-knife in the bark of one of the walnut-trees that also come into my dream.[5] Suddenly, to my unspeakable terror, I noticed that I had cut through the little finger of my (right or left?) hand, so that it was only hanging on by its skin. I felt no pain, but great fear. I did not venture to say anything to my nurse, who was only a few paces distant, but I sank down on the nearest seat and sat there incapable of casting another glance at my finger. At last I grew calm, took a look at the finger, and saw that it was entirely uninjured."

We soon agreed that, in spite of what he had thought, he could not have told me the story of this vision or hallucination before. He was very well aware that I could not have failed to exploit such evidence as this of his having had a *fear of castration* at the age of five. The episode broke down his resistance against assuming the existence of a castration complex; but he raised the question: "Why did I feel so certain of having told you this recollection before?"

It then occurred to both of us that repeatedly and in various connections he had brought out the following trivial recollection, and each time without our deriving any profit from it:

"Once when my uncle went away on a journey he asked

---

[5] Cf. "The Occurrence in Dreams of Material from Fairy-Tales" (1913), *Character and Culture*, essay VI, Collier Books edition BS 193V. In telling the story again on a later occasion he made the following correction: "I don't believe I was cutting the tree. That was a confusion with another recollection, which must also have been hallucinatorily falsified, of having made a cut upon a tree with my knife and of *blood* having come out of the tree."

me and my sister what we should like him to bring us back. My sister asked for a book, and I asked for a pocket-knife." We now understood that this association which had emerged months before had in reality been a screen-memory for the repressed recollection, and had been an attempt (rendered abortive by the resistance) at telling the story of his imagined loss of his little finger—an unmistakable penis-equivalent. The knife which his uncle did in fact bring him back was, as he clearly remembered, the same one that made its appearance in the episode which had been suppressed for so long.

It seems unnecessary to add anything in the way of an interpretation of this little occurrence, so far as it throws light upon the phenomenon of *"fausse reconnaissance."* As regards the subject-matter of the patient's vision, I may remark that, particularly in relation to the castration complex, similar hallucinatory falsifications are of not infrequent occurrence, and that they can just as easily serve the purpose of correcting unwelcome perceptions.

The following notes upon their author's childhood were put at my disposal in 1911. The writer, with whom I am unacquainted and whose age is unknown to me, is a man of university education residing in a university town in Germany:

"In the course of reading your *Kindheitserinnerung des Leonardo da Vinci*, I was moved to internal dissent by the observations contained upon pages 29 to 31. Your assertion that male children are dominated by an interest in their own genitals provoked me to make a counter-assertion to the effect that 'if that is the general rule, I at all events am an exception to it.' I then went on to read the passage that follows (page 31 to the top of page 32) with the utmost amazement, such amazement as one feels when one comes across a fact of an entirely novel character. In the midst of my amazement a recollection occurred to me which showed me, to my own surprise, that the fact could not be by any means so novel as it had seemed. For, at the time at which I was passing through the period of 'infantile sexual inquiry,' a lucky chance gave me the opportunity of inspecting the female genitals in a little girl of my own age, and in doing so *I quite clearly observed a penis of the same kind as my own.* Soon afterwards I was plunged into fresh confusion by the sight of some female statues and nudes; and in order to get over this 'scientific' discrepancy I devised the following experiment. By pressing my thighs together I succeeded in making my genitals disappear between them; and I was glad to find that in that way all differences between my own appearance and that of a female nude could be got rid of. Evidently, I thought to myself, the genitals have been made to disappear in a similar way in female nudes.

"At this point another recollection occurred to me, which has always been of the greatest importance to me, in so far as it is *one* of the three recollections which constitute all that I can remember of my mother, who died when I was very young. My mother is standing in front of the wash-hand-stand and cleaning the glasses and washing-basin, while I am playing in the same room and committing some misdemeanour. As a punishment my hand is soundly slapped. Then to my very great terror I see that my little finger is falling off; and in fact it falls into the pail. Knowing that my mother is angry, I do not venture to say anything; but my terror grows still more intense when I see the pail carried off soon afterwards by the servant-maid. For a long time I was convinced that I had lost a finger—up to the time, I believe, at which I learnt to count.

"I have often tried to interpret this recollection, which, as I have already mentioned, has always been of the greatest importance to me on account of its connection with my mother; but none of my interpretations has satisfied me. It is only now, after reading your book, that I begin to have a suspicion of a simple and satisfying answer to the conundrum."

There is another kind of *fausse reconnaissance* which not infrequently makes its appearance at the close of a treatment, much to the physician's satisfaction. After he has succeeded in forcing the repressed event (whether it was of a real or of a psychical nature) upon the patient's acceptance in the teeth of all resistances, and has succeeded, as it were, in rehabilitating it—the patient may say: *"Now I feel as though I had known it all the time."* With this the problem of the analysis has been solved.

XI

Further Recommendations in the Technique of Psychoanalysis[1] (1913)

ON BEGINNING THE TREATMENT. THE QUESTION OF THE FIRST COMMUNICATIONS. THE DYNAMICS OF THE CURE.

He who hopes to learn the fine art of the game of chess from books will soon discover that only the opening and closing moves of the game admit of exhaustive systematic description, and that the endless variety of the moves which develop from the opening defies description; the gap left in the instructions can only be filled in by the zealous study of games fought out by master-hands. The rules which can be laid down for the practical application of psychoanalysis in treatment are subject to similar limitations.

I intend now to try to collect together for the use of practising analysts some of the rules for the opening of the treat-

---

[1] First published in *Zeitschrift*, Bd. I., 1913; reprinted in *Sammlung*, Vierte Folge. [Translated by Joan Riviere.]

ment. Among them there are some which may seem to be mere details, as indeed they are. Their justification is that they are simply rules of the game, acquiring their importance by their connection with the whole plan of the game. I do well, however, to bring them forward as "recommendations" without claiming any unconditional acceptance for them. The exceptional diversity in the mental constellations concerned, the plasticity of all mental processes, and the great number of the determining factors involved prevent the formulation of a stereotyped technique, and also bring it about that a course of action, ordinarily legitimate, may be at times ineffective, while one which is usually erroneous may occasionally lead to the desired end. These circumstances do not prevent us from establishing a procedure for the physician which will be found most generally efficient.

Some years ago I set forth the considerations of chief importance in the selection of patients, which I shall therefore not repeat here[2]; since that time other psychoanalysts have confirmed their validity. I will add, though, that since then, when I know little of a case, I have formed the practice of first undertaking it only provisionally for one or two weeks. If one breaks off within this period the patient is spared the distress of an unsuccessful attempt at cure; it was only "taking a sounding" in order to learn more about the case and to decide whether it was a suitable one for psychoanalysis. No other kind of preliminary examination is possible; the most lengthy discussions and questionings in ordinary consultation are no substitute. This experiment, however, is in itself the beginning of an analysis, and must conform to its rules; there may perhaps be this difference in that on the whole one lets the patient talk, and explains nothing more than is absolutely necessary to keep him talking.

For the purposes of diagnosis, also, it is an advantage to begin with a period of a few weeks designed as an experiment. Often enough, when one sees a case of neurosis with hysterical or obsessional symptoms, mild in character and of short duration (just the type of case, that is, which one would re-

2 "On Psychotherapy" (1904), above, pp. 70-71.

gard as suitable for the treatment), a doubt which must not be overlooked arises whether the case may not be one of incipient dementia praecox, so called (schizophrenia, according to Bleuler; paraphrenia, as I prefer to call it), and may not sooner or later develop well-marked signs of this disease. I do not agree that it is always possible to effect the distinction so easily. I know that there are psychiatrists who hesitate less often in their differential diagnosis, but I have been convinced that they are just as often mistaken. For the psychoanalyst, however, the mistake is more serious than for a so-called clinical psychiatrist. The latter has little of value to offer either to the one type of case or to the other; he merely runs the risk of a theoretical mistake, and his diagnosis has but an academic interest. In an unsuitable case, however, the psychoanalyst has committed a practical error; he has occasioned useless expense and discredited his method of treatment; he cannot fulfil his promise of cure if the patient is suffering from paraphrenia instead of from hysteria or obsessional neurosis, and therefore he has particularly strong motives for avoiding mistakes in diagnosis. In an experimental course of a few weeks suspicious signs will often be observed which will decide him not to pursue the attempt further. Unfortunately I cannot assert that an attempt of this kind will invariably ensure certainty; it is but one more useful precaution.[3]

Lengthy preliminary discussions before the beginning of the treatment, previous treatment by another method, and also previous acquaintance between physician and patient, have certain disadvantageous consequences for which one must be prepared. They result in the patient entering upon the analysis with a transference already effected, which must then

[3] There is much to be said on the subject of this uncertainty in diagnosis, on the prospects of analysis in the milder forms of paraphrenia, and on the explanation of the similarity between the two diseases, which I cannot bring forward in this connection. I should be willing to contrast hysteria and the obsessional neurosis, under the name of "transference neuroses," with the paraphrenic group, under the name of "introversion neuroses," in accordance with Jung's formula, if the term "introversion" (of the libido) were not alienated by such usage from its only legitimate meaning.

be slowly uncovered by the physician; whereas otherwise he is in a position to observe the growth and development of it from the outset. By this means the patient gains a start upon us which we do not willingly grant him in the treatment.

One must distrust all those who wish to put off beginning the treatment. Experience shows that at the appointed time they fail to return, even though their motive for the delay (that is, their rationalization of the intention) appears to the novice to be above suspicion.

Special difficulties arise when friendship or acquaintance already exists between the physician and the patient, or their families. The psychoanalyst who is asked to undertake treatment of the wife or child of a friend must be prepared for it to cost him the friendship, no matter what the outcome of the treatment; nevertheless he must make the sacrifice unless he can propose a trustworthy substitute.

Both the general public and medical men—still fain to confound psychoanalytic with suggestive treatment—are inclined to attribute great importance to the expectations which the patient brings to the new treatment. They often believe that one patient will not give much trouble because he has a great belief in psychoanalysis and is fully convinced of its truth and curative power; and that another patient will doubtless prove more difficult because he is of a sceptical nature and will not believe until he has experienced good results in his own person. Actually, however, this attitude on the part of the patient has very little importance; his preliminary belief or disbelief is almost negligible compared with the inner resistances which hold the neurosis fast. A blissful trustfulness on the patient's part makes the relationship at first a very pleasant one; one thanks him for it, but warns him that this favourable prepossession will be shattered by the first difficulty arising in the analysis. To the sceptic one says that the analysis requires no faith; that he may be as critical and suspicious as he pleases; that one does not regard his attitude as the effect of his judgement at all, for he is not in a position to form a reliable judgement on the matter; his distrust is but a symptom like his other symptoms and will not interfere if he conscientiously carries out what the rule of the treatment requires of him.

Whoever is familiar with the nature of neurosis will not be astonished to hear that even a man who is very well able to carry out analysis upon others can behave like any other mortal and be capable of producing violent resistances as soon as he himself becomes the object of analytic investigation. When this happens it serves to remind us again of the dimensions which the mind has in regard to its depth, and it does not surprise us to find that a neurosis is rooted in mental strata that were never penetrated by an intellectual study of analysis.

Points of importance for the beginning of the treatment are the arrangements about time and money. In regard to time, I adhere rigidly to the principle of leasing a definite hour. A certain hour of my available working day is appointed to each patient; it is his, and he is liable for it, even if he does not make use of it. This arrangement, which is regarded as a matter of course for teachers of music or languages among our upper classes, perhaps seems too rigorous for a medical man, or even unworthy of the profession. All the many accidents which may prevent the patient from attending every day at the same hour will be referred to, and some allowance will be expected for the numerous intercurrent ailments which may arise in the course of a lengthy analytic treatment. My only answer is: No other way is practicable. Under a less stringent régime the "occasional" non-attendances accumulate so greatly that the physician's material existence is threatened; whereas strict adherence to the arrangement has the effect that accidental hindrances do not arise at all and intercurrent illnesses but seldom. One is hardly ever put in the position of enjoying a leisure hour which one is paid for and would be ashamed of; the work continues without interruptions, and one is spared the disheartening and bewildering experience that an unexpected pause in the work always occurs just when it promises to be especially important and productive. Nothing brings home to one with such overwhelming conviction the significance of the psychogenic factor in the daily life of mankind, the frequency of fictitious "indispositions," and the non-existence of chance as the practice of psychoanalysis for some years strictly on the principle of hire by the hour. In cases of indubitable organic illness, the occurrence of which cannot be excluded in spite of interest in the psychical work, I break off the treatment, regard myself as entitled to dispose otherwise of the hour which becomes free, and take the patient back again when he has recovered and I again have a free hour.

I work with my patients every day, except Sundays and public holidays, that is, usually six days a week. For slight cases, or the continuation of a treatment already well advanced, three days in the week will suffice. Otherwise, restriction of the time expended brings no advantage to physician or patient; it is not to be thought of at the beginning. Even short interruptions have a disconcerting effect on the work; we used to speak jokingly of the "Monday-crust" when we began work again after the rest on Sunday; with more frequent intervals the risk arises that one will not be able to keep pace with the patient's real life, that the analysis will lose contact with the present and be forced into by-paths. Occasionally one meets with patients to whom one must give more than the average time of one hour a day, because the best part of an hour is gone before they begin to open out and to communicate anything at all.

An unwelcome question which the patient asks the physician at the outset is: How long will the treatment last? What length of time will you require to relieve me of my trouble? If one has proposed an experimental course of a few weeks one can avoid a direct reply to this question by undertaking to give a more trustworthy answer later on. The answer is like that of Aesop in the fable of the Wanderer; on being asked the length of the journey he answered "Go," and gave the explanation that he must know the pilgrim's pace before he could tell the time his journey would take him. This explanation helps one over the difficulty at the start, but the comparison is not a good one, for the neurotic can easily alter his pace and at times make but very slow progress. The question of the probable duration of the treatment is hardly to be answered at all, in fact.

As a result of the lack of insight on the part of patients combined with the lack of straightforwardness on the part of physicians, analysis is expected to realize the most boundless claims in the shortest time. As an example I will give some details from a letter which I received a few days ago from a lady in Russia. Her age is fifty-three; her illness began twenty-three years ago; for the last ten years she has been incapable of continued work; "various cures in homes" have not succeeded in making an "active life" possible for her. She hopes to be completely cured by psychoanalysis, of which she has read, but her illness has already cost her family so much that she cannot undertake a visit of more than six weeks or two months to Vienna. In addition to this there is another difficulty: she wishes to "explain herself" from the beginning in writing, since any discussion of her complexes would excite an attack or render her "temporarily dumb." No one would expect a man to lift a heavy table with two fingers as if it were a little stool, or to build a large house in the time it would take to put up a wooden hut, but as soon as it becomes a question of the neuroses (which mankind seems not yet to have fitted into the general scheme of his ideas) even intelligent people forget the necessity for proportion between work, time and success—a comprehensible result, too, of the deep ignorance which prevails concerning the aetiology of neuroses. Thanks to this ignorance a neurosis is generally regarded as a sort of "maiden from afar"; the world knows not whence it comes, and therefore expects it to vanish away some day.

Medical men support this happy belief; even the experienced among them often fail to estimate properly the severity of nervous disorders. A friend and colleague of mine, to whose credit I account it that after several decades of scientific work on other principles he has betaken himself to the recognition of psychoanalysis, once wrote to me: What we need is a short, convenient form of treatment for out-patients suffering from obsessional neurosis. I could not supply him with it, and felt ashamed; so I tried to excuse myself with the remark that probably physicians would also be very glad of a treatment for consumption or cancer which combined these advantages.

To speak more plainly, psychoanalysis is always a matter of long periods of time, of six months or a year, or more— a longer time than the patient expects. It is therefore a duty to explain this fact to the patient before he finally resolves upon the treatment. I hold it to be altogether more honourable, and also more expedient, to draw his attention, without alarming him unduly but from the very beginning, to the difficulties and sacrifices involved by analytic treatment; thereby depriving him of the right to assert later on that he had been inveigled into a treatment the implications and extent of which he did not realize. The patient who lets himself be dissuaded by these considerations would later on have shown himself unsuitable; it is a good thing to institute a selection in this way before the beginning of the treatment. With the progress of understanding among patients the number of those who stand this first test increases.

I do not bind patients to continue the treatment for a certain length of time; I permit each one to break off whenever he likes, though I do not conceal from him that no success will result from a treatment broken off after only a small amount of work, and that it may easily, like an unfinished operation, leave him in an unsatisfactory condition. In the early years of my practice of psychoanalysis I had the greatest difficulty in prevailing upon patients to continue; this difficulty has long since altered; I must now anxiously exert myself to induce them to give it up.

The shortening of the analytic treatment remains a reasonable wish, the realization of which, as we shall hear, is being sought after in various ways. Unfortunately, it is opposed by a very important element in the situation—namely, the slowness with which profound changes in the mind bring themselves about, fundamentally the same thing as the "inappreciation of time" characteristic of our unconscious processes. When the patients are confronted with the great expenditure of time required for the analysis they often bethink themselves of suggesting a makeshift way out of the difficulty. They divide up their complaints and describe some as unendurable and others as secondary, saying, "If only you will relieve me of this (for instance, a headache or a particular fear) I will manage by myself to endure life with the other trouble." They exaggerate the selective capacity of the analysis in this. The analyst is certainly able to do a great deal, but he cannot determine beforehand exactly what results he will effect. He sets in operation a certain process, the "loosening" of the existing repressions: he can watch over it, further it, remove difficulties in the way of it, and certainly do much also to vitiate it; but on the whole, once begun, the process goes its own way and does not admit of prescribed direction, either in the course it pursues or in the order in which the various stages to be gone through are taken. The power of the analyst over the symptoms of disease is comparable in a way to sexual potency; the strongest man can beget a whole child, it is true, but he cannot effect the production of a head alone, or an arm, or a leg in the female organ, he cannot even prescribe the sex of the child. He, too, only sets in operation a highly complicated process, determined by foregone events, and ending with the severance of the child from the mother. Again, a neurosis has the character of an organism; its component manifestations are not independent of one another, they each condition and mutually support the others; a man can only suffer from one neurosis, never from several accidentally combined in his person. Suppose one had freed the patient, according to his wish, from the one unendurable symptom, he might then have discovered that a symptom which was previously negligible had increased until it in turn had become intolerable. In general, the analyst who wishes the results to be as independent as possible of the influence of suggestion from himself (that is, of transference) will do best to refrain from using even the fraction of selective influence upon the results of the cure which is perhaps open to him. The patients who are most welcome to the psychoanalyst will be those who desire complete health so far as they are capable of it, and who will place as much time at his disposal for the cure as the process requires. Naturally, such favourable conditions are to be met with only in the minority of cases.

The next point to be decided on beginning the treatment is the money question, the physician's fee. The analyst does not dispute that money is to be regarded first and foremost as the means by which life is supported and power is obtained, but he maintains that, besides this, powerful sexual factors are involved in the value set upon it; he may expect, therefore, that money questions will be treated by cultured people in the same manner as sexual matters, with the same inconsistency, prudishness and hypocrisy. He is therefore determined beforehand not to concur in this attitude, and in his dealings with patients to treat of money matters with the same matter-of-course frankness that he wishes to induce in them towards matters relating to sexual life. By voluntarily introducing the subject of fees and stating the price for which he gives his time, he shows the patient that he himself has cast aside false shame in these matters. Ordinary prudence then demands that the sums to be paid should not be allowed to accumulate until they are very large, but that payment should be made at fairly short regular intervals (every month or so). (It is well known that the value of the treatment is not enhanced in the patient's eyes if a very low fee is asked.) This is of course not the usual practice of neurologists or other physicians in our European cities. But the psychoanalyst may put himself in the position of surgeons, who are both honest and expensive because they deal in measures which can be of aid. In my opinion it is more dignified and ethically less open to objection to acknowledge one's actual claims and needs rather than, as the practice is now among medical men, to act the part of the disinterested philanthropist, while that enviable situation is denied to one and one grumbles in secret, or animadverts loudly, over the lack of consideration or the miserliness shown by patients. In estimating his fee the analyst must allow for the fact that, in spite of strenuous work, he can never earn as much as other medical specialists.

For the same reasons he may refrain from giving treatment gratuitously, making no exceptions to this in favour of his colleagues or their relatives. This last requisition seems to conflict with the claims of professional fellow-feeling; one must consider, however, that gratuitous treatment means much more to a psychoanalyst than to other medical men—namely, the dedication of a considerable portion (an eighth or a seventh part, perhaps) of the time available for his livelihood over a period of several months. Another treatment conducted gratuitously at the same time would rob him of a quarter or a third of his earning capacity, which would be comparable to the effects of some serious accident.

Then the question arises whether the advantage to the patient would not outweigh the physician's sacrifice. I may rely on my own judgement in this matter, since I have given an hour daily, and sometimes two, for ten years to gratuitous treatment, because I wished, for the purpose of studying the neuroses, to work with the fewest possible hindrances. The advantages which I sought in this way were not forthcoming. Gratuitous treatment enormously increases many neurotic resistances, such as the temptations of the transference-relationship for young women, or the opposition to the obligatory gratitude in young men arising from the father-complex, which is one of the most troublesome obstacles to the treatment. The absence of the corrective influence in payment of the professional fee is felt as a serious handicap; the whole relationship recedes into an unreal world; and the patient is deprived of a useful incentive to exert himself to bring the cure to an end.

One may stand quite aloof from the ascetic view of money as a curse and yet regret that analytic therapy is almost unattainable for the poor, both for external and for internal reasons. Little can be done to remedy this. Perhaps there is some truth in the widespread belief that those who are forced by necessity to a life of heavy labour succumb less easily to neurosis. But at all events experience shows without a doubt that, in this class, a neurosis once acquired is only with very great difficulty eradicated. It renders the sufferer too good service in the struggle for existence; the accompanying secondary "epinosic gain" has here too much importance. The pity which the world has refused to his material distress the sufferer now claims by right of his neurosis and absolves himself from the obligation of combating his poverty by work. Any one who tries to deal by psychotherapeutic means with a neurosis in a poor person usually makes the discovery that what is really required of him in such a case is a very different, material kind of therapy—the sort of healing which, according to tradition, Emperor Joseph II used to dispense. Naturally one does occasionally meet with people of worth who are helpless from no fault of their own, in whom unpaid treatment leads to excellent results without exciting any of the difficulties mentioned.

For the middle classes the necessary expense of psychoanalysis is only apparently excessive. Quite apart from the fact that restored health and capacity for life on the one hand, and a moderate outlay in money on the other, cannot be measured in the same category; if one contrasts a computation of the never-ceasing costs of nursing homes and medical treatment with the increase of capacity to live well and earn well after a successful analytic treatment, one may say that the patient has made a good bargain. Nothing in life is so expensive as illness—and foolishness.

Before I conclude these remarks on beginning the analytic treatment a word must be said about a certain ceremonial observance regarding the position in which the treatment is carried out. I adhere firmly to the plan of requiring the patient to recline upon a sofa, while one sits behind him out of his sight. This arrangement has an historic meaning; it is the last vestige of the hypnotic method out of which psychoanalysis was evolved; but for many reasons it deserves to be retained. The first is a personal motive, one that others may share with me, however. I cannot bear to be gazed at for eight hours a day (or more). Since, while I listen, I resign myself to the control of my unconscious thoughts I do not wish my expression to give the patient indications which he may interpret or which may influence him in his communications. The patient usually regards being required to take up this position as a hardship and objects to it, especially when scoptophilia plays an important part in the neurosis. I persist in the measure, however, for the intention and result of it are that all imperceptible influence on the patient's associations by the transference may be avoided, so that the transference may be isolated and clearly outlined when it appears as a resistance. I know that many analysts work in a different way, though I do not know whether the main motive of their departure is the ambition to work in a different way or an advantage which they gain thereby.

The conditions of the treatment being now regulated in

this manner, the question arises at what point and with what material it shall begin.

What subject-matter the treatment begins with is on the whole immaterial, whether with the patient's life-story, with a history of the illness or with recollections of childhood; but in any case the patient must be left to talk, and the choice of subject left to him. One says to him, therefore, "Before I can say anything to you, I must know a great deal about you; please tell me what you know about yourself."

The only exception to this concerns the fundamental rule of the psychoanalytic technique which the patient must observe. This must be imparted to him at the very beginning: "One thing more, before you begin. Your talk with me must differ in one respect from an ordinary conversation. Whereas usually you rightly try to keep the threads of your story together and to exclude all intruding associations and side-issues, so as not to wander too far from the point, here you must proceed differently. You will notice that as you relate things various ideas will occur to you which you feel inclined to put aside with certain criticisms and objections. You will be tempted to say to yourself: 'This or that has no connection here, or it is quite unimportant, or it is nonsensical, so it cannot be necessary to mention it.' Never give in to these objections, but mention it even if you feel a disinclination against it, or indeed just because of this. Later on you will perceive and learn to understand the reason for this injunction, which is really the only one that you have to follow. So say whatever goes through your mind. Act as if you were sitting at the window of a railway train and describing to some one behind you the changing views you see outside. Finally, never forget that you have promised absolute honesty, and never leave anything unsaid because for any reason it is unpleasant to say it."[4]

---

[4] Much might be said about our experience with the fundamental rule of psychoanalysis. One meets occasionally with people who behave as if they had instituted this rule for themselves; others offend against it from the beginning. It is indispensable, and also advantageous, to mention it at the first stage of the treatment; later, under

Patients who date their illness from a particular time usually concentrate upon the events leading up to it; others who themselves recognize the connection of their neurosis with their childhood often begin with an account of their whole life-story. A consecutive narrative should never be expected and nothing should be done to encourage it. Every detail of the story will later have to be related afresh, and only with this repetition will additional matter appear enabling the significant connections which are unknown to the patient to be traced.

the influence of resistances, obedience to it weakens and there comes a time in every analysis when the patient disregards it. One must remember how irresistible was the temptation in one's self-analysis to yield to those cavilling pretexts for rejecting certain thoughts. The feeble effect of the patient's agreement to the bargain made with him about the "fundamental rule" is regularly demonstrated when something of an intimate nature about a third person rises to his mind for the first time; the patient knows that he must say everything, but he makes a new obstacle out of the discretion required on behalf of others. "Must I really say everything? I thought that only applied to what concerns myself." It is naturally impossible to carry out an analysis if the patient's relations with other people and his thoughts about them are excluded. *Pour faire une omelette il faut casser des oeufs.* An honourable man readily forgets such of the private affairs of strangers as do not seem important for him to know. Names, too, cannot be excepted from communication; otherwise the patient's narratives become rather shadowy, like the scenes of Goethe's *Natural Daughter*, and do not remain in the physician's memory; moreover, the names withheld cover the approach to all kinds of important connections. One may perhaps leave names until the patient has become more familiar with the physician and the process of analysis. It is a most remarkable thing that the whole undertaking becomes lost labour if a single concession is made to secrecy. If at any one spot in a town the right of sanctuary existed, one can well imagine that it would not be long before all the riff-raff of the town would gather there. I once treated a high official who was bound by oath not to communicate certain State secrets, and the analysis came to grief as a consequence of this restriction. The psychoanalytic treatment must override everything which comes in its way, because the neurosis and the resistances are equally relentless.

There are patients who from the first hour carefully prepare their communications, ostensibly so as to make better use of the time given to treatment. This appears to be eagerness on their part, but it is resistance. One must disallow this preparation; it is employed to guard against the appearance of unwelcome thoughts;[5] the patient may believe ever so honestly in his praiseworthy intention, but resistance will play its part in this kind of considered preparation and will see to it that in this way the most valuable part of the communication escapes. One will soon find that the patient invents yet other methods by which the required material may be withheld from analysis. He will perhaps talk over the treatment every day with some intimate friend, and in this discussion bring out all the thoughts which should occur to him in the presence of the physician. The treatment then suffers from a leak which lets through just what is most valuable. It will then soon be time to recommend the patient to treat the analysis as a matter between himself and his physician, and to exclude everyone else from sharing in it, no matter how closely bound to him or how inquisitive they may be. In later stages of the treatment the patient is not usually tempted in this way.

Certain patients wish their treatment kept secret, often because they have kept their neurosis secret, and I put no obstacle in the way of this. That in consequence the world hears nothing of some of the most brilliantly successful cures is of course a consideration not to be taken into account. Obviously the patient's decision in favour of secrecy at once reveals one feature of his inner history.

In advising at the beginning of treatment that as few persons as possible shall be informed of it, one protects patients to some extent from the many hostile influences seeking to detach them from the analysis. Such influences may be very mischievous at the outset of the cure; later they are usually immaterial, or even useful in bringing into prominence resistances which are attempting concealment.

[5] Exceptions may be made only of such data as the family relationships, visits, operations, and so on.

If during the course of the analysis the patient requires temporarily some other medical or special treatment, it is far wiser to call in some colleague outside analytic work than to administer this treatment oneself. Analysis combined with other treatment, for neurotic maladies with a strong organic connection, is nearly always impracticable; the patients withdraw their interest from the analysis when there is more than one way leading them to health. Preferably one postpones the organic treatment until after the conclusion of the mental; if the former were tried first, in most cases it would do no good.

To return to the beginning of the treatment. Patients are occasionally met with who begin the treatment with an absolute disclaimer of the existence of any thoughts in their minds which they could utter, although the whole field of their life-history and their neurosis lies before them untrodden. One must accede this first time as little as at any other to their request that one should propose something for them to speak of. One must bear in mind what it is that confronts one in these cases. A formidable resistance has come out into the open in order to defend the neurosis; one takes up its challenge then and there, and grips it by the throat. Emphatic and repeated assurance that the absence of all ideas at the beginning is an impossibility, and that there is some resistance against the analysis, soon brings the expected confessions from the patient or else leads to the first discovery of some part of his complexes. It is ominous if he has to confess that while listening to the rule of the analysis he formed a determination in spite of it not to communicate this or that; not quite so bad if he only has to declare the distrust he has of the treatment or the appalling things he has heard about it. If he denies these and similar possibilities when they are suggested to him, further pressure will constrain him to acknowledge that he has neglected certain thoughts which are occupying his mind. He was thinking of the treatment itself but not in a definite way, or else the appearance of the room he is in occupied him, or he found himself thinking of the objects round him in the consulting-room, or of the fact that he is lying on a sofa; for all of which thoughts he has substituted "nothing." These indications are surely intelligible; everything connected with the situation of the moment represents a transference to the physician which proves suitable for use as resistance. It is necessary then to begin by uncovering this transference; thence the way leads rapidly to penetration of the pathogenic material in the case. Women who are prepared by events in their past lives for a sexual overture, or men with unusually strong, repressed homosexuality, are the most prone to exhibit this denial of all ideas at the outset of the analysis.

The first symptoms or chance actions of the patient, like the first resistance, have a special interest and will betray one of the governing complexes of the neurosis. A clever young philosopher, with leanings towards aesthetic exquisiteness, hastens to twitch the crease in his trousers into place before lying down for the first sitting; he reveals himself as an erstwhile coprophiliac of the highest refinement, as was to be expected of the developed aesthete. A young girl on the same occasion hurriedly pulls the hem of her skirt over her exposed ankle; she has betrayed the kernel of what analysis will discover later, her narcissistic pride in her bodily beauty and her tendencies to exhibitionism.

Very many patients object especially to the arrangement of reclining in a position where the physician sits out of sight behind them; they beg to be allowed to undergo analysis in some other position, mostly because they do not wish to be deprived of a view of the physician. Permission is invariably refused; one cannot prevent them, however, from contriving to say a few words before the beginning of the "sitting itself," and after one has signified its termination and they have risen from the sofa. In this way they make in their own minds a division of the treatment into an official part, in which they behave in a very inhibited manner, and an informal "friendly" part, in which they really speak freely and say a good deal that they do not themselves regard as belonging to the treatment. The physician does not fall in for long with this division of the time, he makes a note of what is said before or after the sitting, and in bringing it up at the next opportunity he tears down the partition which the patient has tried to erect. It again is a structure formed from the material of a transference-resistance.

So long as the patient continues to utter without obstruction the thoughts and ideas rising to his mind, the theme of the transference should be left untouched. One must wait until the transference, which is the most delicate matter of all to deal with, comes to be employed as resistance.

The next question with which we are confronted is a main one. It runs: When shall we begin our disclosures to the patient? When is it time to unfold to him the hidden meaning of his thoughts and associations, to initiate him into the postulates of analysis and its technical devices?

The answer to this can only be: Not until a dependable transference, a well-developed *rapport*, is established in the patient. The first aim of the treatment consists in attaching him to the treatment and to the person of the physician. To ensure this one need do nothing but allow him time. If one devotes serious interest to him, clears away carefully the first resistances that arise and avoids certain mistakes, such an attachment develops in the patient of itself, and the physician becomes linked up with one of the imagos of those persons from whom he was used to receive kindness. It is certainly possible to forfeit this primary success if one takes up from the start any standpoint other than that of understanding, such as a moralizing attitude, perhaps, or if one behaves as the representative or advocate of some third person, maybe the husband or wife, and so on.

This answer of course involves a condemnation of that mode of procedure which consists in communicating to the patient the interpretation of the symptoms as soon as one perceives it oneself, or of that attitude which would account it a special triumph to hurl these "solutions" in the face at the first interview. It is not difficult for a skilled analyst to read the patient's hidden wishes plainly between the lines of his complaints and the story of his illness; but what a measure of self-complacency and thoughtlessness must exist in one who can upon the shortest acquaintance inform a stranger, who is entirely ignorant of analytical doctrines, that he is bound

by an incestuous love for his mother, that he harbours wishes
for the death of the wife he appears to love, that he conceals
within himself the intention to deceive his chief, and so forth!
I have heard that analysts exist who plume themselves upon
these kinds of lightning-diagnoses and "express"-treatments,
but I warn everyone against following such examples. Such
conduct brings both the man and the treatment into discredit and arouses the most violent opposition, whether the
interpretations be correct or not; yes, and the truer they are
actually the more violent is the resistance they arouse. Usually
the therapeutic effect at the moment is nothing; the resulting
horror of analysis, however, is ineradicable. Even in later
stages of the analysis one must be careful not to communicate
the meaning of a symptom or the interpretation of a wish until the patient is already close upon it, so that he has only a
short step to take in order to grasp the explanation himself.
In former years I often found that premature communication
of interpretations brought the treatment to an untimely end,
both on account of the resistances suddenly aroused thereby
and also because of the relief resulting from the insight so
obtained.

The following objection will be raised here: Is it then our
task to lengthen the treatment, and not rather to bring it to
an end as rapidly as possible? Are not the patient's sufferings
due to his lack of knowledge and understanding, and is it not
a duty to enlighten him as soon as possible, that is, as soon as
the physician himself knows the explanations? The answer to
this question requires a short digression concerning the significance of knowledge and the mechanism of the cure in psychoanalysis.

In the early days of analytic technique it is true that we regarded the matter intellectually and set a high value on the
patient's knowledge of that which had been forgotten, so that
we hardly made a distinction between our knowledge and his
in these matters. We accounted it specially fortunate if it
were possible to obtain information of the forgotten traumas
of childhood from external sources, from parents or nurses,
for instance, or from the seducer himself, as occurred occasionally; and we hastened to convey the information and

proofs of its correctness to the patient, in the certain expectation of bringing the neurosis and the treatment to a rapid end by this means. It was a bitter disappointment when the expected success was not forthcoming. How could it happen that the patient, who now had the knowledge of his traumatic experience, still behaved in spite of it as if he knew no more than before? Not even would the recollection of the repressed trauma come to mind after it had been told and described to him.

In one particular case the mother of an hysterical girl had confided to me the homosexual experience which had greatly influenced the fixation of the attacks. The mother herself had come suddenly upon the scene and had been a witness of it; the girl, however, had totally forgotten it, although it had occurred not long before puberty. Thereupon I made a most instructive observation. Every time that I repeated the mother's story to the girl she reacted to it with an hysterical attack, after which the story was again forgotten. There was no doubt that the patient was expressing a violent resistance against the knowledge which was being forced upon her; at last she simulated imbecility and total loss of memory in order to defend herself against what I told her. After this, there was no alternative but to abandon the previous attribution of importance to knowledge in itself, and to lay the stress upon the resistances which had originally induced the condition of ignorance and were still now prepared to defend it. Conscious knowledge, even if it were not again expelled, was powerless against these resistances.

This disconcerting ability in patients to combine conscious knowledge with ignorance remains unexplained by what is called normal psychology. By reason of the recognition of the unconscious, psychoanalysis finds no difficulty in it; the phenomenon described is, however, one of the best confirmations of the conception by which mental processes are approached as being differentiated topographically. The patients are aware, in thought, of the repressed experience, but the connection between the thought and the point where the repressed recollection is in some way imprisoned is lacking. No change is possible until the conscious thought-process has pen-

etrated to this point and has overcome the resistances of the
repression there. It is just as if a decree were promulgated by
the Ministry of Justice to the effect that juvenile misdemean-
ours should be dealt with by certain lenient methods. As long
as this concession has not come to the knowledge of the individual magistrates, or in the event of their not choosing to
make use of it but preferring to deal justice according to their
own lights, nothing will be changed in the treatment accorded
to youthful delinquents. For the sake of complete accuracy,
though, it may be added that communicating to the patient's
consciousness information about what is repressed does not
entirely fail of any effect at all. It does not produce the hoped-
for result of abolishing the symptoms, but it has other consequences. It first arouses resistances, but when these are
overcome it sets a mental process in action, in the course of
which the desired influence upon the unconscious memory is
eventually effected.

At this point we should review the play of forces brought
into action by the treatment. The primary motive-power used
in therapy is the patient's suffering and the wish to be cured
which arises from it. The volume of this motive-force is diminished in various ways, discoverable only in the course of
the analysis, above all by what we call the "epinosic gain";
the motive-power itself must be maintained until the end of
the treatment; every improvement effects a diminution of it.
Alone, however, the force of this motive is insufficient to overcome the illness; two things are lacking in it, the knowledge
of the paths by which the desired end may be reached, and
the amount of energy needed to oppose the resistances. The
analytic treatment helps to supply both these deficiencies. The
accumulation of energy necessary to overcome the resistances is supplied by analytic utilization of the energies which
are always ready to be "transferred"; and by timely communications to the patient at the right moment analysis points
out the direction in which these energies should be employed.
The transference alone frequently suffices to bring about a
disappearance of the symptoms of the disease, but this is
merely temporary and lasts only as long as the transference
itself is maintained. The treatment is then nothing more than

suggestion, not a psychoanalysis. It deserves the latter name
only when the intensity of the transference has been utilized
to overcome the resistances; only then does illness become
impossible, even though the transference is again dissolved as
its function in the treatment requires.

In the course of the treatment another helpful agency is
roused—the patient's intellectual interest and understanding.
But this alone is hardly worth consideration by the side of
the other forces engaged in the struggle, for it is always in
danger of succumbing to the clouding of reasoning power under the influence of resistances. Hence it follows that the new
sources of strength for which the sufferer is indebted to the
analyst resolve themselves into transference, and instruction
(by explanation). The patient only makes use of the instruction, however, in so far as he is induced to do so by the
transference; and therefore until a powerful transference is
established the first explanation should be withheld; and likewise, we may add, with each subsequent one, we must wait
until each disturbance of the transference by the transference-
resistances arising in succession has been removed.

XII

Further Recommendations in the Technique of Psychoanalysis[1] (1914)

RECOLLECTION, REPETITION AND WORKING THROUGH

It seems to me not unnecessary constantly to remind students of the far-reaching changes which psychoanalytic technique has undergone since its first beginnings. Its first phase was that of Breuer's catharsis, direct concentration upon the events exciting symptom-formation and persistent efforts on this principle to obtain reproduction of the mental processes involved in that situation, in order to bring about a release of them through conscious operations. The aims pursued at that time, by the help of the hypnotic condition, were "recollection" and "abreaction." Next, after hypnosis had been abandoned, the main task became that of divining from the patient's free associations what he failed to remember. Resistances were to be circumvented by the work of interpretation and by

[1] First published in *Zeitschrift*, Bd. II., 1914; reprinted in *Sammlung*, Vierte Folge. [Translated by Joan Riviere.]

making its results known to the patient; concentration on
the situations giving rise to symptom-formation and on those
which lay behind the outbreak of illness was retained, while
abreaction receded and seemed to be replaced by the work
the patient had to do in overcoming his critical objections to
his associations, in accordance with the fundamental psychoanalytic rule. Finally, the present-day technique evolved itself, whereby the analyst abandons concentration on any
particular element or problem, contents himself with studying
whatever is occupying the patient's mind at the moment, and
employs the art of interpretation mainly for the purpose of
recognizing the resistances which come up in regard to this
material and making the patient aware of them. A rearrangement of the division of labour results from this; the physician
discovers the resistances which are unknown to the patient;
when these are removed the patient often relates the forgotten
situations and connections without any difficulty. The aim of
these different procedures has of course remained the same
throughout: descriptively, to recover the lost memories; dy-
namically, to conquer the resistances caused by repression.

One is bound to be grateful still to the old hypnotic technique for the way in which it unrolled before us certain of the
mental processes of analysis in an isolated and schematic
form. Only this could have given us the courage to create
complicated situations ourselves in the analytic process and to
keep them perspicuous.

Now in those days of hypnotic treatment "recollection"
took a very simple form. The patient put himself back into an
earlier situation, which he seemed never to confound with the
present, gave an account of the mental processes belonging
to it, in so far as they were normal, and appended to this
whatever conclusions arose from making conscious what had
before been unconscious.

I will here interpolate a few observations which every analyst has found confirmed in his experience. The forgetting
of impressions, scenes, events, nearly always reduces itself to
"dissociation" of them. When the patient talks about these
"forgotten" matters he seldom fails to add: "In a way I have
always known that, only I never thought of it." He often ex-

presses himself as disappointed that not enough things come into his mind which he can hail as "forgotten," which he has never thought of since they happened. Even this desire on his part is fulfilled, however, particularly in cases of conversion-hysteria. The "forgotten" material is still further circumscribed when we estimate at their true value the screen-memories which are so generally present. In many cases I have had the impression that the familiar childhood-amnesia, which is theoretically so important to us, is entirely outweighed by the screen-memories. Not merely is much that is essential in childhood preserved in them, but actually all that is essential. Only one must understand how to extract it from them by analysis. They represent the forgotten years of childhood just as adequately as the manifest content represents the dream-thoughts.

The other group of mental processes, the purely internal mental activities, such as phantasies, relations between ideas, impulses, feelings, connections, may be contrasted with impressions and events experienced, and must be considered apart from them in its relation to forgetting and remembering. With these processes it particularly often happens that something is "remembered" which never could have been "forgotten," because it was never at any time noticed, never was conscious; as regards the fate of any such "connection" in the mind, moreover, it seems to make no difference whatever whether it was conscious and then was forgotten or whether it never reached consciousness at all. The conviction which a patient obtains in the course of analysis is quite independent of remembering it in that way.

In the manifold forms of obsessional neurosis particularly, "forgetting" consists mostly of a falling away of the links between various ideas, a failure to draw conclusions, an isolating of certain memories.

No memory of one special kind of highly important experience can usually be recovered: these are experiences which took place in very early childhood, before they could be comprehended, but which were *subsequently* interpreted and understood. One gains a knowledge of them from dreams, and is compelled to believe in them on irresistible evidence in the structure of the neurosis; moreover, one can convince oneself that after his resistances have been overcome the patient no longer invokes the absence of any memory of them (sensation of familiarity) as a ground for refusing to accept them. This matter, however, is one demanding so much critical caution and introducing so much that is novel and startling that I will reserve it for special discussion in connection with suitable material.[2]

To return to the comparison between the old and the new techniques; in the latter there remains very little, often nothing, of this smooth and pleasing course of events belonging to the former. There are cases which, under the new technique, conduct themselves up to a point like those under the hypnotic technique and only later abandon this behaviour; but others behave differently from the beginning. If we examine the latter class in order to define this difference, we may say that here the patient *remembers* nothing of what is forgotten and repressed, but that he expresses it in *action*. He reproduces it not in his memory but in his behaviour; he *repeats* it, without of course knowing that he is repeating it.

For instance, the patient does not say that he remembers how defiant and critical he used to be in regard to the authority of his parents, but he behaves in that way towards the physician. He does not remember how he came to a helpless and hopeless deadlock in his infantile searchings after the truth of sexual matters, but he produces a mass of confused dreams and associations, complains that he never succeeds at anything, and describes it as his fate never to be able to carry anything through. He does not remember that he was intensely ashamed of certain sexual activities, but he makes it clear that he is ashamed of the treatment to which he has submitted himself, and does his utmost to keep it a secret; and so on.

Above all, the beginning of the treatment sets in with a repetition of this kind. When one announces the fundamental psychoanalytical rule to a patient with an eventful life-history and a long illness behind him, and then waits for him to pour

2 [Cf. Freud, "From the History of an Infantile Neurosis," *Three Case Histories*, essay III, Collier Books edition BS 191V.]

forth a flood of information, the first thing that happens often is that he has nothing to say. He is silent and declares that nothing comes into his mind. That is of course nothing but the repetition of a homosexual attitude, which comes up as a resistance against remembering anything. As long as he is under treatment he never escapes from this compulsion to repeat; at last one understands that it is his way of remembering.

The relation between this compulsion to repeat and the transference and resistance is naturally what will interest us most of all. We soon perceive that the transference is itself only a bit of repetition, and that the repetition is the transference of the forgotten past not only on to the physician, but also on to all the other aspects of the current situation. We must be prepared to find, therefore, that the patient abandons himself to the compulsion to repeat, which is now replacing the impulse to remember, not only in his relation with the analyst but also in all other matters occupying and interesting him at the time, for instance, when he falls in love or sets about any project during the treatment. Moreover, the part played by resistance is easily recognized. The greater the resistance the more extensively will expressing in action (repetition) be substituted for recollecting. The ideal kind of recollection of the past which belongs to hypnosis is indeed a condition in which resistance is completely abrogated. If the treatment begins under the auspices of a mild and unpronounced positive transference, it makes an unearthing of memories like that in hypnosis possible to begin with, while the symptoms themselves are for the time quiescent; if then, as the analysis proceeds, this transference becomes hostile or unduly intense, consequently necessitating repression, remembering immediately gives way to expression in action. From then onward the resistances determine the succession of the various repetitions. The past is the patient's armoury out of which he fetches his weapons for defending himself against the progress of the analysis, weapons which we must wrest from him one by one.

The patient reproduces instead of remembering, and he reproduces according to the conditions of the resistance; we may now ask what it is exactly that he reproduces or expresses in action. The answer is that he reproduces everything in the reservoirs of repressed material that has already permeated his general character—his inhibitions and disadvantageous attitudes of mind, his pathological traits of character. He also repeats during the treatment all his symptoms. And now we can see that our special insistence upon the compulsion to repeat has not yielded any new fact, but is only a more comprehensive point of view. We are only making it clear to ourselves that the patient's condition of illness does not cease when his analysis begins, that we have to treat his illness as an actual force, active at the moment, and not as an event in his past life. This condition of present illness is shifted bit by bit within the range and field of operation of the treatment, and while the patient lives it through as something real and actual, we have to accomplish the therapeutic task, which consists chiefly in translating it back again into terms of the past.

Causing memories to be revived under hypnosis gives the impression of an experiment in the laboratory. Allowing "repetition" during analytic treatment, which is the latest form of technique, constitutes a conjuring into existence of a piece of real life, and can therefore not always be harmless and indifferent in its effects on all cases. The whole question of "exacerbation of symptoms during treatment," so often unavoidable, is linked up with this.

The very beginning of the treatment above all brings about a change in the patient's conscious attitude towards his illness. He has contented himself usually with complaining of it, with regarding it as nonsense, and with underestimating its importance; for the rest, he has extended the ostrich-like conduct of repression which he adopted towards the sources of his illness on to its manifestations. Thus it happens that he does not rightly know what are the conditions under which his phobia breaks out, has not properly heard the actual words of his obsessive idea or not really grasped exactly what it is his obsessive impulse is impelling him to do. The treatment of course cannot allow this. He must find the courage to pay attention to the details of his illness. His illness itself must no longer seem to him contemptible, but must become an enemy worthy of his mettle, a part of his personality, kept up by good motives, out of which things of value for his future life have to be derived. The way to reconciliation with the repressed part of himself which is coming to expression in his symptoms is thus prepared from the beginning; yet a certain tolerance towards the illness itself is induced. Now if this new attitude towards the illness intensifies the conflicts and brings to the fore symptoms which till then had been indistinct, one can easily console the patient for this by pointing out that these are only necessary and temporary aggravations, and that one cannot overcome an enemy who is absent or not within range. The resistance, however, may try to exploit the situation to its own ends, and abuse the permission to be ill. It seems to say: "See what happens when I really let myself go in these things! Haven't I been right to relegate them all to repression?" Young and childish persons in particular are inclined to make the necessity for paying attention to their illness a welcome excuse for luxuriating in their symptoms.

There is another danger, that in the course of the analysis, other, deeper-lying instinctual trends which had not yet become part of the personality may come to be "reproduced." Finally, it is possible that the patient's behaviour outside the transference may involve him in temporary disasters in life, or even be so designed as permanently to rob the health he is seeking of all its value.

The tactics adopted by the physician are easily justified. For him recollection in the old style, reproduction in the mind, remains the goal of his endeavours, even when he knows that it is not to be obtained by the newer method. He sets about a perpetual struggle with the patient to keep all the impulses which he would like to carry into action within the boundaries of his mind, and when it is possible to divert into the work of recollection any impulse which the patient wants to discharge in action, he celebrates it as a special triumph for the analysis. When the transference has developed to a sufficiently strong attachment, the treatment is in a position to prevent all the more important of the patient's repetition-actions and to make use of his intentions alone, *in statu nascendi*, as material for the therapeutic work. One best protects the patient from disasters brought about by carrying his impulses into action by making him promise to form no important decisions affecting his life during the course of the treatment, for instance, choice of a profession or of a permanent love-object, but to postpone all such projects until after recovery.

At the same time one willingly accords the patient all the freedom that is compatible with these restrictions, nor does one hinder him from carrying out projects which, though foolish, are not of special significance; one remembers that it is only by dire experience that mankind ever learns sense. There are no doubt persons whom one cannot prevent from plunging into some quite undesirable project during the treatment and who become amenable and willing to submit the impulse to analysis only afterwards. Occasionally, too, it is bound to happen that the untamed instincts assert themselves before there is time for the curbing-rein of the transference to be placed on them, or that an act of reproduction causes the patient to break the bond that holds him to the treatment. As an extreme example of this, I might take the case of an elderly lady who had repeatedly fled from her house and her husband in a twilight state, and gone no one knew where, without having any idea of a motive for this "elopement." Her treatment with me began with a marked positive transference of affectionate feeling, which intensified itself with uncanny rapidity in the first few days, and by the end of a week she had "eloped" again from me, before I had time to say anything to her which might have prevented this repetition.

The main instrument, however, for curbing the patient's compulsion to repeat and for turning it into a motive for remembering consists in the handling of the transference. We render it harmless, and even make use of it, by according it the right to assert itself within certain limits. We admit it into the transference as to a playground, in which it is allowed to let itself go in almost complete freedom and is required to display before us all the pathogenic impulses hidden in the depths of the patient's mind. If the patient does but show compliance enough to respect the necessary conditions of the analysis we can regularly succeed in giving all the symptoms of the neurosis a new transference-colouring, and in replacing his whole ordinary neurosis by a "transference-neurosis" of which he can be cured by the therapeutic work. The transference thus forms a kind of intermediary realm between illness and real life, through which the journey from the one to the other must be made. The new state of mind has absorbed all the features of the illness; it represents, however, an artificial illness which is at every point accessible to our interventions. It is at the same time a piece of real life, but adapted to our purposes by specially favourable conditions, and it is of a provisional character. From the repetition-reactions which are exhibited in the transference the familiar paths lead back to the awakening of the memories, which yield themselves without difficulty after the resistances have been overcome.

I might break off at this point but for the title of this paper, which requires me to discuss a further point in analytic technique. The first step in overcoming the resistance is made, as we know, by the analyst's discovering the resistance, which is never recognized by the patient, and acquainting him with it. Now it seems that beginners in analytic practice are inclined to look upon this as the end of the work. I have often been asked to advise upon cases in which the physician complained that he had pointed out his resistance to the patient and that all the same no change had set in; in fact, the resistance had only then become really pronounced and the whole situation had become more obscure than ever. The treatment seemed to make no progress. This gloomy foreboding always proved mistaken. The treatment was as a rule progressing quite satisfactorily; only the analyst had forgotten that naming the resistance could not result in its immediate suspension. One must allow the patient time to get to know this resistance of which he is ignorant, to "work through" it, to overcome it, by continuing the work according to the analytic rule in defiance of it. Only when it has come to its height can one, with the patient's co-operation, discover the repressed instinctual trends which are feeding the resistance; and only by living them through in this way will the patient be convinced of their existence and their power. The physician has nothing more to do than to wait and let things take their course, a course which cannot be avoided nor always be hastened. If he holds fast to this principle, he will often be spared the disappointment of failure in cases where all the time he has conducted the treatment quite correctly.

This "working through" of the resistances may in practice amount to an arduous task for the patient and a trial of patience for the analyst. Nevertheless, it is the part of the work that effects the greatest changes in the patient and that distinguishes analytic treatment from every kind of suggestive treatment. Theoretically one may correlate it with the "abreaction" of quantities of affect pent-up by repression, without which the hypnotic treatment remained ineffective.

XIII

Further Recommendations in the Technique of Psychoanalysis[1]
(1915)

OBSERVATIONS ON TRANSFERENCE-LOVE

Every beginner in psychoanalysis probably feels alarmed at first at the difficulties in store for him when he comes to interpret the patient's associations and deal with the reproduction of repressed material. When the time comes, however, he soon learns to look upon these difficulties as insignificant and instead becomes convinced that the only serious difficulties are encountered in handling the transference.

Among the situations to which the transference gives rise, one is very sharply outlined, and I will select this, partly because it occurs so often and is so important in reality and partly because of its theoretical interest. The case I mean is that in which a woman or girl patient shows by unmistakable allusions or openly avows that she has fallen in love, like any other mortal woman, with the physician who is analysing her.

[1] First published in *Zeitschrift*, Bd. III., 1915; reprinted in *Sammlung*, Vierte Folge. [Translated by Joan Riviere.]

This situation has its distressing and its comical aspects as well as its serious ones; it is so complicated, and conditioned by so many factors, so unavoidable and so difficult to dissolve, that discussion of it has long been a pressing need of analytic technique. But since those who mock at the failings of others are not always themselves free from them, we have hardly been inclined to rush in to the fulfilment of this task. The obligation of professional discretion, which cannot be disregarded in life but which is useless in our science, makes itself felt here again and again. In so far as psychoanalytical publications are a part of life, we have here an insoluble conflict. I have recently disregarded this matter of discretion for once[2] and shown how this same transference situation at first retarded the development of psychoanalytic therapy for ten years.

To a cultivated layman—and in their relation to psychoanalysis the attitude of such men is the best we encounter—matters concerned with love cannot be measured by the same standards as other things: it is as though they were written on a page by themselves which would not take any other script. If a patient falls in love with her doctor, then, such a man will think only two outcomes are possible—one comparatively rare, in which all the circumstances allow of a permanent legal union between them, and the other much commoner, in which physician and patient part, and abandon the work begun which should have led to her recovery, as though it had been prevented by some elemental phenomenon. There is certainly a third conceivable way out, which even appears compatible with continuing the treatment, and that is a love-relationship between them of an illicit character, not intended to last permanently; but both conventional morality and professional dignity surely make this impossible. In any event our layman would beg the analyst to reassure him as unambiguously as possible that this third alternative is out of the question.

It is clear that the analyst's point of view must be different from this.

---

[2] "On the History of the Psychoanalytic Movement" (1914). [Collier Books edition AS 580V.]

Let us take the case of the second possible alternative. After the patient has fallen in love with the physician, they part; the treatment is given up. But very soon the patient's condition necessitates her making another attempt at cure with another physician; the next thing that happens is that she feels she has fallen in love with the second physician, and just the same again when she had broken off and begun again with a third, and so on. This phenomenon, which occurs with such regularity and is one of the foundations of psychoanalytical theory, may be regarded from two points of view, that of the physician analysing and that of the patient in need of analysis.

To the physician it represents an invaluable explanation and a useful warning against any tendency to counter-transference which may be lurking in his own mind. He must recognize that the patient's falling in love is induced by the analytic situation and is not to be ascribed to the charms of his person, that he has no reason whatever therefore to be proud of such a "conquest," as it would be called outside analysis. And it is always well to be reminded of this. For the patient, however, there are two alternatives: either she must abandon her analytic treatment or she must make up her mind to being in love with physicians as to an inevitable destiny.[3]

I have no doubt that the patient's relatives and friends would decide as emphatically in favour of the first of the two alternatives as the analyst would for the second. In my opinion, however, this is a case in which the decision cannot be left to the tender—or rather, the jealous egoistic—mercies of the relatives and friends. The patient's welfare alone should decide. The love of her relatives cannot cure her neurosis. It is not necessary for the psychoanalyst to force himself upon anyone, but he may take up the stand that for certain purposes he is indispensable. Anyone who takes up Tolstoy's attitude to this problem can remain in undisputed possession of his wife or daughter, but must try to put up with her retaining

---

[3] We know that the transference can express itself by other less tender feelings, but I do not propose to go into that side of the matter here.

her neurosis and with the disturbance it involves in her capacity for love. After all, it is the same situation as that of a gynecological treatment. Incidentally, the jealous father or husband makes a great mistake if he thinks the patient will escape falling in love with the physician if he hands her over to some other kind of treatment than that of analysis in order to get rid of her neurosis. The difference will be, on the contrary, that her falling in love in a way which is bound to remain unexpressed and unanalysed can never render that aid to her recovery which analysis would have extracted from it.

It has come to my knowledge that certain physicians who practise analysis frequently prepare their patients for the advent of a love-transference or even instruct them to "go ahead and fall in love with the analyst so that the treatment may make progress." I can hardly imagine a more nonsensical proceeding. It robs the phenomenon itself of the element of spontaneity which is so convincing and it lays up obstacles ahead which are extremely difficult to overcome.

At the first glance it certainly does not look as if any advantage to the treatment could result from the patient's falling in love in the transference. No matter how amenable she has been up till then, she now suddenly loses all understanding of and interest in the treatment, and will not hear or speak of anything but her love, the return of which she demands; she has either given up her symptoms or else she ignores them; she even declares herself well. A complete transformation ensues in the scene—it is as though some make-believe had been interrupted by a real emergency, just as when the cry of fire is raised in a theatre. Any physician experiencing this for the first time will not find it easy to keep a grasp of the analytic situation and not to succumb to the illusion that the treatment is really at an end.

On reflection one realizes the true state of things. One remembers above all the suspicion that everything impeding the progress of the treatment may be an expression of resistance. It certainly plays a great part in the outbreak of passionate demands for love. One has long noticed in the patient the signs of an affectionate transference on to the physician and could with certainty ascribe to this attitude her docility, her acceptance of the analytic explanations, her remarkable comprehension and the high degree of intelligence which she displayed during this period. This is now all swept away; she has become completely lacking in understanding and seems to be swallowed up in her love; and this change always came over her just as one had to bring her to the point of confessing or remembering one of the particularly painful or heavily repressed vicissitudes in her life-history. She had been in love, that is to say, for a long time; but now the resistance is beginning to make use of it in order to hinder the progress of the treatment, to distract her interest from the work and to put the analyst into a painful and embarrassing position.

If one looks into the situation more closely one can recognize that more complicated motives are also at work, of which some are connected with the falling in love, and others are particular expressions of resistance. To the first belong the patient's efforts to re-assure herself of her irresistibility, to destroy the physician's authority by bringing him down to the level of a lover, and to gain all the other advantages which she foresees as incidental to gratification of her love. With regard to the resistance, one may presume that at times it uses the declarations of love as a test for the strait-laced analyst, so that compliance on his part would call down on him a reprimand. But above all one obtains the impression that the resistance acts as an *agent provocateur*, intensifying the love of the patient and exaggerating her readiness for the sexual surrender, in order thereby to vindicate the action of her repression more emphatically by pointing to the dangers of such licentiousness. All this by-play, which in less complicated cases may not be present at all, has as we know been regarded by A. Adler as the essential element in the whole process.

But how is the analyst to behave in this situation if he is not to come to grief and yet believes that the treatment should be continued through this love-transference and in spite of it?

It would be very simple for me now, on the score of conventional morality, emphatically to insist that the analyst must never in any circumstances accept or return the tender passion proffered him—that instead he must watch for his chance to urge the infatuated woman to take the moral path and see the necessity of renunciation, and induce her to overcome the animal side of her nature and subdue her passion, so as to continue the analytic work.

I shall not fulfil these expectations, however—neither the first nor the second. Not the first, because I am writing not for patients, but for physicians who have serious difficulties to contend with, and also because in this instance I can go behind moral prescriptions to the source of them, namely, to utility. I am on this occasion in the happy position of being able to put the requirements of analytic technique in the place of a moral decree without any alteration in the results.

Even more emphatically, however, do I decline to fulfil the second of the expectations suggested above. To urge the patient to suppress, to renounce and to sublimate the promptings of her instincts, as soon as she has confessed her love-transference, would be not an analytic way of dealing with them, but a senseless way. It would be the same thing as to conjure up a spirit from the underworld by means of a crafty spell and then to dispatch him back again without a question. One would have brought the repressed impulses out into consciousness only in terror to send them back into repression once more. Nor should one deceive oneself about the success of any such proceeding. When levelled at the passions, lofty language achieves very little, as we all know. The patient will only feel the humiliation, and will not fail to revenge herself for it.

Just as little can I advocate a middle course which would recommend itself to some as especially ingenious; this would consist in averring one's response to the patient's feelings of affection, but in refraining from all the physical accompaniments of these tender feelings, until one could guide the situation along calmer channels and raise it on to a higher level. Against this expedient I have to object that the psychoanalytic treatment is founded on truthfulness. A great part of its educative effect and its ethical value lies in this very fact. It is dangerous to depart from this sure foundation. When a man's life has become bound up with the analytic technique, he finds himself at a loss altogether for the lies and the guile which are otherwise so indispensable to a physician, and if for once with the best intentions he attempts to use them he is likely to betray himself. Since we demand strict truthfulness from our patients, we jeopardize our whole authority if we let ourselves be caught by them in a departure from the truth. And besides, this experimental adoption of tender feeling for the patient is by no means without danger. One cannot keep such complete control of oneself as not one day suddenly to go further than was intended. In my opinion, therefore, it is not permissible to disavow the indifference one has developed by keeping the counter-transference in check.

I have already let it be seen that the analytic technique requires the physician to deny the patient who is longing for love the satisfaction she craves. The treatment must be carried through in a state of abstinence; I do not mean merely corporal abstinence, nor yet deprivation of everything desired, for this could perhaps not be tolerated by any sick person. But I would state as a fundamental principle that the patient's desire and longing are to be allowed to remain, to serve as driving forces for the work and for the changes to be wrought, and that one must beware of granting this source of strength some discharge by surrogates. Indeed, one could not offer the patient anything but surrogates, for until the repressions are lifted her condition makes her incapable of true satisfaction.

Let us admit that this principle—of carrying through the analytic treatment in a state of renunciation—extends far beyond the case we are discussing, and that it needs close consideration in order to define the limits of its possible application. But we will refrain from going into this question now and will keep as closely as possible to the situation we started from. What would happen if the physician were to behave differently, and avail himself of a freedom perhaps available to them both to return the love of the patient and to appease her longing for tenderness from him?

If he had been guided in his decision by the argument that compliance on his part would strengthen his power over the patient so that he could influence her to perform the tasks required by the treatment, that is, could achieve a permanent cure of her neurosis by this means, experience would teach him that he had miscalculated. The patient would achieve her aim, but he would never achieve his. There is an amusing story about a pastor and an insurance agent which describes what would happen. An ungodly insurance agent lay at the point of death and his relatives fetched the holy man to convert him before he died. The interview lasted so long that those outside began to have some hope. At last the door of the sick chamber opened. The free-thinker had not been converted—but the pastor went away insured.

If her advances were returned, it would be a great triumph for the patient, but a complete overthrow for the cure. She would have succeeded in what all patients struggle for, in expressing in action, in reproducing in real life, what she ought only to remember, to reproduce as the content of her mind and to retain within the mental sphere.[4] In the further course of the love-relationship all the inhibitions and pathological reactions of her love-development would come out, yet there would be no possibility of correcting them, and the painful episode would end in remorse and a strengthening of her tendency to repression. The love-relationship actually destroys the influence of the analytic treatment on the patient; a combination of the two would be an inconceivable thing.

It is therefore just as disastrous for the analysis if the patient's craving for love prevails as if it is suppressed. The way the analyst must take is neither of these; it is one for which there is no prototype in real life. He must guard against ignoring the transference-love, scaring it away or making the patient disgusted with it; and just as resolutely must he withhold any response to it. He must face the transference-love boldly but treat it like something unreal, as a condition which must be gone through during the treatment and traced back to its unconscious origins, so that it shall assist in bringing to light all that is most hidden in the development of the patient's erotic life, and help her to learn to control it. The more plainly the analyst lets it be seen that he is proof against every temptation, the sooner will the advantage from the sit-

4 Cf. pp. 114 and 160 et seq.

uation accrue to the analysis. The patient, whose sexual repressions are of course not yet removed but merely pushed
into the background, will then feel safe enough to allow all
her conditions for loving, all the phantasies of her sexual desires, all the individual details of her way of being in love to
come to light, and then will herself open up the way back
from them to the infantile roots of her love.

With one type of woman, to be sure, this attempt to preserve the love-transference for the purposes of analytic work
without gratifying it will not succeed. These are women of an
elemental passionateness; they tolerate no surrogates; they
are children of nature who refuse to accept the spiritual instead of the material; to use the poet's words, they are amenable only to the "logic of gruel and the argument of dump-
lings." With such people one has the choice: either to return
their love or else to bring down upon oneself the full force
of the mortified woman's fury. In neither event can one safe-
guard the interests of the treatment. One must acknowledge
failure and withdraw; and may at leisure study the problem
how the capacity for neurosis can be combined with such an
intractable craving for love.

Many analysts must have discovered the way in which
other women, less violent in their love, can be brought round
gradually to the analytic point of view. Above all, the unmistakable element of resistance in their "love" must be insisted upon. Genuine love would make the patient docile and
intensify her readiness to solve the problems of her case,
simply because the man she loved expected it. A woman who
was really in love would gladly choose the road to completion
of the cure, in order to give herself a value in the physician's
eyes and to prepare herself for real life where her feelings of
love could find their proper outlet. Instead of this, she is
showing a stubborn and rebellious spirit, has thrown up all
interest in her treatment, and clearly too all respect for the
physician's well-founded judgement. She is bringing out a resistance, therefore, under the guise of being in love; and in
addition to this, she has no compunction about trying to lead
him into a cleft stick. For if he refuses her love, as duty and
his understanding compel him to do, she can take up the atti-

tude that she has been humiliated and, out of revenge and resentment, make herself inaccessible to cure by him, just as she is now doing ostensibly out of love.

As a second argument against the genuineness of this love one advances the fact that it shows not a single new feature connecting it with the present situation, but is entirely composed of repetitions and *"rechauffés"* of earlier reactions, including childish ones. One then sets about proving this by detailed analysis of the patient's behaviour in love.

When the necessary amount of patience is added to these arguments it is usually possible to overcome the difficult situation and to continue the work, the patient having either moderated her love or transformed it; the aim of the work then becomes the discovery of the infantile object-choice and of the phantasies woven round it. I will now, however, examine these arguments critically and put the question whether they really represent the truth or whether by employing them we are not in our desperation resorting to prevarication and misrepresentation. In other words: can the love which is manifested in analytic treatment not truly be called real?

I think that we have told the patient the truth, but not the whole truth without regard for consequences. Of our two arguments the first is the stronger. The part taken by resistance in the transference-love is unquestionable and very considerable. But this love was not created by the resistance; the latter finds it ready to hand, exploits it and aggravates the manifestations of it. Nor is its genuineness impugned by the resistance. The second argument is far weaker; it is true that the love consists of new editions of old traces and that it repeats infantile reactions. But this is the essential character of every love. There is no love that does not reproduce infantile prototypes. The infantile conditioning factor in it is just what gives it its compulsive character which verges on the pathological. The transference-love has perhaps a degree less of freedom than the love which appears in ordinary life and is called normal; it displays its dependence on the infantile pattern more clearly, is less adaptable and capable of modification, but that is all and that is nothing essential.

By what other signs can the genuineness of a love be recognized? By its power to achieve results, its capacity to accomplish its aim? In this respect the transference-love seems to give place to none; one has the impression that one could achieve anything by its means.

Let us resume, therefore: One has no right to dispute the "genuine" nature of the love which makes its appearance in the course of analytic treatment. However lacking in normality it may seem to be, this quality is sufficiently explained when we remember that the condition of being in love in ordinary life outside analysis is also more like abnormal than normal mental phenomena. The transference-love is characterized, nevertheless, by certain features which ensure it a special position. In the first place, it is provoked by the analytic situation; secondly, it is greatly intensified by the resistance which dominates this situation; and thirdly, it is to a high degree lacking in regard for reality, is less sensible, less concerned about consequences, more blind in its estimation of the person loved, than we are willing to admit of normal love. We should not forget, however, that it is precisely these departures from the norm that make up the essential element in the condition of being in love.

The first of these three characteristics of the transference-love is what determines the physician's course of action. He has evoked this love by undertaking analytic treatment in order to cure the neurosis; for him it is an unavoidable consequence of the medical situation, as inevitable as the exposure of a patient's body or being told some life-and-death secret. It is therefore plain to him that he is not to derive any personal advantage from it. The patient's willingness makes no difference whatever; it merely throws the whole responsibility on him. Indeed, as he must know, the patient had from the beginning entertained hopes of this way of being cured. After all the difficulties are overcome she will often confess to a phantasy, an expectation that she had had as she began the treatment—"if she behaved well, she would be rewarded in the end by the doctor's love for her."

For the physician there are ethical motives which combine with the technical reasons to hinder him from according the patient his love. The aim that he has to keep in view is that this woman, whose capacity for love is disabled by infantile fixations, should attain complete access over this function which is so inestimably important for her in life, not that she should fritter it away in the treatment, but preserve it for real life, if so be that after her cure life makes that demand on her. He must not let the scene of the race between the dogs be enacted, in which the prize was a chaplet of sausages and which a funny fellow spoilt by throwing one sausage on to the course; the dogs fell upon it and forgot about the race and the chaplet in the distance luring them on to win. I do not mean to say that it is always easy for the physician to keep within the bounds prescribed by technique and ethics. Younger men especially, who are not yet bound by a permanent tie, may find it a hard task. The love between the sexes is undoubtedly one of the first things in life, and the combination of mental and bodily satisfaction attained in the enjoyment of love is literally one of life's culminations. Apart from a few perverse fanatics, all the world knows this and conducts life accordingly; only science is too refined to confess it. Again, when a woman sues for love, to reject and refuse is a painful part for a man to play; and in spite of neurosis and resistance there is an incomparable fascination about a noble woman who confesses her passion. It is not the grossly sensual desires of the patient that constitute the temptation. These are more likely to repel and to demand the exercise of toleration in order to regard them as a natural phenomenon. It is perhaps the finer impulses, those "inhibited in their aim," which lead a man into the danger of forgetting the rules of technique and the physician's task for the sake of a wonderful experience.

And yet the analyst is absolutely debarred from giving way. However highly he may prize love, he must prize even more highly the opportunity to help his patient over a decisive moment in her life. She has to learn from him to overcome the pleasure-principle, to give up a gratification which lies to hand but is not sanctioned by the world she lives in, in favour of a distant and perhaps altogether doubtful one, which is, however, socially and psychologically unimpeachable. To achieve this mastery of herself she must be taken through the primordial era of her mental development and in this way reach that greater freedom within the mind which distinguishes conscious mental activity—in the systematic sense—from unconscious.

The analytic psychotherapist thus has a threefold battle to wage—in his own mind against the forces which would draw him down below the level of analysis; outside analysis against the opponents who dispute the importance he attaches to the sexual instinctual forces and hinder him from making use of them in his scientific method; and in the analysis against his patients, who at first behave like his critics but later on disclose the over-estimation of sexual life which has them in thrall, and who try to take him captive in the net of their socially ungovernable passions.

The lay public, of whose attitude to psychoanalysis I spoke at the outset, will certainly seize the opportunity given it by this discussion of the transference-love to direct the attention of the world to the dangers of this therapeutic method. The psychoanalyst knows that the forces he works with are of the most explosive kind and that he needs as much caution and conscientiousness as a chemist. But when has it ever been forbidden to a chemist, on account of its danger, to occupy himself with the explosives which, just because of their effectiveness, are so indispensable? It is remarkable that psychoanalysis has to win for itself afresh all the liberties which have long been accorded to other medical work. I certainly do not advocate that the harmless methods of treatment should be abandoned. For many cases they suffice, and when all is said, the *furor sanandi* is no more use to human society than any other kind of fanaticism. But it is grossly to undervalue both the origins and the practical significance of the psychoneuroses to suppose that these disorders are to be removed by pottering about with a few harmless remedies. No; in medical practice there will always be room for the "*ferrum*" and the "*ignis*" as well as for the "*medicina*," and there a strictly regular, unmodified psychoanalysis, which is not afraid to handle the most dangerous forces in the mind and set them to work for the benefit of the patient, will be found indispensable.

XIV

Turnings in the Ways of Psychoanalytic
Therapy[1]
(1919)

You know that we have never been proud of the fullness and
finality of our knowledge and our capacity; as at the beginning, we are ready now to admit the incompleteness of our
understanding, to learn new things and to alter our methods in
any way that yields better results.

Now that we are met together once more after the long and
difficult years of separation we have lived through, I feel
drawn to review the position of our therapy, for to it indeed
we owe our position, and to take a survey of the new directions in which it may develop.

We have formulated our therapeutic task as one of bringing
to the knowledge of the patient the unconscious, repressed
impulses existing in his mind and, to this end, of uncovering
the resistances that oppose themselves to this extension of his

[1] Address delivered before the Fifth International Psychoanalyti-
cal Congress, in Budapest, September 1918. First published in
Zeitschrift, Bd. V., 1919; reprinted in *Sammlung*, Fünfte Folge.
[Translated by Joan Riviere.]

182   THERAPY AND TECHNIQUE

knowledge about himself. Now when we speak of uncovering
these resistances, do we also mean that they are thereby
overcome? Certainly not always; but our hope is to achieve
this by exploiting the patient's transference to the person of
the physician, so as to induce him to adopt our conviction
of the inexpediency of the repressive processes established in
childhood and of the impossibility of conducting life on the
pleasure-principle. I have expounded elsewhere[2] the dynamic
conditions in the new conflict we lead the patient through,
which we have substituted in him for the previous conflict of
his illness. I know of nothing there to alter at present.

The work by which we bring the repressed material in his
mind into the patient's consciousness has been called by us
psychoanalysis. Why "analysis," which means divellication and
dissection and, by analogy with the work of chemists, suggests the substances they find existing in nature and bring into
their laboratories? Because in an important respect there is
really an analogy between the two. The patient's symptoms
and pathological manifestations, like all his mental processes,
are of a very elaborately organized nature; their elements at
bottom consist of motives, of instinctual impulses. But the patient knows nothing of these elemental motives or not nearly
enough. Now we teach him to understand the structure of
these highly complicated formations in his mind; we trace the
symptoms back to the instinctual impulses which motivate
them; we point out to the patient these instinctual motives in
his symptoms of which he has hitherto been unaware—just
as a chemist segregates the fundamental substance, the chemical "element," out of the salt in which it had been combined
with other elements and was thus unrecognizable. In the same
way with expressions of his personality that were not regarded
as pathological, we show the patient that he was only to a
certain extent conscious of their motivation, that other instinctual impulses of which he had remained in ignorance had
co-operated in forming them.

We have also thrown light on the sexual force in man, too,
by separating it into its component elements, and when we in-

2 [Cf. "The Dynamics of the Transference," supra, p. 105 —Trans.]

terpret a dream we proceed by ignoring the dream as a whole and instituting associations to its single elements.

Now this well-founded comparison of the psychoanalytic medical procedure with a chemical procedure might suggest a new direction for our therapy. We have *analysed* the patient, *i.e.* separated his mental processes into their constituent parts and demonstrated these instinctual elements in him singly and in isolation; what could be more natural than a request that we should also help him to make a new and a better re-combination of them? You know that this demand has actually been put forward. We have heard that after the analysis of the diseased mental organism a synthesis of it must follow! And, close upon this, concern was expressed that the patient might be given too much analysis and too little synthesis; and then there followed a move to put all the weight on this synthesis as the main factor in the psychotherapeutic effect— seeing in it a kind of revivification of something destroyed by vivisection.

I cannot imagine, however, that any new task for us is to be found in this psychosynthesis. If I were to permit myself to be honest and uncivil I should say it was nothing but a meaningless phrase. I will limit myself to remarking that it is only pushing a comparison so far that it ceases to have any foundation, or, if you prefer, that it is an unjustifiable exploitation of a name. A name, however, is only a label applied to it to distinguish a thing from other similar things, not a syllabus, a description of its content or a definition. And the two objects in a comparison need only touch at a single point and may be entirely different from each other in all else. The life of the mind is a thing so unique and peculiar to itself that no one comparison can reflect its nature. The work of psychoanalysis suggests analogies with chemical analysis, but just as much with the incursions of the surgeon or the manipulations of the orthopaedist or the influence of the pedagogue. The comparison with chemical analysis has its limits, in this way: in mental life we have to deal with forces that are under a compulsion towards unification and combination. When we succeed in dissolving a symptom into its elements, in freeing an instinct from one concatenation, it does not remain in isolation, but immediately enters into combination again with something else.[3]

On the contrary, indeed! The neurotic human being brings us his mind racked and rent by resistances; whilst we are working at analysis of it and at removing the resistances, this mind of his begins to grow together; that great unity which we call his ego fuses into one all the instinctual trends which before had been split off and barred away from it. The psychosynthesis is thus achieved during analytic treatment without our intervention, automatically and inevitably. We have created the conditions for it by dissolving the symptoms into their elements and by removing the resistances. There is no truth in the idea that when the patient's mind is dissolved into its elements it then quietly waits until somebody puts it together again.

Developments in our therapy will surely proceed in a different direction, therefore; above all, in that which Ferenczi[4] has lately characterized as "activity" on the part of the analyst.

Let us hasten to agree upon what we mean by this activity. We defined our therapeutic task as consisting of two things: making conscious the repressed material and uncovering the resistances. In that we are active enough, to be sure. But are we to leave it to the patient to deal alone with the resistances we have pointed out to him? Can we give him no other help in this besides the stimulus he gets from the transference? Does it not seem natural that we should help him also in another way, by putting him into the mental situation most favourable to solution of the conflict, which is our aim? After all, what he can achieve depends partly on a number of external circumstances which converge in their influence on him. Should we hesitate to alter this combination by intervening

[3] Even in chemical analysis something very similar occurs. Simultaneously with the isolation of the various elements, which the chemist forces upon them, syntheses which are no part of his intention come into existence, owing to the liberation of the elective affinities in their substances.

[4] Ferenczi, *Technische Schwierigkeiten einer Hysterieanalyse.*

in a suitable manner? I think activity of such a kind on the part of the physician analysing is unobjectionable and entirely justifiable.

You observe that this opens up a new vein in analytic technique, which will require close application in order to work it out and which will yield very definite rules. I shall not attempt to introduce you to-day to this new technique which is still being evolved, but will content myself with enunciating a fundamental principle which will probably be the guiding force in our work on this new problem. It runs as follows: *Analytic treatment should be carried through, as far as is possible, under privation—in a state of abstinence.*

How far it is possible to determine this must be left for more detailed discussion. By abstinence, however, is not to be understood doing without any and every satisfaction—that would of course not be practicable; nor do we mean what it popularly connotes, refraining from sexual intercourse; it means something else which has far more to do with the dynamics of illness and recovery.

You will remember that it was a *frustration* that made the patient ill, and that his symptoms serve him as substitutive gratifications. It is possible to observe during the treatment that every improvement in his condition reduces the rate at which he recovers and diminishes the instinctual energy impelling him towards cure. But this instinctual propelling force is indispensable for cure; reduction of it endangers our aim, the patient's restoration to health. What is the conclusion that forces itself inevitably upon us? Harsh though it may sound, we must see to it that the patient's sufferings, to a degree that is in some way or other effective, do not prematurely come to an end. When the symptoms have been dissected and the value of them thus discounted, his sufferings become moderated, and then we must set up a sufficiently distressing privation again in some other sensitive spot, or else we run the risk of never achieving any further improvement except quite insignificant and transitory ones.

As far as I can see, danger threatens from two directions. On the one hand, when the illness has been broken down by the analysis the patient applies his most assiduous endeavours to creating for himself in place of his symptoms new substitutive gratifications, now lacking in the feature of suffering. He makes use of the colossal capacity for displacement in the libido that is now partly liberated, in order to invest with libido and promote to the position of substitutive gratifications the most diverse kinds of activities, pleasures, interests, habits, including those that he already possessed. He continually finds new distractions of this kind, into which the energy necessary to complete the cure escapes, and he knows how to keep them secret for a time. It is the analyst's task to detect these by-paths and to require him every time to abandon them, however harmless the performance which leads to satisfaction may be in itself. The half-cured person may also undertake escapades that are not so harmless, as when, for instance, if he is a man, he seeks prematurely to bind himself to a woman. It may be observed, incidentally, that unhappy marriage and bodily infirmity are the two things that most often dissolve a neurosis. They both gratify especially the sense of guilt (need for punishment) which binds many neurotics so fast to their neuroses. By a foolish choice in marriage they punish themselves; a long organic illness they regard as a punishment by fate and then often cease to keep up their neurosis.

In all such situations activity on the part of the physician must take the form of energetic opposition to premature substitutive gratifications. It is easier for him, however, to prevent the second danger, one not to be under-estimated, which jeopardizes the propelling forces of the analysis. The patient looks for his substitutive gratification above all in the treatment itself, in his transference-relationship with the physician, and he may even strive to compensate himself through this means for all the other privations laid upon him. A certain amount must of course be permitted to him, more or less according to the nature of the case and the patient's individuality. But it is not good to let it become too much. Any analyst who out of the fullness of his heart and his readiness to help perhaps extends to the patient all that one human being may hope to receive from another, commits the same economic error which our non-analytic institutions for nerv-ous patients are guilty of. They exert themselves only to make everything as pleasant as possible for the patient, so that he may feel well there and gladly take flight back there again away from the trials of life. In so doing they entirely forgo making him stronger for life and more capable of car-rying out the actual tasks of his life. In analytic treatment all such cosseting must be avoided. As far as his relations with the physician are concerned, the patient must have unfulfilled wishes in abundance. It is expedient to deny him precisely those satisfactions which he desires most intensely and ex-presses most importunately.

I do not think I have exhausted the range of useful activ-ity on the part of the physician with the statement that a con-dition of privation is to be kept up during the treatment. Ac-tivity in another direction during analytic treatment has already, as you will remember, been a point at issue between us and the Swiss school. We rejected most emphatically the view that we should convert into our own property the pa-tient who puts himself into our hands in seek of help, should carve his destiny for him, force our own ideals upon him, and with the arrogance of a Creator form him in our own image and see that it was good. I still to-day maintain this attitude of rejection, and I think that this is the place for that medical discretion which we have had to ignore in other connections; I have learnt, too, that such a far-reaching activity towards patients is not at all requisite for therapeutic aims. For I have been able, without affecting their individuality, to help people with whom I had nothing in common, neither national-ity, education, social position nor outlook upon life in general. At the time of the controversy I spoke of, I had the impres-sion, to be sure, that the objections of our spokesmen—I think it was Ernest Jones who took the chief part—were too harsh and uncompromising. We cannot avoid also taking for treatment patients who are so helpless and incapable of or-dinary life that for them one has to combine analytic with educative influence; and even with the majority now and then occasions arise in which the physician is bound to take up the position of teacher and mentor. But it must always be done with great caution, and the patient should be educated to liberate and fulfil his own nature, and not to resemble ourselves.

Our honoured friend, J. J. Putnam, in the land of America which is now so hostile to us, must forgive us if we cannot accept his proposal either, namely, that psychoanalysis should place itself in the service of a particular philosophical outlook on the world and should urge this upon the patient in order to ennoble him. I would say that after all this is only tyranny, even though disguised by the most honourable motives.

Lastly, another quite different kind of activity is necessitated by the gradually growing appreciation that the various forms of disease treated by us cannot all be dealt with by the same technique. It would be premature to discuss this in detail, but I can give two examples of the way in which a new kind of activity comes into question. Our technique grew up in the treatment of hysteria and is still directed principally to the cure of this affection. But the phobias have already made it necessary for us to go beyond our former limits. One can hardly ever master a phobia if one waits till the patient lets the analysis influence him to give it up. He will never in that case bring for the analysis the material indispensable for a convincing solution of the phobia. One must proceed differently. Take the example of agoraphobia; there are two classes of it, one slight and the other severe. Patients belonging to the first indeed suffer from anxiety when they go about alone, but they have not yet given up going out alone on that account; the others protect themselves from the anxiety by altogether giving up going about alone. With these last one succeeds only when one can induce them through the influence of the analysis to behave like the first class, that is, to go about alone and to struggle with their anxiety while they make the attempt. One first achieves, therefore, a considerable moderation of the phobia, and it is only when this has been attained by the physician's recommendation that the associations and memories come into the patient's mind enabling the phobia to be solved.

In severe cases of obsessive acts a passive waiting attitude seems even less well adapted; indeed in general these cases incline to favour an asymptomatic process of cure, an interminable protraction of the treatment; in their analysis there is always the danger of a great deal coming to light without its effecting any change in them. I think there is little doubt that here the correct technique can only be to wait until the treatment itself has become a compulsion, and then with this counter-compulsion forcibly to suppress the compulsion of the disease. You will understand, however, that these two instances I have given you are only samples of the new developments towards which our therapy is tending.

And now in conclusion I will cast a glance at a situation which belongs to the future—one that will seem fantastic to many of you, but which I think, nevertheless, deserves that we should be prepared for it in our minds. You know that the therapeutic effects we can achieve are very inconsiderable in number. We are but a handful of people, and even by working hard each one of us can deal in a year with only a small number of persons. Against the vast amount of neurotic misery which is in the world, and perhaps need not be, the quantity we can do away with is almost negligible. Besides this, the necessities of our own existence limit our work to the well-to-do classes, accustomed to choose their own physicians, whose choice is diverted away from psychoanalysis by all kinds of prejudices. At present we can do nothing in the crowded ranks of the people, who suffer exceedingly from neuroses.

Now let us assume that by some kind of organization we were able to increase our numbers to an extent sufficient for treating large masses of people. Then on the other hand, one may reasonably expect that at some time or other the conscience of the community will awake and admonish it that the poor man has just as much right to help for his mind as he now has to the surgeon's means of saving life; and that the neuroses menace the health of a people no less than tuberculosis, and can be left as little as the latter to the feeble handling of individuals. Then clinics and consultation-departments will be built, to which analytically trained physicians will be appointed, so that the men who would otherwise give way to drink, the women who have nearly succumbed under their

190

burden of privations, the children for whom there is no choice
but running wild or neurosis, may be made by analysis able to
resist and able to do something in the world. This treatment
will be free. It may be a long time before the State regards
this as an urgent duty. Present conditions may delay its ar-
rival even longer; probably these institutions will first be
started by private beneficence; some time or other, however,
it must come.

The task will then arise for us to adapt our technique to
the new conditions. I have no doubt that the validity of our
psychological assumptions will impress the uneducated too,
but we shall need to find the simplest and most natural expression for our theoretical doctrines. We shall probably discover that the poor are even less ready to part with their
neuroses than the rich, because the hard life that awaits them
when they recover has no attraction, and illness in them
gives them more claim to the help of others. Possibly we
may often only be able to achieve something if we combine
aid for the mind with some material support, in the manner
of Emperor Joseph. It is very probable, too, that the application of our therapy to numbers will compel us to alloy the
pure gold of analysis plentifully with the copper of direct suggestion; and even hypnotic influence might find a place in it
again, as it has in the treatment of war-neuroses. But whatever
form this psychotherapy for the people may take, whatever
the elements out of which it is compounded, its most effective
and most important ingredients will assuredly remain those
borrowed from strict psychoanalysis which serves no ulterior
purpose.

XV

A Note on the Prehistory of the Technique of Analysis[1]
(1920)

A recent book by Havelock Ellis (so justly admired for his researches into sexual science, and an eminent critic of psychoanalysis), which bears the title of *The Philosophy of Conflict* (1919), includes an essay on "Psychoanalysis in Relation to Sex." The aim of this essay is to show that the writings of the creator of analysis should be judged not as a piece of scientific work but as an artistic production. We cannot but regard this view as a fresh turn taken by resistance and as a repudiation of analysis, even though it is disguised in a friendly, indeed in too flattering a manner. We are inclined to meet it with a most decided contradiction.

It is not, however, with a view to contradicting him on this point that we are now concerned with Havelock Ellis's essay, but for another reason. His wide reading has enabled

---

[1] ["Zur Vorgeschichte der analytischen Technik." First published anonymously, over the signature "F," *Int. Z. Psychoanal.*, 6 (1920), 79; reprinted *Ges. Schr.*, 6, 148, and *Ges. W.*, 12, 309. Translation by James Strachey.]

him to bring forward an author who practised and recommended free association as a technique, though for purposes other than ours, and thus has a claim to be regarded as a forerunner of psychoanalysis.

In 1857, Dr. J. J. Garth Wilkinson, more noted as a Swedenborgian mystic and poet than as a physician, published a volume of mystic doggerel verse written by what he considered "a new method," the method of "Impression." "A theme is chosen or written down," he stated; "as soon as this is done the first impression upon the mind which succeeds the act of writing the title is the beginning of the evolution of that theme, no matter how strange or alien the word or phrase may seem." "The first mental movement, the first word that comes" is "the response to the mind's desire for the unfolding of the subject." It is continued by the same method, and Garth Wilkinson adds: "I have always found it lead by an infallible instinct into the subject." The method was, as Garth Wilkinson viewed it, a kind of exalted *laissez-faire*, a command to the deepest unconscious instincts to express themselves. Reason and will, he pointed out, are left aside; you trust to "an influx," and the faculties of the mind are "directed to ends they know not of." Garth Wilkinson, it must be clearly understood, although he was a physician, used this method for religious and literary, and never for scientific or medical ends; but it is easy to see that essentially it is the method of psychoanalysis applied to oneself, and it is further evidence how much Freud's method is an artist's method.

Those who are familiar with psychoanalytic literature will recall at this point the interesting passage in Schiller's correspondence with Körner[2] in which (1788) the great poet and thinker recommends anyone who desires to be productive to adopt the method of free association. It is to be suspected that what is alleged to be Garth Wilkinson's new technique had

---

[2] Pointed out by Otto Rank and quoted in my *Interpretation of Dreams* (1900) [English translation, revised ed. (1932), 111-12].

already occurred to the minds of many others and that its systematic application in psychoanalysis is not evidence so much of Freud's artistic nature as of his conviction, amounting almost to a prejudice, that all mental events are completely determined. It followed from this view that the first and most likely possibility was that a free association would be related to the subject designated; and this was confirmed by experience in analysis except in so far as too great resistances made the suspected connection unrecognizable.

Meanwhile it is safe to assume that neither Schiller nor Garth Wilkinson had in fact any influence on the choice of psychoanalytic technique. It is from another direction that there are indications of a personal influence at work.

A short time ago in Budapest Dr. Hugo Dubowitz drew Dr. Ferenczi's attention to a short essay covering only four and a half pages, by Ludwig Börne. This was written in 1823 and was reprinted in the first volume of the 1862 edition of his collected works. It is entitled "The Art of Becoming an Original Writer in Three Days," and shows the familiar stylistic features of Jean Paul, of whom Börne was at that time a great admirer. He ends the essay with the following sentences:

> And here follows the practical application that was promised. Take a few sheets of paper and for three days on end write down, without fabrication or hypocrisy, everything that comes into your head. Write down what you think of yourself, of your wife, of the Turkish War, of Goethe, of Fonk's trial, of the Last Judgement, of your superiors—and when three days have passed you will be quite out of your senses with astonishment at the new and unheard-of thoughts you have had. This is the art of becoming an original writer in three days.

When Professor Freud came to read this essay of Börne's, he brought forward a number of facts that may have an important bearing on the question that is under discussion here as to the prehistory of the psychoanalytic use of free associations. He said that when he was fourteen he had been given

Börne's works as a present, that he still possessed the book now, fifty years later, and that it was the only one that had survived from his boyhood. Börne, he said, had been the first author into whose writings he had penetrated deeply. He could not remember the essay in question, but some of the others that were contained in the same volume—such as "A Tribute to the Memory of Jean Paul," "The Artist in Eating," and "The Fool at the White Swan Inn"—kept on recurring to his mind for no obvious reason over a long period of years. He was particularly astonished to find expressed in the advice to the original writer some opinions which he himself had always cherished and vindicated. For instance: "A disgraceful cowardliness in regard to thinking holds us all back. The censorship of governments is less oppressive than the censorship exercised by public opinion over our intellectual productions." (Moreover there is a reference here to a "censorship," which reappears in psychoanalysis as the dream-censorship.) "It is not lack of intellect but lack of character that prevents most writers from being better than they are. . . . Sincerity is the source of all genius, and men would be cleverer if they were more moral. . . ."

Thus it seems not impossible that this hint may have brought to light the fragment of cryptomnesia which in so many cases may be suspected to lie behind apparent originality.

XVI

A Dream which Bore Testimony[1]
(1913)

A lady suffering from doubting mania and obsessive ceremonials made a rule that her nurses should never let her out of sight for a single moment: otherwise she would begin to brood about forbidden actions that she might conceivably have committed during this relaxation of vigilance. One evening whilst resting on the sofa she thought she saw that the nurse on duty had fallen asleep. On calling out, "Have you seen me?" the latter started up and replied, "Of course I have." This aroused a fresh doubt in the patient's mind, and after a time she repeated her question, which the nurse met with renewed protestations; just at that moment a maidservant came in bringing the patient's supper.

This incident occurred one Friday evening. Next morning the nurse recounted a dream which had the effect of dispelling the patient's doubt.

Dream: *Some one entrusted a child to her whilst the mother was absent on a journey and she had lost it. Going along the street, she inquired from various people whether they had seen the child. Then she came to a large expanse of water and*

1 First published in the *Zeitschrift*, Bd. I., 1913; reprinted in *Sammlung*, Vierte Folge. [Translated by Edward Glover.]

crossed a narrow bridge. (Supplementing this later: *Suddenly there appeared before her on this bridge, like a* fata Morgana, *the figure of another nurse.*) *Then she found herself in some familiar place where she met a woman she had known as a girl: the latter had in those days been saleswoman in a provision-shop and later had got married. She was standing in front of her door and the dreamer asked her, "Have you seen the child?" The woman paid no attention to the question but informed her that she had been divorced, adding that even marriage is not always happy. She woke up feeling reassured and thought: the child will turn up in a neighbour's house.*

Analysis: The patient concluded that this dream was connected with the incident of falling asleep which the nurse had denied; from additional information volunteered by the latter she was able to interpret the dream in a fashion which, although incomplete in many respects, was sufficient for all practical purposes. For myself, not having interviewed the nurse, I have only the lady's report to go on; first of all I shall quote the patient's interpretation, supplementing this afterwards as far as possible from our general understanding of the laws governing dream-formation.

"Nurse told me that the child in the dream reminded her of a case the treatment of which had given her the most lively satisfaction. It was that of a child who was unable to see on account of inflammation of the eyes (blennorrhoea). The mother, however, was not away: she helped to look after the child. On the other hand, I know that my husband thinks highly of this nurse; when he went away he left me in her care and she promised him to look after me—as she would a child!"

On the other hand, we know from the patient's analysis that by insisting on being kept in sight she had put herself once again in the position of a child.

"That she had lost the child," continued our patient, "signified that she had not watched me; she had lost sight of me. It was an admission that she had actually gone to sleep for the time and had not told me the truth later."

She was quite in the dark about the meaning of that fragment of dream where the nurse inquired from people in the street whether they had seen the child: on the other hand she was able to elucidate subsequent details of the manifest dream.

"The expanse of water made nurse think of the Rhine; she added, however, that it was much larger. Then she remembered that on the previous evening I had read her the story of Jonah and the whale, and had told her that I once saw a whale in the English Channel. I fancy that the water represents the sea and is an allusion to the story of Jonah.

"I think, too, that the narrow bridge comes from the same story, which is told wittily in dialect. A religious instructor describes to his pupils the wonderful adventure of Jonah, whereupon a boy points out that it cannot be true, since the teacher himself had told them before that whales could swallow only the smallest creatures owing to the narrowness of their throats. The teacher got out of the difficulty by saying that Jonah was a Jew, and that Jews would squeeze themselves in anywhere. My nurse is very religious but inclined to scepticism, and I reproached myself that my story-telling might perhaps have stirred her religious doubts.

"Now on this narrow bridge she saw the figure of another nurse whom she knew. From what she said it appears that this nurse drowned herself in the Rhine after being discharged from a case owing to some neglect or other.[2] She herself

---

[2] I was here guilty of a condensation of the material, which I was able to put right when I read my account to the patient. The nurse who appeared on the bridge had not been discharged on account of neglect. She was discharged because the child's mother, who had to leave home at the time, wanted to leave her child in charge of an older—*i.e.* after all, a more trustworthy!—attendant. This was followed by a reference to yet another nurse who had actually been discharged on account of neglect, but who had not drowned herself. The material necessary for interpretation of the dream element comes, as is often the way, from two sources. My memory completed the synthesis leading to interpretation. For the rest, this story of the drowned nurse contains the element of a mother's departure, which the patient connected with the departure of her husband. We thus have here an overdetermination which detracts somewhat from the elegance of the interpretation.

had feared, therefore, that she would be discharged for having fallen asleep. Moreover, on the day following the incident and after relating the dream, nurse cried bitterly, and when I asked why, replied quite rudely: 'You know why as well as I do: you won't trust me any more!' "

Since the appearance of the drowned nurse was an after-thought and an especially distinct item, we should have advised the patient to begin her dream-interpretation at this point. According to the dreamer's report, too, the first half of her dream was accompanied by acute anxiety; the second part paved the way for that feeling of reassurance with which she awoke.

"I regard the next part of the dream," said the lady, continuing her analysis, "as certain corroboration of my view that the dream had to do with what happened on Friday evening, for the person who had formerly been a saleswoman in a provision-shop can only have referred to the servant who brought in the supper on that occasion. I noticed, too, that nurse complained of nausea all day long. The question she puts to this woman, 'Have you seen the child?' is obviously traceable to my question, 'Have you seen me?' I put this question to her for the second time, just as the servant came in with the dishes."

In the dream, too, inquiry after the child is made on two occasions. The fact that the woman does not reply and shows no sign of interest we shall regard as an aspersion on this other servant made in the dreamer's own interest: she represents herself in the dream as being superior to the other, just because she herself has to face reproach on account of her own lack of attention.

"The woman who appears in the dream is not in actual fact divorced from her husband. The situation is taken from an incident in the life of the other servant, who has been separated from her lover—'separated,' divorced—by her parent's veto. The remark that even marriage is not always happy was in all probability a consoling remark made in the course of conversation between the two servants. On it is modelled the concluding sentence of the dream: the child will turn up.

"I concluded from this dream, however, that on the evening in question nurse really did fall asleep and that she was afraid of being dismissed for this reason. I had no more doubt about the accuracy of my powers of perception. Moreover, after relating the dream, nurse added that she was very sorry she had no dream-book at hand. To my comment that such books were full of the most ignorant superstitions, she replied that, although she was not at all superstitious, still all the unpleasant happenings of her life had taken place on a Friday. I must add that at the present moment her treatment of me is not at all satisfactory; she is touchy and irritable and makes scenes about nothing."

I think we must credit the lady with having accurately interpreted and appreciated her nurse's dream. As so often happens with dream-interpretation during analysis, the translation of the dream does not depend solely on associative material, but in addition on the circumstances of its narration, the behaviour of the patient before and after analysis, together with every remark or disclosure made by the patient at the time—during the same analytic session. If we take into account this nurse's touchiness, her attitude to unlucky Fridays, etc., we should confirm the conclusion that the dream contained a confession; in spite of her denial, she had actually fallen asleep and was afraid she would be sent away from her "foster-child."[3]

This dream, however, which had a practical bearing for the lady, stimulates our theoretical interest in two directions. It took the form of a consolation, but essentially it represented a significant *avowal* in regard to the nurse's relation to her patient. How does it come about that a dream, which should surely serve the purpose of a wish-fulfilment, can represent a confession which is not even in any way advantageous to the dreamer? Must we concede the existence of confession-dreams as distinct from wish- (and anxiety-) dreams, or again of warning-dreams, reflection-dreams, adaptation-dreams, and so on?

[3] As a matter of fact, a few days later the nurse confessed to a third person that she had fallen asleep, thus confirming the lady's interpretation.

I must confess I still do not quite understand why the objections I gave to any such course in my *Traumdeutung* have given rise to misgivings in the minds of so many psychoanalysts, among them some of repute. It seems to me that the differentiation of wish-, avowal-, warning- and adaptation-dreams, and so on, has not much greater value than the differentiation, accepted perforce, of medical specialists into gynecologists, children's specialists, dentists. Let me recapitulate here as briefly as possible the discussion of this question as set forth in my *Traumdeutung*.[4]

The so-called "residues from the previous day" can act as disturbers of sleep and dream-producers; they are thought-processes from the previous day which have retained affective cathexis and to some extent withstood the general lowering of energy through sleep. These residues are discovered by tracing back the manifest dream to the latent dream-thoughts; they constitute portions of the latter, belong, that is to say, to the activities of waking life—whether they are conscious or unconscious—which are able to persist during sleep. In accordance with the multiformity of thought-processes in the conscious and preconscious systems, these day-residues are present in numerous forms with the most varying significance: they may be wishes or fears that have not been disposed of, or resolutions, reflections, warnings, attempts to adapt one-self to current situations, and so on. To this extent the question of this particular characteristic of dreams would seem to be confirmed by the content discovered on interpretation of them. These residues from the previous day, however, are not the dream itself: they even lack the most essential constituent of a dream. They could not of themselves form a dream. They are, strictly speaking, only the psychical material which the dream-work employs, just as sensory and somatic stimuli, either incidental or produced under experimental conditions, constitute the somatic material for the dream-work. To attribute to them the main part in dream-formation is simply to repeat in a new guise the pre-analytical error by which dreams were explained on the hypothesis of

---

[4] Dritte Auflage, p. 367 *et seq*.

stomach trouble or skin-pressure. Scientific errors indeed have many lives, and even when refuted are ready to creep in again under new guises.

In so far as we comprehend the state of affairs, the conclusion has been forced on us that the essential factor in dream-formation is an unconscious wish—as a rule, an infantile wish—now in a state of repression; this can come to expression through the somatic or psychic material (therefore also through the day-residues), and thus it can provide these with the energy by which they can force themselves through to consciousness even during the nocturnal suspension of thought. Whatever else it may contain, warning, reflection, or avowal, whatever part of the rich content of preconscious waking life remains unsatisfied and arises during the night, the dream is in every case the fulfilment of *this* unconscious wish. It is *this* unconscious wish that gives the dream-work its peculiar characteristic of an unconscious elaboration of preconscious material. For a psychoanalyst dreams can only be characterized as productions of the dream-work; in spite of the fact that the latent dream-thoughts may only be found after dream-interpretation, he cannot reckon them as part of the dream; they are a part of preconscious thinking. (Secondary elaboration by the conscious system is reckoned as part of the dream-work. Even if one were to regard it separately, this would not involve any alteration in our conception. The definition would then run: Dreams considered in the analytical sense include the actual dream-work together with the secondary elaboration of the product of this work.) The conclusion to be drawn from these considerations is that one cannot put the dream-characteristic of wish-fulfilment in the same category with dream-characteristics such as warnings, avowals, attempts at solution, etc., without denying the concept of psychic dimensions of depth, that is to say, without rejecting the psychoanalytical standpoint.

At this point we may revert to the dream related by the nurse, in order to demonstrate the dimensional character of the wish-fulfilment contained therein. We already know that the lady's interpretation of this dream was by no means complete; there were portions of the day-content which she was unable to appraise accurately. Moreover she suffered from an obsessional neurosis, a condition which seems to me to make it harder for the patient to understand dream-symbols, in contrast with dementia praecox in which the reverse is true.

Nevertheless our knowledge of dream-symbolism enables us to understand uninterpreted portions of this dream and to perceive a deeper significance behind the interpretations already given. We cannot but observe how some of the material employed by the nurse comes from the complex of giving birth, of having children. The expanse of water (the Rhine, the Channel where the whale was seen) is certainly the water out of which children come. She too comes to the water "in search of a child." The Jonah legend behind this determination of the water, the question how Jonah (the child) could get through such a narrow passage, belong to the same association. The nurse, too, who out of mortification threw herself into the Rhine, found some comfort in her despair of life by the sexual-symbolic mode of her death—by going into water. The narrow bridge on which the nurse makes her appearance is in all probability also a genital symbol, although I must admit that here we lack more precise knowledge.

The wish to have a child seems therefore to be the unconscious creator of the dream in this instance; no other would be better calculated to comfort the nurse for the painful state of affairs in real life. "I shall be discharged: I shall lose my foster-child. What matter? I shall get a real child of my own instead." That uninterpreted portion of the dream where she questions everyone in the street about the child perhaps belongs here; the interpretation would then run, "and even if I have to offer myself on the streets I know how to get a child for myself." A strain of defiance in the dreamer hitherto disguised suddenly declares itself here: her avowal fits in here for the first time. "What if I have shut my eyes and compromised my professional reputation for conscientiousness and lost my post? Shall I be such a fool as to drown myself like Nurse X? Not I: I'll give up nursing altogether and get married: I'll be a woman and have a real child; nothing shall prevent me." This interpretation is justified by the consideration that "having children" is really the infantile expression of a desire for sexual intercourse: indeed it can be consciously chosen as an euphemistic expression of this shocking wish.

In her waking life itself the dreamer showed some tendency to confess; in the dream a confession which would be detrimental to her interests is made possible; one of the nurse's latent character-traits makes use of the confession to bring about an infantile wish-fulfilment. We may surmise that this character has a close connection—in regard both to time and to content—with the wish for a child and for sexual enjoyment.

Subsequent inquiry of the lady to whom I owe the first part of this interpretation afforded some unexpected information about the previous career of the nurse. Before she took up nursing she had wished to marry a man who had courted her assiduously; she had then abandoned this projected marriage on account of the opposition of an aunt towards whom her relations were a curious mixture of dependence and defiance. This aunt who prevented the marriage was the superintendent of a nursing association, and was regarded by the nurse as the pattern on which she modelled her life. The latter expected to be her aunt's heir, and was dependent on her in this way; nevertheless she thwarted the aunt by not entering the particular branch of nursing the latter had destined her for. The defiance shown in the dream was therefore directed against the aunt. We have ascribed an anal-erotic origin to this character-trait, and may take into consideration that the interests binding her to the aunt are of a financial nature; we are also reminded that children favour the anal theory of birth.

This factor of infantile defiance may perhaps allow us to assume a closer relation between the first and last scenes in the dream. The former saleswoman in a provision-shop represents in the dream the servant who brought the lady's supper into the room just when she was asking the question, "Have you seen me?" It appears, however, that she is intended in every way to play the part of hostile rival. Depreciation of her nursing capacity is indicated by the fact that she takes not the slightest interest in the lost child, her answer dealing with her own private affairs. The dreamer had thus displaced on to this figure the indifference about her patient which applied to herself. The unhappy marriage and divorce which the former dreaded in connection with her most secret wishes are attributed to the same person. We know, however, that it was the aunt who had separated the nurse and her fiancé. Hence the "provision-seller" (a figure not lacking in infantile symbolic significance) may represent the aunt-superintendent, who was in fact not much older than the nurse and who had played the necessary part of mother-rival in the nurse's life. A satisfactory confirmation of this interpretation is to be found in the fact that the "familiar" district where she comes upon this person standing in front of her door was the place where her aunt carried out her official duties.

Owing to the lack of contact between the analyst and the object of the analysis, it is scarcely advisable to penetrate deeper into the structure of the dream. It may perhaps be stated that even in the slight degree to which interpretation was possible the dream showed itself rich in corroborative material and in new problems.

XVII

Remarks Upon the Theory and Practice
of Dream-Interpretation[1]
(1923)

The accidental circumstance that the last editions of my *Interpretation of Dreams* (1900) have been printed from stereotype plates has led me to issue the following remarks in an independent form, instead of introducing them into the text as modifications or additions.

1

In interpreting a dream during an analysis a choice lies open to one between several technical procedures.

One can (*a*) proceed chronologically and get the dreamer to bring up his associations to the elements of the dream in the order in which those elements occurred in his account of

---

[1] ["Bemerkungen zur Theorie und Praxis der Traumdeutung." First published *Int. Z. Psychoanal.*, 9, 1; reprinted *Ges. Schr.*, 3, 305, and *Ges. W.*, 13, 301. Translation, reprinted from *Int. J. Psycho-Anal.*, 24 (1943), 66, by James Strachey.]

the dream. This is the original, classical method, which I still regard as the best if one is analysing one's own dreams.

Or one can (b) start the work of interpretation from some one particular element of the dream which one picks out from the middle of it. For instance, one can choose the most striking piece of it, or the piece which shows the greatest clarity or sensory intensity; or, again, one can start off from some spoken words in the dream, in the expectation that they will lead to the recollection of some spoken words in waking life.

Or one can (c) begin by entirely disregarding the manifest content and instead ask the dreamer what events of the previous day are associated in his mind with the dream he has just described.

Finally, one can (d) if the dreamer is already familiar with the technique of interpretation, avoid giving him any instructions and leave it to him to decide with which associations to the dream he shall begin.

I cannot lay it down that one or the other of these techniques is preferable or in general yields better results.

2

What is of far greater importance is the question of whether the work of interpretation proceeds under a pressure of resistance which is high or low—a point upon which the analyst never remains long in doubt. If the pressure is high, one may perhaps succeed in discovering what the things are with which the dream is concerned, but one cannot make out what it says about these things. It is as though one were trying to listen to a conversation taking place at a distance or in a very low voice. In that case, one can feel confident that there is not much prospect of collaborating with the dreamer, one decides not to bother too much about it and not to give him much help, and one is content to put before him a few translations of symbols that seem probable.

The majority of dreams in a difficult analysis are of this kind; so that one cannot learn much from them about the nature and mechanism of dream-formation. Least of all can one learn anything from them upon the recurring question of where the dream's wish-fulfilment may lie hidden. When the pressure of resistance is quite extremely high, one meets with the phenomenon of the dreamer's associations broadening instead of deepening. In place of the desired associations to the dream that has already been narrated, there appear a constant succession of new fragments of dream, which in their turn remain without associations.

It is only when the resistance is kept within moderate limits that the familiar picture of the work of interpretation comes into view: the dreamer's associations begin by *diverging* widely from the manifest elements, so that a great number of subjects and ranges of ideas are touched upon, after which, a second series of associations suddenly *converge* from these on to the dream-thoughts that are being looked for. When this is so, collaboration between the analyst and the dreamer becomes possible; whereas under a high pressure of resistance it would not even be of any advantage.

A number of dreams which occur during analyses are untranslatable even though they do not actually make much show of the resistance that is there. They exhibit free renderings of the latent dream-thoughts behind them and are comparable to successful creative writings which have been artistically worked over and in which the basic themes are still recognizable though they have been subjected to any amount of rearrangement and transformation. Dreams of this kind serve in the treatment as an introduction to thoughts and memories of the dreamer without their own actual content coming into account.

3

It is possible to distinguish between dreams *from above* and dreams *from below*, provided the distinction is not made too sharply. Dreams from below are those which are provoked by the strength of an unconscious (repressed) wish which has found a means of being represented in some of the day's residues. They may be regarded as inroads of the repressed into waking life. Dreams from above correspond to thoughts or intentions of the day before which have contrived during the night to obtain reinforcement from repressed material which is debarred from the ego. When this is so, analysis as a rule disregards this unconscious ally and succeeds in inserting the latent dream-thoughts into the complex of waking thought. This distinction calls for no modification in the theory of dreams.

4

In some analyses, or in some periods of an analysis, a divorce may become apparent between dream-life and waking life, like the divorce between the activity of phantasy and waking life which is found in the "continued story" (a novel in day-dreams). In that case one dream leads off from another, taking as its central point some element which was lightly touched upon in its predecessor, and so on. But we find far more frequently that dreams are not attached to one another but are interpolated into a successive series of fragments of waking thought.

5

The interpretation of a dream falls into two phases: the phase in which it is translated and the phase in which it is judged or has its value assessed. During the first phase one must not allow oneself to be influenced by any consideration whatever for the second phase. It is as though one had before one a chapter from some work in a foreign language—by Livy, for instance. The first thing one wants to know is what Livy says in the chapter; and it is only after this that the discussion arises of whether what one has read is an historical narrative or a legend or a digression on the part of the author.

What conclusions can one draw from a correctly translated dream? I have an impression that analytic practice has not always avoided errors and over-estimates on this point, partly owing to an exaggerated respect for the "mysterious unconscious." It is only too easy to forget that a dream is as a rule merely a thought like any other, made possible by an easing-up of the censorship and by unconscious intensification, and distorted by the operation of the censorship and by unconscious elaboration.

Let us take as an example the so-called dreams of recovery. If a patient has had a dream of this kind, in which he seems to abandon the restrictions of his neurosis—if, for instance, he overcomes some phobia or gives up some emotional attachment—we are inclined to think that he has made a great step forward, that he is ready to take his place in a new condition of life, that he has begun to reckon upon his recovery, etc. This may often be true, but quite as often such dreams of recovery only have the value of dreams of convenience: they signify a wish to be well at last, in order to avoid another portion of the work of analysis which is felt to lie ahead. In this sense, dreams of recovery very frequently occur, for instance, when the patient is about to enter upon a new and disagreeable phase of the transference. He is behaving just like some neurotics who after a few hours of analysis declare they have been cured—because they want to escape all the unpleasantness that is bound to come up for discussion in the analysis. Sufferers from war neuroses, too, who gave up their symptoms because the therapy adopted by the army doctors succeeded in making being ill even more uncomfortable than serving at the front—these sufferers, too, were following the same economic laws, and in both cases alike the cures have proved to be only temporary.

6

It is by no means easy to arrive at general conclusions upon the value of correctly translated dreams. If a conflict of ambivalence is taking place in a patient, then the emergence in him of a hostile thought certainly does not imply a permanent overcoming of his affectionate impulse, that is to say, a resolution of the conflict: neither does any such implication follow from a *dream* with a similarly hostile content. During a conflict of ambivalence such as this, there are often two dreams every night, each of them representing an opposite attitude. In that case the progress lies in the fact that a complete isolation of the two contrasted impulses has been achieved and that each of them, with the help of its unconscious intensifications, can be followed and understood to its extreme limits. And if it sometimes happens that one of the two ambivalent dreams has been forgotten, one must not be deceived into assuming that a decision has been made in favour of the one side. The fact that one of the dreams has been forgotten shows, it is true, that for the moment one tendency is in the ascendant, but that is true only of the one day, and may be changed. The next night may perhaps bring the opposite expression into the foreground. The true state of the conflict can only be determined by taking into account all the other indications, including those of waking life.

7

The question of the value to be assigned to dreams is intimately related to the other question of their susceptibility to influence from "suggestion" by the physician. Analysts may at first be alarmed at the mention of this possibility. But on further reflection this alarm will give place to the realization that the influencing of the patient's dreams is no more a blunder on the part of the analyst or disgrace to him than the guiding of the patient's conscious thoughts.

The fact that the manifest content of dreams is influenced by the analytic treatment stands in no need of proof. It follows from our knowledge that dreams are dependent upon waking life and work over material derived from it. Occurrences during analytic treatment are of course among the impressions of waking life and soon become some of the most powerful of these. So it is not to be wondered at that patients should dream of things which the analyst has discussed with them and of which he has aroused expectations in them. At least it is no more to be wondered at than what is implied in the familiar fact of "experimental" dreams.

And, from here, our interest proceeds to the question whether the latent dream-thoughts that have to be arrived at by interpretation can also be influenced or suggested by the analyst. And to this the answer must once more be that they obviously can be. For a portion of these latent dream-thoughts correspond to preconscious thought-formations, perfectly capable of being conscious, with which the dreamer might quite well have reacted to the physician's remarks in his waking state too—whether the patient's reactions were favourable to those remarks or in opposition to them. In fact, if we replace the dream by the dream-thoughts which it contains, the question of how far one can suggest dreams coincides with the more general question of how far a patient in analysis is accessible to suggestion.

On the mechanism of dream-formation itself, on the dream-work in the strict sense of the word, one never exercises any influence: of that one may be quite sure.

Besides that portion of the dream which we have already discussed—the preconscious dream-thoughts—every true dream contains indications of the repressed wishful impulses to which it owes the possibility of its formation. The doubter will reply that they appear in the dream because the dreamer knows that he ought to produce them—that they are expected by the analyst. The analyst himself will rightly think otherwise.

If a dream brings up situations that can be interpreted as referring to scenes from the dreamer's past, it seems especially important to ask whether the physician's influence can also play a part in such elements as those. And this question is most urgent of all in the case of what are called "confirmatory" dreams, dreams which, as it were, lag after the analysis. With some patients these are the only dreams that one obtains. Such patients reproduce the forgotten experiences of their childhood only after one has constructed them from their symptoms, associations and other signs and has propounded these constructions to them. Then follow the confirmatory dreams, concerning which, however, the doubt arises whether they may not be entirely without evidential value, since they may have been imagined in compliance with the physician's words instead of having been brought to light from the dreamer's unconscious. This ambiguous position cannot be escaped in the analysis, since with these patients unless one interprets, constructs and propounds, one never obtains access to what is repressed in them.

The situation takes a favourable turn if the analysis of a confirmatory, lagging dream of this sort is immediately followed by feelings of remembering what has hitherto been forgotten. But even then the sceptic can fall back upon an assertion that the recollections are illusory. Moreover, such feelings are for the most part absent. The repressed material is only allowed through bit by bit; and every lack of completeness inhibits or delays the forming of a sense of conviction. Furthermore, what we are dealing with may not be the reproduction of a real and forgotten event but the emergence of an unconscious phantasy, about which no feeling of memory is ever to be expected, though the possibility may sometimes remain of a sense of subjective conviction.

Is it possible, then, that confirmatory dreams are really the result of suggestion, that they are compliant dreams? The patients who produce only confirmatory dreams are the same patients in whom doubt plays the principal part in resistance. One makes no attempt at shouting down this doubt by means of one's authority or at reducing it by arguments. It must persist until it is brought to an end in the further course of the analysis. The analyst, too, may himself retain a doubt of the same kind in some particular instances. What makes him certain in the end is precisely the complication of the problem before him, which is like the solution of a jig-saw puzzle. A coloured picture, pasted upon a thin sheet of wood and fitting exactly into a wooden frame, is cut into a large number of pieces of the most irregular and crooked shapes. If one succeeds in arranging the confused heap of fragments, each of which bears upon it an unintelligible piece of drawing, so that the picture acquires a meaning, so that there is no gap anywhere in the design and so that the whole fits into the frame—if all these conditions are fulfilled, then one knows that one has solved the puzzle and that there is no alternative solution.

An analogy of this kind can of course have no meaning for a patient while the work of analysis is still uncompleted. At this point I recall a discussion which I was led into with a patient whose exceptionally ambivalent attitude was expressed in the most intense compulsive doubt. He did not dispute my interpretations of his dreams and was very much struck by their agreement with the hypotheses which I put forward. But he asked whether these confirmatory dreams might not be an expression of his compliance towards me. I pointed out that the dreams had also brought up a quantity of details of which I could have had no suspicion and that his behaviour in the treatment apart from this had not been precisely characterized by compliance. Whereupon he switched over to another theory and asked whether his narcissistic wish to be cured might not have caused him to produce these dreams, since, after all, I had held out to him a prospect of recovery if he were able to accept my constructions. I could only reply that I had not yet come across any such mechanism of dream-formation. But a decision was reached by another road. He recollected some dreams which he had had before starting analysis and indeed before he had known anything about it; and the analysis of these dreams, which were free from all suspicion of suggestion, led to the same interpretations as the later ones. It is true that his obsession for contradiction once more found a way out in the idea that the earlier dreams had been less clear than those that occurred during the treatment; but I was satisfied with their similarity. I think that in general it is a good plan occasionally to bear in mind the fact that people were in the habit of dreaming before there was such a thing as psychoanalysis.

8

It may well be that dreams during psychoanalysis succeed in bringing to light what is repressed to a greater extent than dreams outside that situation. But it cannot be proved, since the two situations are not comparable; the employment of dreams in analysis is something very remote from their original purpose. On the other hand, it cannot be doubted that within an analysis far more of the repressed is brought to light in connection with dreams than by any other method. In order to account for this, there must be some motive power, some unconscious force, which is better able to lend support to the purposes of analysis during the state of sleep than at other times. What is here in question cannot well be any factor other than the patient's compliance towards the analyst which is derived from his parental complex—in other words, the positive portion of what we call the transference; and in fact, in many dreams which recall what has been forgotten and repressed, it is impossible to discover any other unconscious wish to which the motive force for the formation of the dream can be attributed. So that if anyone wishes to maintain that most of the dreams that can be made use of in analysis are compliant dreams and owe their origin to suggestion, nothing can be said against that opinion from the point of view of analytical theory. I need only add a reference to what I have said in my *Introductory Lectures* [(1916-17) Lecture XXVIII], where I have dealt with the relation between transference and suggestion and shown how little the trustworthiness of our results is affected by a recognition of the operation of suggestion in our sense of the word.

In *Beyond the Pleasure Principle* [(1920), trans., 1922, 17ff.; new trans., 1950, 18ff.] I have dealt with the economic problem of how what are in every respect distressing experiences of the early infantile sexual period can succeed in forcing their way through to any kind of reproduction. I was obliged to ascribe to them an extraordinarily strong upward drive in the shape of the "compulsion to repeat"—a force able to overcome the repression which, in the service of the pleasure principle, weighs down upon them—though not until "the work of the treatment, operating in the same direction, has loosened the repression." Here we may add that it is the positive transference that gives this assistance to the compulsion to repeat. Thus an alliance has been made between the treatment and the compulsion to repeat, an alliance which is directed in the first instance against the pleasure principle but of which the ultimate purpose is the establishment of the dominion of the reality principle. As I have shown in the passage to which I am referring, it happens only too often that the compulsion to repeat throws over its obligations under this alliance and is not content with the return of the repressed merely in the form of dream-pictures.

9

So far as I can at present see, dreams that occur in a traumatic neurosis are the only *genuine* exceptions, and punishment dreams are the only *apparent* exceptions, to the rule that dreams are directed towards wish-fulfilment. In the latter class of dreams we are met by the remarkable fact that actually nothing belonging to the latent dream-thoughts is taken up into the manifest content of the dream. Something quite different appears instead, which must be described as a reaction-formation against the dream-thoughts, a rejection and complete contradiction of them. Such offensive action as this against the dream can only be ascribed to the critical function of the ego and it must therefore be assumed that the latter, provoked by the unconscious wish-fulfilment, has been temporarily re-established even during the sleeping state. It might have reacted to the undesirable content of the dream by waking up; but it has found a means, by the construction of the punishment dream, of avoiding an interruption of sleep.

For instance, in the case of the well-known dreams of the poet Rosegger which I have mentioned in *The Interpretation of Dreams* [English translation, revised ed. (1932), 438-440], we must suspect the existence of a suppressed version with an arrogant and boastful text, whereas the actual dream said to him: "You are an incompetent journeyman-tailor." It would, of course, be useless to look for a repressed wishful impulse as the motive power for a manifest dream such as this; one must be content with the fulfilment of the wish for self-criticism.

A dream-structure of this kind will excite less astonishment if one considers how frequently dream-distortion, acting in the service of the censorship, replaces a particular element by something that is in some sense or other its opposite or contrary. It is only a short step from there to the replacement of a characteristic portion of the content of the dream by a defensive denial, and one further step will lead to the whole objectionable dream-content being replaced by the punishment dream. I should like to give a couple of characteristic examples of the intermediate phase in the falsification of the manifest content.

Here is an extract from the dream of a girl with a strong fixation to her father, who had difficulty in talking during the analysis. She was sitting in a room with a girl friend, and dressed only in a kimono. A gentleman came in and she felt embarrassed. But the gentleman said: "Why, this is the girl we once saw dressed so nicely!"—The gentleman stood for me, and, further back, for her father. But we can make nothing of the dream unless we make up our mind to replace the most important element in the gentleman's speech by its contrary: "This is the girl I once saw *undressed* and who looked so nice then!" When she was a child of three or four she had for some time slept in the same room as her father and everything goes to suggest that she used then to throw back her clothes in her sleep in order to look pleasing to her father. The subsequent repression of her pleasure in exhibiting herself was the motive for her secretiveness in the treatment, her dislike of showing herself openly.

And here is another scene from the same dream. She was reading her own case history, which she had before her in print. In it was a statement that a young man murdered his *fiancée*—cocoa—that comes under anal erotism. This last phrase was a thought that she had in the dream at the mention of cocoa.—The interpretation of this piece of the dream was even more difficult than the former one. It emerged at last that before going to sleep she had been reading my "History of an Infantile Neurosis" [*Three Case Histories*, Collier Books edition BS 191V], the central point of which is the real or imagined observation by a patient of his parents copulating. She had already once before related this case history to her own, and this was not the only indication that in her case as well there was a question of an observation of the same kind. The young man murdering his *fiancée* was a clear reference to a sadistic view of the scene of copulation. But the next element, the cocoa, was very remote from it. Her only association to cocoa was that her mother used to say that co-coa gave one a headache, and she maintained that she had heard the same thing from other women. Moreover she had at one time identified herself with her mother by means of head-aches like hers. Now I could find no link between the two ele-ments of the dream except by supposing that she wanted to make a diversion from the consequences of the observation of coitus. No, she was saying, coitus had nothing to do with the procreation of children; children came from something one ate (as they do in fairy tales); and the mention of anal erotism, which looks like an attempt in the dream at interpretation, supplemented the infantile theory which she had called to her help, by adding anal birth to it.

10

Astonishment is sometimes expressed at the fact that the dreamer's ego can appear two or more times in the manifest dream, once as himself and again disguised behind the figures of other people. During the course of the construction of the dream, the secondary elaboration has evidently sought to obliterate this multiplicity of the ego, which cannot fit in with any possible scenic situation; but it is re-established by the work of interpretation. In itself this multiplicity is no more remarkable than the multiple appearance of the ego in a waking thought, especially when the ego divides itself into subject and object, puts one part of itself as an observing and critical agency in contrast to the other, or compares its present nature with its recollected past, which was also ego once; for instance, in such sentences as "When *I* think what *I*'ve done to this man" or "When *I* think that *I* too was a child once." But I should reject as a meaningless and unjustifiable piece of speculation the notion that *all* figures that appear in a dream are to be regarded as fragmentations and rep-resentatives of the dreamer's own ego. It is enough that we should keep firmly to the fact that the separation of the ego from an observing, critical, punishing agency (an ego-ideal) must be taken into account in the interpretation of dreams.

XVIII

Some Additional Notes on Dream-Interpretation as a Whole[1] (1925)

(A) THE LIMITS TO THE POSSIBILITY OF INTERPRETATION

It may be asked whether it is possible to give a complete and assured translation into the language of waking life (that is, an interpretation) of every product of dream-life. This question will not be treated here in the abstract but with reference to the conditions under which one works at interpreting dreams.

Our mental activities pursue either a useful aim or the immediate attainment of pleasure. In the former case what we

---

[1] ["Einige Nachträge zum Ganzen der Traumdeutung" appeared for the first time in 1925 in *Ges. Schr.*, 3, 172; reprinted *Ges. W.*, 1. The three notes were evidently intended for inclusion in the eighth edition of *Traumdeutung* (1930). For some reason, however, they were omitted from it and were consequently also omitted from the Revised Edition of the English translation based upon it in 1932. Present translation, reprinted from *Int. J. Psycho-Anal.*, 24 (1943), 71, by James Strachey.]

are dealing with are intellectual judgements, preparations for action or the conveyance of information to other people. In the latter case we describe these activities as play or phantasy. What is useful is itself (as is well known) only a circuitous path to pleasurable satisfaction. Now, dreaming is an activity of the second kind, which is indeed, from the point of view of evolution, the earlier one. It is misleading to say that dreams are concerned with the tasks of life before us or seek to find a solution for the problems of our daily work. That is the business of preconscious thought. Useful work of this kind is as remote from dreams as is any intention of conveying information to another person. When a dream deals with a problem of actual life, it solves it in the manner of an irrational wish and not in the manner of a reasonable reflection. There is only one useful task, only one function, that can be ascribed to a dream, and that is the guarding of sleep from interruption. A dream may be described as a piece of phantasy working on behalf of the maintenance of sleep.

It follows from this that it is on the whole a matter of indifference to the sleeping ego what may be dreamt during the night so long as the dream performs its task, and that those dreams best fulfil their function about which there is nothing to be said after waking. If it so often happens otherwise, if we remember dreams—even after years and decades—it always means that there has been an irruption of the repressed unconscious into the normal ego. Unless the repressed had been pacified in this way, it would not have consented to lend its help to the removal of the threat of disturbance to sleep. We know that it is the fact of this irruption that gives dreams their importance for psychopathology. If we can uncover a dream's motivating force, we shall obtain unsuspected information about the repressed impulses in the unconscious; and on the other hand, if we can undo its distortions, we shall overhear preconscious thought taking place in states of internal reflection which would not have attracted consciousness to themselves during the daytime.

No one can practice the interpretation of dreams as an isolated activity: it remains a part of the work of analysis. In analysis we direct our interest according to necessity, now to the preconscious content of the dream and now to the unconscious contribution to its formation; and we often neglect the one element in favour of the other. Nor would it be of any avail for anyone to endeavour to interpret dreams outside analysis. He would not succeed in escaping the conditions of the analytic situation; and if he worked at his own dreams, he would be undertaking a self-analysis. This comment would not apply to someone who did without the dreamer's collaboration and sought to interpret dreams by intuitive insight. But dream-interpretation of such a kind, without reference to the dreamer's associations, would in the most favourable case remain a piece of unscientific virtuosity of the most doubtful value.

If one practises dream-interpretation according to the sole justifiable technical procedure, one soon notices that success depends entirely upon the tension of resistance between the awakened ego and the repressed unconscious. Work under a "high pressure of resistance" demands (as I have explained elsewhere [p. 206 *supra*]) a different attitude on the part of the analyst from work under a low pressure. In analysis one has for long periods at a time to deal with strong resistances which are still unknown to one and which it will in any case be impossible to overcome so long as they remain unknown. It is therefore not to be wondered at that only a certain portion of a patient's dream-products can be translated and made use of, and even at that not completely. Even if, owing to one's own experience, one is in a position to understand many dreams to the interpretation of which the dreamer has contributed little, one must always remember that the certainty of such interpretations remains in doubt and one hesitates to press one's conjectures upon the patient.

Critical voices will now be raised. It will be objected that, since it is not possible to interpret every dream that is dealt with, one should cease asserting more than one can establish and should be content to say that *some* dreams can be shown by interpretation to have a meaning but that as to the rest we are in ignorance. But the very fact that success in interpretation depends upon the resistance absolves the analyst from the necessity for such modesty. He may have the experience of a dream which was at first unintelligible becoming clear during the very same hour after some fortunate piece of analytic work has got rid of one of the dreamer's resistances. A portion of the dream which he had hitherto forgotten may suddenly occur to him and may bring the key to the interpretation; or a new association may emerge which may throw light upon the darkness. It sometimes happens, too, that, after months or years of analytic labour, one returns to a dream which at the beginning of the treatment seemed meaningless and incomprehensible but which is now, in the light of knowledge obtained in the meantime, completely elucidated. And if one further takes into consideration the argument from the theory of dreams that the model dreams produced by children invariably have a clear meaning and are easy to interpret, then it will be justifiable to assert that dreams are quite generally mental structures that are capable of interpretation, though the situation may not always allow of an interpretation being reached.

When the interpretation of a dream has been discovered, it is not always easy to decide whether it is a "complete" one—that is, whether further preconscious thoughts may not also have found expression in the same dream. In that case we must consider the meaning proved which is based upon the dreamer's associations and our estimate of the situation, without on that account feeling bound to reject the other meaning. It remains possible, though unproven: one must become accustomed to a dream being thus capable of having many meanings. Moreover, the blame for this is not always to be laid upon incompleteness of the work of interpretation; it may just as well be inherent in the latent dream-thoughts themselves. Indeed it may happen in waking life, quite apart from the situation of dream-interpretation, that one is uncertain whether some remark that one has heard or some piece of information that one has received justifies one in coming to such and such a conclusion or whether it is hinting at something else beyond its obvious meaning.

One interesting occurrence which has been insufficiently investigated is to be seen where the same manifest dream-content gives simultaneous expression to a set of concrete ideas and to an abstract line of thought based upon them. It is of course difficult for the dream-work to find a means for representing abstract thoughts.

(B) MORAL RESPONSIBILITY FOR THE CONTENT OF DREAMS

In the introductory chapter of this book [*The Interpretation of Dreams*] (which deals with "The Scientific Literature of Dream-Problems") I have shown the way in which writers have reacted to what is felt as the distressing fact that the unbridled content of dreams is so often at odds with the moral sense of the dreamer. (I deliberately avoid speaking of "criminal" dreams, as such a description, which would overstep the limits of psychological interest, seems to me quite unnecessary.) The immoral character of dreams has naturally provided a fresh motive for denying them any psychological value: if dreams are the meaningless product of disordered mental activity, then there can be no ground for assuming responsibility for their apparent content.

The problem of responsibility for the manifest content of dreams has been fundamentally shifted and indeed disposed of by the explanations given in my *Interpretation of Dreams*.

We know now that the manifest content is an illusion, a *façade*. It is not worth while to submit it to an ethical examination or to take its breaches of morality any more seriously than its breaches of logic or mathematics. When the "content" of the dream is spoken of, what must be referred to can only be the content of the preconscious thoughts and of the repressed wishful impulse which are revealed behind the *façade* of the dream by the work of interpretation. Nevertheless, this immoral *façade* has a question to put to us. We have heard that the latent dream-thoughts have to submit to a severe censorship before they are allowed access to the manifest content. How can it happen, then, that this censorship, which makes difficulties over more trivial things, breaks down so completely over these manifestly immoral dreams?

The answer is not easy to come by and may perhaps not

seem completely satisfying. If, in the first place, one submits these dreams to interpretation, one finds that some of them have given no offence to the censorship because *au fond* they have no bad meaning. They are innocent boastings or identifications that put up a mask of pretence; they have not been censored because they do not tell the truth. But others of them—and, it must be admitted, the majority—really mean what they say and have undergone no distortion from the censorship. They are an expression of immoral, incestuous and perverse impulses or of murderous and sadistic lusts. The dreamer reacts to many of these dreams by waking up in a fright, in which case the situation is no longer obscure to us. The censorship has neglected its task, this has been noticed too late, and the development of anxiety is a substitute for the distortion that has been omitted. In still other instances of such dreams, even that expression of emotion is absent. The objectionable matter is carried along by the height of the sexual excitement that has been reached during the sleep, or it is viewed with the same tolerance with which even a waking person can regard a fit of rage, an angry mood or the indulgence in cruel phantasies.

But our interest in the genesis of these *manifestly* immoral dreams is greatly reduced when we find from analysis that the majority of dreams—innocent dreams, dreams without affect and anxiety dreams—are revealed, when the distortions of the censorship have been undone, as the fulfilments of immoral—egoistic, sadistic, perverse or incestuous—wishful impulses. As in the world of waking life, these masked criminals are far commoner than those with their vizors raised. The straightforward dream of sexual relations with one's mother, which Jocasta alludes to in the *Oedipus Rex*, is a rarity in comparison with all the multiplicity of dreams which psychoanalysis must interpret in the same sense.

I have dealt so exhaustively in these pages with this characteristic of dreams, which indeed provides the motive for their distortion, that I can pass at once from this topic to the problem that lies before us: Must one assume responsibility for the content of one's dreams? For the sake of completeness, it must, however, be added that dreams do not always offer immoral wish-fulfilments, but often energetic reactions against them in the form of "punishment dreams." In other words, the dream-censorship can not only express itself in distortions and the development of anxiety, but can go so far as to blot out the immoral subject-matter completely and replace it by something else that serves as an atonement, though it allows one to see what lies behind. But the problem of responsibility for the immoral content of dreams no longer exists for us as it formerly did for writers who knew nothing of latent dream-thoughts and the repressed part of our mental life. Obviously one must hold oneself responsible for the evil impulses of one's dreams. In what other way can one deal with them? Unless the content of the dream (rightly understood) is inspired by alien spirits, it is a part of my own being. If I seek to classify the impulses that are present in me according to social standards into good and bad, I must assume responsibility for both sorts; and if, in defence, I say that what is unknown, unconscious and repressed in me is not my "ego," then I shall not be basing my position upon psychoanalysis, I shall not have accepted its conclusions and I shall perhaps be taught better by the criticisms of my fellowmen, by the disturbances in my actions and the confusion of my feelings. I shall perhaps learn that what I am repudiating not only "is" in me but sometimes "acts" from out of me as well.

It is true that in the metapsychological sense this bad repressed content does not belong to my "ego"—that is, assuming that I am a morally blameless individual—but to an "id" upon which my ego is seated. But this ego developed out of the id, it forms with it a single biological unit, it is only a specially modified peripheral portion of it, it is subject to the influences and obeys the suggestions that arise from the id. For any vital purpose, a separation of the ego from the id would be a hopeless undertaking.

Moreover, if I were to give way to my moral pride and tried to decree that for purposes of moral valuation I might disregard the evil in the id and need not make my ego responsible for it, what use would that be to me? Experience shows me that I nevertheless do take that responsibility, that I am somehow compelled to do so. Psychoanalysis has made us familiar with a pathological condition, the obsessional neurosis, in which the poor ego feels itself responsible for all sorts of evil impulses of which it knows nothing, impulses which are brought up against it in consciousness but which it is unable to acknowledge. Something of this is present in every normal person. It is a remarkable fact that the more moral he is the more sensitive is his "conscience." It is just as though we could say that the healthier a man is, the more liable he is to contagions and to the effects of injuries. This is no doubt because conscience is itself a reaction-formation against the evil that is perceived in the id. The more the latter is suppressed the more active is the conscience.

The ethical narcissism of humanity should rest content with the knowledge that the fact of distortion in dreams, as well as the existence of anxiety dreams and punishment dreams, afford just as clear evidence of his moral nature as dream-interpretation gives of the existence and strength of his evil nature. If anyone is dissatisfied with this and would like to be "better" than he was created, let him see whether he can attain more in life than hypocrisy or inhibition.

The physician will leave it to the jurist to construct a responsibility that is artificially limited to the metapsychological ego. It is notorious that the greatest difficulties are encountered by attempts to derive from such a construction any practical consequences not in contradiction to human feelings.

(C) THE OCCULT SIGNIFICANCE OF DREAMS[2]

There seems to be no end to the problems of dream-life. But

[2] [This subject and much of this actual material was dealt with by Freud at greater length in a posthumously published but hitherto untranslated paper "Psychoanalyse und Telepathie" (1921), *Ges. W.*, 17, 27; as well as in "Dreams and Telepathy" (1922), *The Uncanny and Other Papers on Parapsychology,* Collier Books edition AS 583V, and in Lecture XXX ("Dreams and the Occult") of his *New Introductory Lectures* (1932).]

this can only be surprising if we forget that all the problems of mental life are repeated in dreams with the addition of a few new ones arising from the special nature of dreams. But many of the things that we study in dreams, because we meet with them there, have little or nothing to do with the psychological peculiarity of dreams. Thus, for instance, symbolism is not a dream-problem, but a topic connected with our archaic thinking—our "root-language," as it was aptly called by the paranoic Schreber. [Cf. Freud (1911b), "Psychoanalytic Notes Upon an Autobiographical Account of Paranoia," *Three Case Histories,* Collier Books edition BS 191V.] It dominates myths and religious ritual no less than dreams, and dream-symbolism can scarcely even claim as a peculiarity the fact of its concealing more particularly what is important sexually. Again, it is not to be expected that the explanation of anxiety dreams will be found in the theory of dreams. Anxiety is a problem rather of neurosis, and all that remains to be discussed is how it comes about that anxiety can arise under dream conditions.

The position is just the same, I think, in the matter of the occult world. But, since dreams themselves have always been mysterious things, they have been brought into intimate connection with the other unknown mysteries. No doubt, too, they have a historic claim to that position, since in primaeval ages, when our mythology was being formed, dream-pictures may have played a part in the origin of ideas about spirits.

There would seem to be two categories of dreams with a claim to being reckoned as occult phenomena: prophetic dreams and telepathic ones. A countless multitude of witnesses speak in favour of both of them, while against both of them there is the obstinate aversion, or maybe prejudice, of science.

There can, indeed, be no doubt that there are such things as prophetic dreams, in the sense that their content gives some sort of picture of the future; the only question is whether these predictions coincide to any noticeable extent with what really happens subsequently. I must confess that upon this point my resolution in favour of impartiality deserts me. The notion that there is any mental power, apart from acute calculation, which can foresee future events in detail is on the one hand too much in contradiction to all the expectations and presumptions of science and on the other hand corresponds too closely to certain ancient and familiar human desires which criticism must reject as unjustifiable pretensions. I am therefore of opinion that after one has taken into account the untrustworthiness, credulity and unconvincingness of most of these reports, together with the possibility of falsifications of memory facilitated by emotional causes[3] and the inevitability of a few lucky shots, it may be anticipated that the spectre of prophetic dreams will disappear into nothing. Personally, I have never experienced anything or learnt of anything that could encourage a more favourable presumption.

It is otherwise with telepathic dreams. But at this point it must be made quite clear that no one has yet maintained that telepathic phenomena—the reception of a mental process by one person from another by means other than sensory perception—are exclusively related to dreams. Thus once again telepathy is not a dream-problem: our judgement upon whether it exists or not need not be based on a study of telepathic dreams.

If reports of telepathic occurences (or, to speak less exactly, of thought-transference) are submitted to the same criticism as stories of other occult events, there remains a considerable amount of material which cannot be so easily neglected. Further, it is much more possible to collect observations and experiences of one's own in this field which justify a favourable attitude to the problem of telepathy, even though they may not be enough to carry an assured conviction. One arrives at a provisional opinion that it may well be that telepathy really exists and that it provides the kernel of truth in many other hypotheses that would otherwise be incredible.

It is certainly right in what concerns telepathy, too, to ad-

---

[3] [Cf. "A Premonitory Dream Fulfilled," *Early Psychoanalytic Writings*, Collier Books edition BS 188V.]

here obstinately to a sceptical position and only to yield grudgingly to the force of evidence. I believe I have found a class of material which is exempt from the doubts which are otherwise justified—namely, unfulfilled prophecies of professional fortune-tellers. Unluckily, I have but few such observations at my disposal; but two among these have made a powerful impression on me. I am not in a position to describe them in such detail as would produce a similar effect upon other people, and I must restrict myself to bringing out a few essential points.

A prediction was made, then, to the people in question (at a strange place and by a strange fortune-teller, who at the same time went through some, presumably irrelevant, performances) that something would happen to them at a particular time, which in fact did *not* happen. The date at which the prophecy should have come true was long past. It was striking that those concerned told of their experience not with derision or disappointment but with obvious satisfaction. Included among what had been told them there were certain quite definite details which seemed capricious and unintelligible and would only have been justified if they had hit the mark. Thus, for instance, the palmist told a woman who was twenty-seven (though she looked much younger) and who had taken off her wedding-ring, that she would be married and have two children before she was thirty-two. The woman was forty-three when, now seriously ill, she told me the story in her analysis: she had remained childless. If one knew her private history (of which the "Professor" in the lounge of the Paris hotel was certainly ignorant) one could understand the two numbers included in the prophecy. The girl had married after an unusually intense attachment to her father and had then had a passionate longing for children, so as to be able to put her husband in the place of her father. After years of disappointment, when she was on the brink of a neurosis, she obtained the prophecy, which promised her—the fate of her mother. For it was a fact that the latter had had two children by the time she was thirty-two. Thus it was only by the help of psychoanalysis that it was possible to give a significant interpretation of the peculiarities of this pretended message from without. But there was then no better explanation of the whole, unequivocally determined chain of events than to suppose that a strong wish on the part of the questioner—the strongest unconscious wish, in fact, of her whole emotional life and the motive force of her impending neurosis—had made itself manifest by being directly transferred to the fortune-teller, whose attention was distracted at the time by the performances he was going through.

I have often had an impression, in the course of experiments in my private circle, that strongly emotionally coloured recollections can be successfully transferred without much difficulty. If one has the courage to submit to an analytical examination the associations of the person to whom the thoughts are supposed to be transferred, correspondences often come to light which would otherwise have remained undiscovered. On the basis of much experience I am inclined to draw the conclusion that thought-transference of this kind comes about particularly easily at the moment at which an idea emerges from the unconscious, or, in theoretical terms, as it passes over from the "primary process" to the "secondary process."

In spite of the caution which is prescribed by the importance, novelty and obscurity of the subject, I feel that I should not be justified in holding back any longer these considerations upon the problem of telepathy. All of this has only this much to do with dreams: if there are such things as telepathic messages, the possibility cannot be dismissed of their reaching someone during sleep and coming to his knowledge in a dream. Indeed, on the analogy of other perceptual and intellectual material, the further possibility arises that telepathic messages received in the course of the day may only be dealt with during a dream of the following night. There would then be nothing contradictory in the material that had been telepathically communicated being modified and transformed in the dream like any other material. It would be satisfactory if with the help of psychoanalysis we could obtain further and better authenticated knowledge of telepathy.

XIX

Analysis Terminable and Interminable[1]
(1937)

1

Experience has taught us that psychoanalytic therapy—the liberation of a human being from his neurotic symptoms, inhibitions and abnormalities of character—is a lengthy business. Hence, from the very beginning, attempts have been made to shorten the course of analysis. Such endeavours required no justification: they could claim to be prompted by the strongest considerations alike of reason and expediency. But there probably lurked in them some trace of the impatient contempt with which the medical profession of an earlier day regarded the neuroses, seeing in them the unnecessary results of invisible lesions. If it had now become necessary to deal with them, they should at least be got rid of with the utmost despatch. Basing his procedure on the theory formulated in *Das Trauma der Geburt* (1924) Otto Rank

[1] ["Die endliche und die unendliche Analyse." First published *Int. Z. Psychoanal.*, 23 (1937), 209; reprinted *Ges. W.*, 16. Translation, reprinted from *Int. J. Psycho-Anal.*, 18 (1937), 373, by Joan Riviere.]

made a particularly determined attempt to shorten analysis. He assumed that the cardinal source of neurosis was the experience of birth, on the ground of its involving a possibility that the infant's "primal fixation" to the mother might not be surmounted but persist in the form of "primal repression." His hope was that, if this primal trauma were overcome by analysis, the whole neurosis would clear up, so that this one small piece of analytic work, for which a few months should suffice, would do away with the necessity for all the rest. Rank's argument was certainly bold and ingenious, but it did not stand the test of critical examination. Moreover, it was a child of its time, conceived under the stress of the contrast between the post-war misery of Europe and the "prosperity" of America, and designed to accelerate the tempo of analytic therapy to suit the rush of American life. We have heard little of the clinical results of Rank's plan. Probably it has not accomplished more than would be done if the men of a fire-brigade, summoned to deal with a house set on fire by an upset oil-lamp, merely removed the lamp from the room in which the conflagration had broken out. Much less time would certainly be spent in so doing than in extinguishing the whole fire. The theory and practice of Rank's experiment are now things of the past—no less than American "prosperity" itself.

Before the war, I myself had already tried another way of speeding up analysis. I had undertaken to treat a young Russian, a rich man spoilt by riches, who had come to Vienna in a state of complete helplessness, accompanied by physician and attendant.[2] It was possible in the course of several years to restore to him a considerable measure of independence, and to awaken his interest in life, while his relations to the principal people in his life were adjusted. But then we came to a full stop. We made no progress in clearing up his childhood's neurosis, which was the basis of his later illness, and it was obvious that the patient found his present situa-

_____

[2] Cf. my paper, published with the patient's consent, "From the History of an Infantile Neurosis" (1918). It contains no detailed account of the young man's adult illness, which is touched on only when its connection with his infantile neurosis requires it. [*Three Case Histories*, essay III, Collier Books edition BS 191V.]

tion quite comfortable and did not intend to take any step which would bring him nearer to the end of his treatment. It was a case of the treatment obstructing itself: the analysis was in danger of failing as a result of its—partial—success. In this predicament I resorted to the heroic remedy of fixing a date for the conclusion of the analysis. At the beginning of a period of treatment I told the patient that the coming year was to be the last of his analysis, no matter what progress he made or failed to make in the time still left to him. At first he did not believe me, but, once he was convinced that I was in dead earnest, the change which I had hoped for began to take place. His resistances crumbled away, and in the last months of treatment he was able to produce all the memories and to discover the connecting links which were necessary for the understanding of his early neurosis and his recovery from the illness from which he was then suffering. When he took leave of me at mid-summer, 1914, unsuspecting as we all were, of what was so shortly to happen, I believed that his cure was complete and permanent.

In a postscript to this patient's case history (1923d) I have already reported that I was mistaken. When, towards the end of the war, he returned to Vienna, a refugee and destitute, I had to help him to master a part of the transference which had remained unresolved. Within a few months this was successfully accomplished and I was able to conclude my postscript with the statement that "since then the patient has felt normal and has behaved unexceptionably, in spite of the war having robbed him of his home, his possessions, and all his family relationships." Fifteen years have passed since then, but this verdict has not proved erroneous, though certain reservations have had to be made. The patient has remained in Vienna and has made good, although in a humble social position. Several times, however, during this period, his satisfactory state of health has broken down, and the attacks of neurotic illness from which he has suffered could be construed only as offshoots of his original neurosis. Thanks to the skill of one of my pupils, Dr. Ruth Mack Brunswick, a short course of treatment has sufficed on each occasion to clear up these attacks. I hope Dr. Mack Brunswick herself will report on this case before long.[3] Some of these relapses were caused by still unresolved residues of the transference; short-lived though the attacks were, they were distinctly paranoic in character. In other instances, however, the pathogenic material consisted of fragments from the history of the patient's childhood, which had not come to light while I was analysing him and which now came away (the comparison is obvious) like sutures after an operation or small pieces of necrotic bone. I have found the history of this man's recovery almost as interesting as that of his illness.

Since then I have employed the method of fixing a date for the termination of analysis in other cases and I have also inquired about the experience of other analysts in this respect. There can be only one verdict about the value of this blackmailing device. The measure is effective, provided that one hits the right time at which to employ it. But it cannot be held to guarantee perfect accomplishment of the task of psychoanalysis. On the contrary, we may be quite sure that, while the force of the threat will have the effect of bringing part of the material to light, another part will be held back and become buried, as it were, and will be lost to our therapeutic efforts. Once the date for discontinuing the treatment has been fixed we must not extend the time; otherwise the patient will lose all his faith in the analyst. The most obvious way out would be to let him continue his treatment with another analyst, although we know that a change of this sort involves a fresh loss of time and the sacrifice of some of the results of the work already done. Nor can any general rule be laid down as to the right time for resorting to this forcible technical method: the analyst must use his own tact in the matter. A mistake, once made, cannot be rectified. The saying that the lion springs once and once only must hold good here.

2

The discussion of the technical problem of how to accelerate the slow progress of an analysis suggests another,

---

[3] [One such report had already appeared: Brunswick (1928b).]

more deeply interesting question: is there such a thing as a natural end to an analysis or is it really possible to conduct it to such an end? To judge by the ordinary talk of analysts we should presume that it is, for we often hear them say, when deploring or excusing the admitted imperfection of some fellow-mortal: "His analysis was not finished" or "He was not completely analysed."

Now we must first decide what is meant by the ambiguous term, "the end of an analysis." From the practical standpoint it is easily defined. An analysis is ended when analyst and patient cease to meet for the analytic session. This happens when two conditions have been approximately fulfilled. First, the patient must no longer be suffering from his former symptoms and must have overcome his various anxieties and inhibitions and, secondly, the analyst must have formed the opinion that so much repressed material has been brought into consciousness, so much that was inexplicable elucidated, and so much inner resistance overcome that no repetition of the patient's specific pathological processes is to be feared. If for external reasons one is prevented from reaching this goal, it is more correct to say that an analysis is imperfect than to say that it has not been completed.

The second definition of the "end" of an analysis is much more ambitious. According to it we have to answer the question whether the effect upon the patient has been so profound that no further change would take place in him if his analysis were continued. The implication is that by means of analysis it is possible to attain to absolute psychical normality and to be sure that it will be maintained, the supposition being that all the patient's repressions have been lifted and every gap in his memory filled. Let us first consult our experience and see whether such things do in fact happen, and then examine our theory and learn whether there is any *possibility* of their happening.

Every analyst will have treated some cases with this gratifying outcome. He has succeeded in clearing up the patient's neurosis, there has been no relapse and no other nervous disturbance has succeeded it. We know something of what determines these results. No noticeable modification had taken place in the patient's ego and the causation of his illness was pre-eminently traumatic. The aetiology of all neuroses is indeed a mixed one; either the patient's instincts are excessively strong and refuse to submit to the taming influence of his ego or else he is suffering from the effects of premature traumas, by which I mean traumas which his immature ego was unable to surmount. Generally there is a combination of the two factors: the constitutional and the accidental. The stronger the constitutional factor the more readily will a trauma lead to fixation, with its sequel in a disturbance of development; the stronger the trauma the more certain is it that it will have injurious effects even when the patient's instinctual life is normal. There can be no doubt that, when the aetiology of the neurosis is traumatic, analysis has a far better chance. Only when the traumatic factor predominates can we look for what psychoanalysis can achieve in such a masterly fashion, namely, the replacement (owing to the strengthening of the ego) of the inadequate decision made in infancy by a correct solution. Only in such a case can one speak of a definitive end to an analysis. When such a result has been attained analysis has done all that can be required of it and need not be continued. If the patient who has made such a good recovery never produces any more symptoms calling for analysis, it still, of course, remains an open question how much of this immunity is due to a benevolent fate which spares him too searching a test.

The factors which are prejudicial to analysis and may cause it to be so long-drawn-out as to be really interminable are a constitutional strength of instinct and an unfavourable modification of the ego in the defensive conflict, a modification comparable to a dislocation or crippling. One is tempted to make the first factor—the strength of the instincts—responsible for the second—the modification of the ego—but it seems that the latter has its own aetiology and indeed it must be admitted that our knowledge of these relations is as yet imperfect. They are only just becoming the object of analytic investigation. I think that here the interest of analysts is quite wrongly orientated. Instead of inquiring *how* analysis effects a cure (a point which in my opinion has been sufficiently elucidated) we should ask what are the obstacles which this cure encounters.

This brings me to two problems which arise directly out of psychoanalytic practice, as I hope to show by the following examples. A certain man, who had himself been a most successful practitioner of analysis, came to the conclusion that his relations with men as well as with women—the men who were his rivals and the woman whom he loved—were not free from neurotic inhibitions, and he therefore had himself analysed by an analyst whom he regarded as his superior. This critical exploration of his own personality was entirely successful. He married the woman whom he loved and became the friend and teacher of the men whom he had regarded as rivals. Many years passed, during which his relation to his former analyst remained unclouded. But then, for no demonstrable external reason, trouble arose. The man who had been analysed adopted an antagonistic attitude to his analyst and reproached him for having neglected to complete the analysis. The analyst, he said, ought to have known and to have taken account of the fact that a transference-relation could never be merely positive; he ought to have considered the possibilities of a negative transference. The analyst justified himself by saying that, at the time of the analysis, there was no sign of a negative transference. But, even supposing that he had failed to observe some slight indication of it, which was quite possible considering the limitations of analysis in those early days, it was still doubtful, he thought, whether he would have been able to activate a psychical theme or, as we say, a "complex," by merely indicating it to the patient, so long as it was not at that moment an actuality to him. Such activation would certainly have necessitated real unfriendly behaviour on the analyst's part. And, he added, every happy relation between an analyst and the subject of his analysis, during and after analysis, was not to be regarded as transference; there were friendly relations with a real basis, which were capable of persisting.

I now pass on to my second example, which raises the

same problem. A girl who had left her childhood behind her had, since puberty, been cut off from life by an inability to walk, owing to acute pain in her legs. Her condition was obviously hysterical in character and it had resisted various kinds of treatment. After an analysis lasting nine months the trouble disappeared and the patient, whose character was truly sound and estimable, was able once more to take her place in life. In the years following her recovery she was consistently unfortunate: there were disasters in her family, they lost their money and, as she grew older, she saw every hope of happiness in love and marriage vanish. But this woman, who had formerly been an invalid, stood her ground valiantly and in difficult times was a support to her people. I cannot remember whether it was twelve or fourteen years after the end of her analysis that she had to undergo a gynaecological examination on account of profuse haemorrhages. A myoma was discovered which made a complete hysterectomy advisable. From the time that this operation took place she relapsed into neurosis. She fell in love with the surgeon and was overwhelmed by masochistic phantasies of the dreadful internal changes which had taken place in her—phantasies in which she disguised her romance. She proved inaccessible to a further attempt at analysis, and to the end of her life she remained abnormal. The successful analytic treatment took place so long ago that we could not expect too much from it; it was in the first years of my work as an analyst. It is no doubt possible that the patient's second neurosis sprang from the same root as the first, which had been successfully overcome, and that it was a different manifestation of repressed tendencies which the analysis had only partially resolved. But I am inclined to think that, but for the fresh trauma, there would have been no second outbreak of neurosis.

These two cases, purposely selected from a large number of similar ones, will suffice to set going a discussion of the problems we are considering. The sceptical, the optimistic and the ambitious will draw very different conclusions from them. Sceptics will say that they prove that even a successful analysis does not prevent the patient who is cured for the time being from subsequently developing another neurosis, or even a neurosis springing from the same instinctual root, that is to say, from a recurrence of his former trouble. The others will maintain that this is not proved. They will object that both the cases I have cited date from the early days of analysis, twenty and thirty years ago, respectively, and that since then we have acquired deeper insight and wider knowledge and, in adapting our technique to our new discoveries, we have modified it in many respects. To-day, they will argue, we may demand and expect that an analytic cure shall be permanent or, at least, that, if a patient falls ill again, his fresh neurosis shall not turn out to be a revival of his earlier instinctual disturbance, manifesting itself in a new guise. Our experience, they will say, is not such that we must limit so severely the demands which we may legitimately make upon psychoanalytic therapy.

Now, of course, my reason for selecting these particular cases as illustrations was precisely that they date so far back. It is obvious that the more recent the result of an analysis the less valuable is it for our theoretical discussion since we have no means of predicting what will happen later to a patient who has been cured. Clearly the expectations of the optimist presuppose a number of things which are not exactly a matter of course. In the first place he assumes that it is really possible to resolve an instinctual conflict (or, more accurately, a conflict between the ego and an instinct) finally and for all time. Secondly, that when we are dealing with one such conflict in a patient, we can, as it were, inoculate him against the possibility of any other instinctual conflicts in the future. And thirdly, that we have the power, for purposes of prophylaxis, to stir up a pathogenic conflict of this sort, when at the moment there is no indication of it, and that it is wise to do so. I merely suggest these questions: I do not propose to answer them now. In any case a definite answer is perhaps not possible at the present time.

Probably some light may be thrown on the subject from the theoretical standpoint. But already another point has become clear: if we wish to fulfil the more exacting demands which are now made upon therapeutic analysis, we shall not shorten its duration whether as a means or an end.

3

My analytic experience, extending now over several decades, and the change which has taken place in the nature and mode of my work encourage me to attempt an answer to the questions before us. In earlier days I dealt with a comparatively large number of patients, who, as was natural, wanted to be cured as quickly as possible. Of late years I have been mainly engaged in training-analyses and I have also had a relatively small number of patients suffering from severe neuroses, whose treatment has been carried on continuously, though with longer or shorter intermissions. In these cases the therapeutic aim is no longer the same as before. There is no question of shortening the treatment: the object has been completely to exhaust the possibilities of illness and to bring about a radical change in the personality.

Of the three factors which, as we have seen, determine the results of analysis—the effect of traumas, the constitutional strength of the instincts and the modification of the ego—we are at this point concerned with the second only: the strength of the instincts. Reflection immediately suggests a doubt as to whether it is necessary to use the qualifying adjective "constitutional" (or "congenital"). It is true that from the very beginning the constitutional factor is of crucial importance, but it is yet conceivable that the same effects might ensue from a reinforcement of instinctual energy at some later period in life. If this were so, we should have to modify our formula and say "the strength of the instincts at a given moment" rather than "the constitutional strength of the instincts." Now the first of our questions was this: is it possible for analysis permanently and definitively to resolve a conflict between instinct and ego or to settle a pathogenic instinctual demand upon the ego? To avoid misunderstanding we must perhaps define more exactly what we mean by the phrase: "a permanent settlement of an instinctual demand." We certainly do not mean that we cause the demand to disappear, so that it never makes itself felt again. As a rule this is impossible and not even desirable. No, we mean something else, something which may be roughly described as the "taming" of the instinct. That is to say, it is brought into harmony with the ego and becomes accessible to the influence of the other trends in the ego, no longer seeking for independent satisfaction. If we are asked how and by what means this result is achieved, we do not find it easy to answer. There is nothing for it but to "summon help from the Witch"[4]—the Witch Metapsychology. Without metapsychological speculation and theorizing—I had almost said "phantasy"—we shall not get a step further. Unfortunately, here as elsewhere, what our Witch reveals is neither very clear nor very exact. We have only a single clue to follow—but a clue the value of which cannot be exaggerated—namely, the antithesis between the primary and the secondary processes, and to this I must refer here.

Reverting to our first question, we find that our new approach to the problem makes a particular conclusion inevitable. The question was as follows: is it possible permanently and definitively to resolve an instinctual conflict—that is to say, to "tame" the instinctual demand? Formulated thus, the question contains no mention whatever of the strength of the instinct, but it is precisely this which determines the issue. Let us assume that what analysis achieves for neurotics is only what normal people accomplish for themselves without its help. But everyday experience teaches us that in a normal person any solution of an instinctual conflict holds good only for a particular strength of instinct, or rather, only where there is a particular relation between the strength of the instinct and the strength of the ego.[5] If the latter becomes enfeebled, whether through illness, exhaustion or for some similar cause, all the instincts which have so far been successfully tamed may renew their demands and strive in abnormal

4 "*So muss denn doch die Hexe dran.*" [Goethe, *Faust*, Part I.]
5 Or, to be perfectly accurate, where that relation falls within particular limits.

ways after substitutive satisfactions.[6] We have irrefutable proof of this statement in what takes place in dreams, when the reaction to the ego's condition in sleep is the awakening of instinctual demands.

The material relating to the strength of the instincts is equally unambiguous. Twice in the course of the development of the individual certain instincts are powerfully reinforced: at puberty and at the menopause in women. We are not in the least surprised if people who were normal before become neurotic at these times. When the instincts were not so strong these individuals succeeded in taming them, but they can no longer do so when the instincts acquire this new strength. The repressions behave like dams in time of flood. What occurs regularly at these two periods, when for physiological reasons the instincts become stronger, may occur sporadically as the result of accidental influences at any other period in life. Factors contributing to the reinforcement of instinct are: fresh traumas, the infliction of frustration and collateral interaction between the various instincts. The result is always the same and it confirms the irresistible importance of the quantitative factor in the causation of illness.

I feel as if I ought to be ashamed of so much ponderous exposition, seeing that all I have said has long been familiar and self-evident. It is a fact that we have always behaved as if we knew these things, yet for the most part our theoretical concepts have failed to give the same importance to the economic as to the dynamic and topographical aspects of the case. So my excuse must be that I am drawing attention to this omission.

Before we decide on an answer to our question, however, we must listen to an objection the force of which lies in the

[6] Here we have a justification of the claim to aetiological importance of such unspecific factors as overwork, shock, etc. These have always been certain of general recognition and psychoanalysis has had to force them into the background. It is impossible to define health except in terms of metapsychology, *i.e.* of the dynamic relations between those agencies of the psychical apparatus, the existence of which psychoanalysis has discovered, or, if it is preferred, has deduced or conjectured.

fact that we are very likely predisposed in its favour. It will be contended that our arguments are all deduced from the spontaneous processes that take place between ego and instinct and that we are assuming that analytic therapy can accomplish nothing which does not occur spontaneously under favourable normal conditions. But is this really so? Is not the claim of our theory precisely that analysis produces a state which never does occur spontaneously within the ego and the creation of which constitutes the main difference between a person who has been analysed and a person who has not? Let us consider on what this claim is based. All repressions take place in early childhood; they are primitive defensive measures adopted by the immature, feeble ego. In later years there are no fresh repressions, but the old ones persist and are used by the ego for the purpose of further mastering instinct. New conflicts are resolved by what we call "after-repression." To these infantile repressions our general statement applies that they depend entirely on the relative strength of the various psychical forces and cannot withstand an increase in the strength of the instincts. But analysis enables the mature ego, which by this time has attained a greater strength, to review these old repressions, with the result that some are lifted, while others are accepted but reconstructed from more solid material. These new dams have a greater tenacity than the earlier ones; we may be confident that they will not so easily give way before the flood-tide of instinct. Thus the real achievement of analytic therapy would be the subsequent correction of the original process of repression, with the result that the supremacy of the quantitative factor is brought to an end.

So far our theory, to which we must adhere unless we are irresistibly compelled to abandon it. And what is the testimony of our *experience*? Perhaps it is not yet wide enough to enable us to come to a definite decision. Quite often it justifies our expectations, but not always. Our impression is that we must not be surprised if the difference between a person who has not and a person who has been analysed is, after all, not so radical as we endeavour to make it and expect and assert that it will be. Thus analysis does indeed sometimes succeed in counteracting the effect of increases in the strength of instinct, but it does not invariably do so. Sometimes its effect is simply to raise the power of the resistance put up by inhibitions, so that after analysis they are equal to a much heavier strain than before the analysis took place or if it had never taken place at all. I really cannot commit myself to a decision on this point nor do I know whether at the present time a decision is possible.

There is another angle from which we may approach this problem of the variability of the effect of analysis. We know that the first step towards the intellectual mastery of the world in which we live is the discovery of general principles, rules and laws which bring order into chaos. By such mental operations we simplify the world of phenomena, but we cannot avoid falsifying it in so doing, especially when we are dealing with processes of development and change. We are trying to discern a qualitative alteration and as a rule we neglect, at any rate at first, the quantitative factor. In reality transitional and intermediate stages are far more common than sharply differentiated opposite states. In studying various developments and changes we focus our attention entirely on the result and we readily overlook the fact that such processes are usually more or less incomplete, that is to say, the changes that take place are really only partial. A shrewd satirist of the old Austria, Johann Nestroy, once said: "Every advance is only half as great as it looks at first." One is tempted to think that this malicious dictum is universally valid. There are almost always vestiges of what has been and a partial arrest at a former stage. When an open-handed Maecenas surprises us by some isolated trait of miserliness or a person whose kind-heartedness has been excessive suddenly indulges in some unfriendly act, these are "vestiges" and are of priceless value for genetic research. They show that these praiseworthy and valuable qualities are based on compensation and overcompensation which, as was only to be expected, have not been absolutely and completely successful. Our first account of libidinal development was that an original oral phase was succeeded by a sadistic-anal, and this in its turn by a phallic-genital phase. Later investigation has not contradicted this view, but we must now qualify our statement by saying that the one phase does not succeed the other suddenly but gradually, so that part of the earlier organization always persists side by side with the later, and that even in normal development the transformation is never complete, the final structure often containing vestiges of earlier libidinal fixations. We see the same thing in quite different connections. There is not one of the erroneous and superstitious beliefs of mankind that are supposed to have been superseded but has left vestiges at the present day in the lower strata of civilized peoples or even in the highest strata of cultivated society. All that has once lived clings tenaciously to life. Sometimes one feels inclined to doubt whether the dragons of primaeval ages are really extinct.

Applying these remarks to our particular problem, I would say that the answer to the question how we explain the variable results or our analytic therapy might well be that our success in replacing insecure repressions by reliable and ego-syntonic controls is not always complete, i.e. is not radical enough. A change does occur but it is often only partial: parts of the old mechanisms remain untouched by analysis. It is difficult to prove that this is really so. We can only judge it by the result which it is supposed to explain. But the impressions we receive during our analytic work do not contradict this hypothesis—rather, they confirm it. We have to be careful not to imagine that the clarity of our own insight is a measure of the conviction we produce in the mind of the patient. This conviction may lack "depth," so to speak; the point in question is always that quantitative factor which is so easily overlooked. If we now have the correct answer to our question, we may say that analysis is always right in theory in its claim to cure neurosis by ensuring control over instinct but that in practice its claim is not always justified. This is because it does not always succeed in laying sufficiently firm foundations for that control. The reason for this partial failure is easy to discover. The quantitative factor of instinctual strength in the past opposed the efforts of the patient's ego to defend itself, and now that analysis has been called in to help, that same factor sets a limit to the efficacy of this new attempt. If the instincts are excessively strong the ego fails in its task, although it is now mature and has the support of analysis, just as it failed in earlier days in its helpless state; its control over instinct is greater but not complete, because the change in the defensive mechanism is only partial. This is not surprising, for the power of analysis is not infinite; it is limited, and the final result always depends on the relative strength of the conflicting psychical agencies.

No doubt it is desirable to shorten analytic treatment, but we shall achieve our therapeutic purpose only when we can give a greater measure of analytic help to the patient's ego. At one time it seemed that hypnotic influence was a splendid way of achieving our end; the reasons why we had to abandon that method are well known. Hitherto no substitute for hypnosis has been discovered, but we can understand from this how such a master of analysis as Ferenczi came to devote his last years to therapeutic experiments which were, alas! in vain.

4

The two further questions—whether, when dealing with one instinctual conflict, we can guard a patient against future conflicts and whether it is practicable and advisable to stir up for purposes of prophylaxis a conflict which is not at the moment manifest—must be treated together; for obviously the first task can be accomplished only if one performs the second, i.e. if one turns a possible future conflict into an actual one and then brings analytic influence to bear upon it. This new problem is really only an extension of the earlier one. In the first instance we were considering how to guard against the return of the *same* conflict: now we are considering the possible substitution of a second conflict for the first. This sounds a very ambitious proposal, but we are in fact only trying to make clear what limits are set to the efficacy of analytic therapy.

Tempting as it may be to our therapeutic ambition to propose such tasks for itself, experience bids us reject them out of hand. If an instinctual conflict is not an actual one and does not manifest itself in any way, it cannot be influenced by analysis. The warning that we should "let sleeping dogs lie"—which we have so often heard in connection with our investigation of the psychical underworld—is peculiarly inapposite when applied to the conditions existing in mental life. For, if the instincts are causing disturbances it is a proof that the dogs are not sleeping and if they seem really to be sleeping, we have not the power to wake them. This last statement, however, does not seem entirely accurate and we must consider it in greater detail. Let us consider the means we have at our disposal for transforming a latent into an actual instinctual conflict. Clearly there are only two things we can do: either we can bring about situations in which the conflict becomes actual or we can content ourselves with discussing it in analysis and pointing out that it may possibly arise. The first of these two alternatives can be accomplished in two different ways, either in reality, or in the transference. In either case we expose the patient to a measure of real suffering through frustration and the damming-up of libido. Now it is true that in ordinary analytic practice we do make use of this technique. Otherwise, what would be the meaning of the rule that analysis must be carried through "in a state of abstinence"? But we use it when we are dealing with a conflict which is already present. We try to bring this conflict to a head and to develop it in its most acute form in order to increase the instinctual energy available for its solution. Analytic experience has taught us that the better is always the enemy of the good and that in every phase of the patient's restoration we have to combat his inertia, which disposes him to be content with a partial solution of his conflicts.

If, however, our aim is the prophylactic treatment of instinctual conflicts which are not actual but merely possible, it is not enough to deal with the suffering which the patient is inevitably undergoing. We must make up our minds to conjure up fresh suffering—a thing which we have so far quite rightly left to fate. We should receive protests from all sides against the presumption of vying with fate in putting wretched human beings to such cruel experiments. And what sort of experiments would they be? Could we, for purposes of pro-

phylaxis, take the responsibility of destroying a happy marriage or causing a patient to give up work upon which his
livelihood depended? Fortunately there is no question of having to justify such interference with real life. We have not the
plenary powers which such intervention would demand and
most certainly the object of this therapeutic experiment would
refuse to co-operate in it. In practice then, this method may
be said to be excluded and there are, besides, theoretical objections to it, for the work of analysis progresses best when
the patient's pathogenic experiences belong to the past so that
the ego can stand at a distance from them. In conditions of
acute crisis it is, to all intents and purposes, impossible to use
analysis. In such states the whole interest of the ego is concentrated on the painful reality, and resists analysis, which
seeks to penetrate below the surface and to discover the influences to which the patient has been exposed in the past.
Thus to create a fresh conflict will only make the analysis
longer and more difficult.

It may be objected that all this discussion is quite superfluous. Nobody imagines that a latent instinctual conflict can
be treated by purposely conjuring up a fresh painful situation. As a prophylactic achievement this would not be much
to boast of. Let us take an example: we know that when a
patient recovers from scarlet fever he has become immune to
a recurrence of that illness. But it never occurs to a physician
on that account to infect a patient with scarlet fever in order to make him immune. It is not the business of prophylactic treatment to produce the same dangerous situation as that
of the illness itself but only something much more mild, as
in the case of vaccination and many similar procedures. Similarly, in the analytic prophylaxis of instinctual conflicts the
only methods which we need really consider are the other
two: the artificial production of new conflicts in the transference (conflicts which lack the character of reality) and the
rousing of such conflicts in the imagination of the patient by
talking to him about them and telling him that they may
possibly arise.

I do not know if we can assert that the first of these two
less drastic procedures is out of the question in analysis. No

experiments have been made in this particular direction. But some difficulties at once suggest themselves which make the success of such an undertaking very problematic. In the first place the choice of such situations for the transference is very limited. The patient himself cannot embody all his conflicts in the transference, nor can the transference-situation be so employed by the analyst as to rouse all the instinctual conflicts in which the patient may possibly become engaged. We may incite him to jealousy or inflict upon him the pain of disappointed love, but no special technical design is necessary for that purpose. These things happen spontaneously in most analyses. But in the second place we must not overlook the fact that any such deliberate procedure would necessitate unkind behaviour on the part of the analyst towards the patient and this would have an injurious effect upon his affectionate attitude towards the analyst, *i.e.* upon the positive transference, which is the patient's strongest motive for co-operating in the work of analysis. So we shall not form any high expectation of the results of such a technique.

This leaves only the other method, which is probably the only one originally contemplated. The analyst will tell the patient about possible instinctual conflicts which may occur and will lead him to expect that they may occur in himself. This is done in the hope that the information and warning will have the effect of activating in the patient one of these conflicts in a moderate degree and yet sufficiently for it to be dealt with. But here experience speaks with no uncertain voice. The result hoped for is not achieved. The patient hears what we say but it rouses no response in his mind. He probably thinks to himself: "That is very interesting, but I see no sign of it in myself." We have increased his knowledge but effected no other change in his mind. We have much the same situation when people read psychoanalytical writings. The reader is "stimulated" only by those passages which he feels apply to himself, *i.e.* which refer to conflicts that are active in him. Everything else leaves him cold. I think we have a similar experience when we enlighten children on matters of sex. I am far from maintaining that this is a harmful or unnecessary thing to do, but it is clear that the prophylactic effect of this liberal measure has been vastly over-estimated. After such enlightenment the children know something that they did not know before but they make no use of the new knowledge imparted to them. We come to the conclusion that they are by no means ready to sacrifice those sexual theories which may be said to be a natural growth and which they have constructed in harmony with and in dependence on their undeveloped libidinal organization—theories about the part played by the stork, about the nature of sexual intercourse and about the way in which children are born. For a long time after they have been enlightened on these subjects they behave like primitive races who have had Christianity thrust upon them and continue in secret to worship their old idols.

5

Our starting-point was the question of how to shorten the tediously long duration of an analysis and, still pursuing the question of time, we went on to consider whether we can achieve permanent cure or prevent illness in the future by prophylactic treatment. We saw that the success of our therapeutic work depended on the influence of traumatic factors in the aetiology of the neurosis, on the relative strength of the instincts which have to be controlled and on something which we called modification of the ego. Only the second of these factors has been discussed in any detail and we have had occasion in so doing to recognize the paramount importance of the quantitative factor and to stress the claim of the metapsychological standpoint to be taken into account in any attempt at explanation.

Of the third factor, the modification of the ego, we have as yet said nothing. The first impression received when we turn our attention to it is that there is much to ask and to answer, and that what we can say on the subject will prove very inadequate. This impression is confirmed when we go into the problem further. We know that the essence of the analytic situation is that the analyst enters into an alliance with the ego of the patient to subdue certain uncontrolled parts of his id, *i.e.* to include them in the synthesis of the ego. The fact that in the case of psychotics this co-operation is never successful brings us to our first definite conclusion. If we want to make a compact with the patient's ego, that ego must be normal. But such a normal ego is, like normality in general, an ideal fiction. The abnormal ego, which is of no use for our purpose, is unfortunately no fiction. Now every normal person is only approximately normal: his ego resembles that of the psychotic in one point or another, in a greater or lesser degree, and its distance from one end of the scale and proximity to the other may provisionally serve as a measure of what we have indefinitely spoken of as "modification of the ego."

If we ask what is the source of the great variety of kinds and degrees of ego-modification we cannot escape the first obvious alternative that such modifications are either congenital or acquired. The second case will be the easier to treat. If they are acquired it must certainly have been during the individual's development from the very beginning of his life. From the very outset the ego has to try to fulfil its task of acting as an intermediary between the id and the external world in the service of the pleasure principle, to protect the id from the dangers of the external world. If, while thus endeavouring, the ego learns to adopt a defensive attitude towards its own id and to treat the instinctual demands of the latter like external dangers, this is at any rate partly because it understands that satisfaction of instinct would lead to conflicts with the external world. Under the influence of its upbringing, the child's ego accustoms itself to shift the scene of the battle from outside to inside and to master the *inner* danger before it becomes *external*. Probably it is generally right in so doing. In this battle on two fronts—later there is a third front as well—the ego makes use of various methods of fulfilling its task, *i.e.*, to put it in general terms, of avoiding danger, anxiety and unpleasure. We call these devices *defensive mechanisms*. Our knowledge of them is as yet incomplete. Anna Freud's book (1936) has given us our first insight into their multiplicity and their manifold significance.

One of these mechanisms, that of repression, provided the

starting-point for the study of neurotic processes in general. There was never any doubt that repression was not the only method which the ego could employ for its purposes. Nevertheless, repression is something quite peculiar, more sharply differentiated from the other mechanisms than these are from one another. I should like to make its relation to these other mechanisms clear by an analogy, but I know that analogies never carry us very far in such matters.

Let us imagine what might have happened to a book at the time when books were not printed in editions but written out separately by hand. We will imagine that such a book contained statements which at a later time were regarded as undesirable—as, for instance, according to Robert Eisler (1929), the writings of Flavius Josephus must have contained passages about Jesus Christ which were offensive to later Christendom. At the present day the only defensive mechanism to which the official censorship would resort would be the confiscation and destruction of every copy of the whole edition. At that time other methods were employed to render the book innocuous. Either the offensive passages were heavily scored through, so that they were illegible, in which case they could not be transcribed and the next copyist of the book produced a text to which no exception could be taken but which had gaps in certain places, probably making the passages in question unintelligible. Or, not satisfied with this, the authorities tried to conceal any indication that the text had been mutilated. They therefore proceeded to tamper with the text. Single words here and there were left out or replaced by others and whole new sentences were interpolated; at best, the passage was completely erased and replaced by another in exactly the opposite sense. When the book was next transcribed the text aroused no suspicion, but had, in fact, been falsified. It no longer contained the author's statement and very probably the correction was not in the interests of truth.

Without pressing the analogy too closely we may say that repression is to the other methods of defence what the omission of words or passages is to the corruption of a text, and in the various forms of this falsification we can discover parallels to the manifold ways in which the ego may be modified.

It may be objected that this analogy breaks down in an essential particular, for the corruption of a text is the work of a purposeful censorship to which we have no counterpart in the development of the ego. But this is not so, for this purpose is amply represented by the compelling force of the pleasure principle. The psychical apparatus is intolerant of unpleasure and strives to ward it off at all costs and, if the perception of reality involves unpleasure, that perception—*i.e.* the truth—must be sacrificed. For quite a long time flight and an avoidance of a dangerous situation serve as expedients in the face of external danger, until the individual is finally strong enough to remove the menace by actively modifying reality. But one cannot flee from oneself and no flight avails against danger from within; hence the ego's defensive mechanisms are condemned to falsify the inner perception, so that it transmits to us only an imperfect and travestied picture of our id. In its relations with the id the ego is paralysed by its restrictions or blinded by its errors, and the result in the sphere of psychical events may be compared to the progress of a poor walker in a country which he does not know.

The purpose of the defensive mechanisms is to avert dangers. It cannot be disputed that they are successful; it is doubtful whether the ego can altogether do without them during its development, but it is also certain that they themselves may become dangerous. Not infrequently it turns out that the ego has paid too high a price for the services which these mechanisms render. The expenditure of energy necessary to maintain them and the ego-restrictions which they almost invariably entail prove a heavy burden on the psychical economy. Moreover these mechanisms are not relinquished after they have helped the ego through the difficult years of its development. Of course, no individual makes use of all the possible mechanisms of defence: each person merely selects certain of them, but these become fixated in his ego, establishing themselves as regular modes of reaction for that particular character, which are repeated throughout life whenever a situation occurs similar to that which originally evoked them. They are, in fact, infantilisms and share the fate of so many institutions which struggle to maintain themselves when they have outlived their usefulness. *"Vernunft wird Unsinn, Wohltat Plage,"*[7] as the poet laments. The adult ego with its greater strength continues to defend itself against dangers which no longer exist in reality and even finds itself impelled to seek out real situations which may serve as a substitute for the original danger, so as to be able to justify its clinging to its habitual modes of reaction. Thus the defensive mechanisms produce an ever-growing alienation from the external world and a permanent enfeeblement of the ego and we can easily understand how they pave the way for and precipitate the outbreak of neurosis.

For the moment, however, we are not concerned with the pathogenic role of the defensive mechanisms. Our purpose is to discover how our therapeutic work is affected by the ego-modification they produce. The material for the answer to this question is contained in Anna Freud's work, to which I have already referred. The main point is that the patient repeats these modes of reaction during analysis itself, exhibiting them, as it were, before our eyes; in fact, that is the only means we have of learning about them. This must not be taken to imply that they make analysis impossible. On the contrary, they constitute half of our analytic task. The other half, the first to be tackled by analysis in its early days, is the revelation of that which is hidden in the id. Our therapeutic work swings to and fro during the treatment like a pendulum, analysing now a fragment of the id and now a fragment of the ego. In the one case our aim is to bring a part of the id into consciousness and in the other to correct something in the ego. The crux of the matter is that the mechanisms of defence against former dangers recur in analysis in the shape of *resistances* to cure. It follows that the ego treats recovery itself as a new danger.

The therapeutic effect of analysis depends on the making conscious what is, in the widest sense, repressed within the id. We prepare the way for this operation by our interpretations

---

[7] ["Reason becomes unreason, kindness torment." Goethe, *Faust,* Part I.]

and constructions, but so long as the ego clings to its former defences and refuses to abandon its resistances we have interpreted merely for ourselves and not for the patient. Now these resistances, although they belong to the ego, are nevertheless unconscious and, in a certain sense, they are segregated within the ego. The analyst recognizes them more easily than the hidden material in the id; one would suppose it would be enough to treat them as parts of the id and to bring them into relation with the rest of the ego by making them conscious. This would mean that half of our analytic task had been accomplished: we are hardly prepared for a resistance to the discovery of resistances. But what takes place is as follows. While we are analysing the resistances, the ego—more or less of set purpose—breaks the compact upon which the analytic situation is based. It ceases to support us in our efforts to reveal the id, it opposes those efforts, disobeys the fundamental rule of analysis and suffers no further derivatives of repressed material to emerge into consciousness. It is too much to expect that the patient should have a firm conviction of the curative power of analysis, but he may have come to the analyst with a certain amount of confidence and this, reinforced by the various factors in the positive transference which it is our business to evoke, makes him capable of doing his share. The effect of the unpleasurable impulses which he feels stirring in him when his defensive conflicts are once more roused may be that negative transferences gain the upper hand and break up the whole analytic situation. The patient now regards the analyst simply as an alien personality who makes disagreeable demands upon him and he behaves towards him exactly like a child who does not like a stranger and has no confidence in him. If the analyst tries to explain to the patient one of the distortions which his defence has produced and to correct it, he meets with a complete lack of comprehension and an imperviousness to valid arguments. We see then that there really *is* a resistance to the discovery of resistances and that the defensive mechanisms do deserve the name which we originally gave them before they had been more closely examined: they are resistances not only to the bringing of id-contents into consciousness but also to the whole process of analysis and so to cure.

The effect which the defensive activities produce within the ego is rightly described as "modification of the ego," if by that we understand the deviation of the ego from an imaginary normal ego which would guarantee unswerving loyalty to the analytic compact. We can well believe what our daily experience suggests, that the outcome of an analysis depends principally upon the strength and depth of the roots of the resistances constituting the ego-modification. Once more we realize the importance of the quantitative factor and once more we are reminded that analysis has only certain limited quantities of energy which it can employ to match against the hostile forces. And it does seem as if victory were really for the most part with the big battalions.

6

Our next question will be whether all modification of the ego (in the sense in which we are using the term) is acquired during the defensive conflicts of early childhood. There can be no doubt about the answer. We have no reason to dispute the existence and importance of primary congenital variations in the ego. A single fact is decisive, namely, that every individual selects only *certain* of the possible defensive mechanisms and invariably employs those which he has selected. This suggests that each individual ego is endowed from the beginning with its own peculiar dispositions and tendencies, though it is true that we cannot predicate their nature and conditioning factors. Moreover, we know that we must not exaggerate the difference between inherited and acquired characteristics into an antithesis; what was acquired by our ancestors is certainly an important part of what we inherit. When we speak of our "archaic heritage" we are generally thinking only of the id and we apparently assume that no ego is yet in existence at the beginning of the individual's life. But we must not overlook the fact that id and ego are originally one, and it does not imply a mystical over-valuation of heredity if we think it credible that, even before the ego exists, its subsequent lines of development, tendencies and reactions are already determined. The psychological peculiarities of families, races and nations, even in their attitude towards analysis, admit of no other explanation. Indeed, analytic experience convinces us that particular psychical contents, such as symbolism, have no other source than hereditary transmission, and research in various fields of social psychology seems to justify the assumption that there are other, no less specialized, deposits from primitive human development present in our archaic heritage.

When we recognize that the peculiarities of the ego which we detect in the form of resistances may be not only acquired in defensive conflicts but determined by heredity, the topographical differentiation between ego and id loses much of its value for our investigations. When we advance a step further in analytic experience we come upon resistances of another type, which we can no longer localize and which seem to be conditioned by certain fundamental characteristics of the mental apparatus. I can give only a few examples of the type of resistance to which I refer: this whole field of inquiry is still bewilderingly strange and has not been sufficiently explored. We come across people, for instance, of whom we should say that they display a peculiar "adhesiveness of libido." The processes which their analysis sets in motion are so much slower than in other people because they apparently cannot make up their minds to detach libidinal cathexes from one object and displace them to another, although we can find no particular reasons for this cathectic fidelity. Then we meet the opposite type, in which libido seems specially mobile: it readily enters upon the new cathexes suggested by the analysis, abandoning its former ones for these. The difference between the two types is comparable to that experienced by a sculptor according as he works in hard stone or soft clay. Unfortunately in the latter type the results of analysis often prove very evanescent; the new cathexes are soon abandoned and one feels not as if one had been working in clay but as if one had been writing on water. *"Wie gewonnen, so zerronnen,"*[8] as the proverb says.

In another group of patients we are surprised by an attitude which we can only put down to a loss of the plasticity we should expect, an exhaustion of the capacity for change and development. We are indeed prepared for a certain degree of psychical inertia in analysis; when new paths are pointed out for the instinctual impulses, we almost invariably see an obvious hesitation in entering upon them. We have described this attitude, though perhaps not quite rightly, as "resistance from the id." But in the cases which I have in mind all the mental processes, relations and distributions of energy are immutable, fixed and rigid. One finds the same state of affairs in very old people, when it is explained by what is described as force of habit, the exhaustion of receptivity through a kind of psychical entropy; but I am thinking of people who are still young. Our theoretical knowledge does not seem adequate to explain these types. Probably some element of a temporal nature is at work here, changes in some rhythm in the development of psychical life which we have not yet apprehended.

In yet another group of cases the patients' resistance to analysis and the obstacles in the way of therapeutic success are probably due to variations in the ego which spring from another and even deeper root. Here we come to the ultimate phenomena to which psychological research has penetrated—the behaviour of the two primal instincts, their distribution, fusion and defusion, things which we cannot imagine to be confined to a single province of the mental apparatus, whether it be id, ego or super-ego. Nothing impresses us more strongly in connection with the resistances encountered in analysis than the feeling that there is a force at work which is defending itself by all possible means against recovery and is clinging tenaciously to illness and suffering. We have recognized that part of this force is the sense of guilt and the need for punishment, and that is undoubtedly correct; we have localized it in the ego's relation to the super-ego. But this is only one

---

[8] ["Easy come, easy go."]

element in it, which may be described as psychically bound by the super-ego and which we thus perceive. We may suppose that other portions of the same force are at work, either bound or free, in some unspecified region of the mind. If we consider the whole picture made up of the phenomena of the masochism inherent in so many people, of the negative therapeutic reaction and of the neurotic's sense of guilt, we shall have to abandon the belief that mental processes are governed exclusively by a striving after pleasure. These phenomena are unmistakable indications of the existence of a power in mental life which, according to its aim, we call the aggressive or destructive instinct and which we derive from the primal death-instinct of animate matter. It is not a question of an optimistic as opposed to a pessimistic theory of life. Only by the concurrent or opposing action of the two primal instincts—Eros and the death-instinct—never by one or the other alone, can the motley variety of vital phenomena be explained.

How the elements of these two species of instinct combine to fulfil the various vital functions, under what conditions such combinations grow looser and break up, what disturbances correspond to these changes and what feelings they evoke in the perceptual scale of the pleasure principle—these are problems whose elucidation would be the most valuable achievement of psychological research. For the moment we must bow to those superior forces which foil our efforts. Even to exert a psychical influence upon a simple case of masochism is a severe tax on our powers.

In studying the phenomena which testify to the activity of the instinct of destruction we are not confined to the observation of pathological material. There are countless facts in normal mental life which require this explanation, and the keener the power of our discernment the greater the abundance in which they present themselves to our notice. The subject is too novel and too important to be treated as a side-issue in this discussion; I will content myself with selecting a few specimens of these phenomena.

Here is an example: It is well known that at all times there have been, as there still are, human beings who can take as their sexual objects persons of either sex without the one trend interfering with the other. We call these people bisexual and accept the fact of their existence without wondering much at it. But we have come to know that all human beings are bisexual in this sense and that their libido is distributed between objects of both sexes, either in a manifest or a latent form. But the following point strikes us. While in the individuals I first mentioned the libidinal impulses can take both directions without producing a clash, in the other and more frequent cases the result is an irreconcilable conflict. A man's heterosexuality will not tolerate homosexuality, and vice versa. If the former tendency is the stronger, it succeeds in keeping the latter in a state of latency and preventing its attaining satisfaction in actuality. On the other hand there is no greater danger for a man's heterosexual function than disturbance by latent homosexuality. We might explain these facts by saying that each individual has only a given quantity of libido at his disposal and that the two rival trends have to contend for it. But it is not clear why these rivals should not regularly divide between them the available quantity of libido, according to their relative strength, since that is what does in fact happen in some cases. We are forced to conclude that there is something peculiar in the tendency to conflict, something which introduces a new element into the situation, independently of the quantity of libido. It is difficult to account for this spontaneous tendency to conflict except as the intervention of an element of free aggressiveness.

If we recognize that the case which I have just described is a manifestation of the destructive or aggressive instinct we are at once confronted with the question whether this notion should not be extended to apply to other instances of conflict, or, indeed, whether we ought not to review all our knowledge of psychical conflict from this new angle. After all, we assume that, in the course of the development of human beings from their primitive state to civilization a considerable part of their aggressiveness is internalized or turned inwards; and, if this is so, internal conflicts would certainly be the correct equivalent of the external conflicts which have now ceased. I am well aware that the dualistic theory, according to which an instinct of death, destruction or aggression claims equal partnership with Eros as manifested in libido, has met with little general acceptance and has not really established itself even among psychoanalysts. My delight was proportionately great when I recently discovered that that theory was held by one of the great thinkers of ancient Greece. For the sake of this confirmation I am happy to sacrifice the prestige of originality, especially as I read so widely in earlier years that I can never be quite certain that what I thought was a creation of my own mind may not really have been an outcome of cryptomnesia.

Empedocles of Acragas (Girgenti),[9] born about 495 B.C., is one of the grandest and most remarkable figures in the history of Greek civilization. The interests of this many-sided personality took the most varied directions. He was a man of science and a thinker, a prophet and a magician, a politician, a philanthropist and a physician versed in natural science. He was said to have freed the town of Selinus from malaria, and his contemporaries worshipped him as a god. The sharpest contrasts seem to have co-existed in his mind; exact and sober in his researches in physics and physiology, he did not recoil from obscure mysticism and he indulged in cosmic speculations of astonishing imaginative boldness. Capelle compares him with Dr. Faust, to whom *"manch Geheimnis wurde kund."*[10] Born at a time when the realm of science was not yet divided into so many provinces, he held some theories which inevitably strike us as primitive. He explained the variety of things by the fusion of the four elements, earth, air, fire and water, and he held that all nature was animate and believed in the transmigration of souls. At the same time, however, he had such modern ideas as that of the gradual evolution of living beings, the survival of the fittest and the recognition of the part played by chance (*tyche*) in this development.

The theory of Empedocles which specially claims our attention is one which approximates so closely to the psycho-

[9] I have based what follows on a work by Wilhelm Capelle (1935).
[10] ["Many a secret was revealed." Goethe, *Faust*, Part I.]

analytical theory of the instincts that we should be tempted
to maintain that the two are identical, were it not for this
difference: the Greek's theory is a cosmic phantasy, while our
own confines its application to biology. At the same time, the
fact that Empedocles ascribed to the whole universe the same
animistic principle as is manifested in each individual organism
makes this difference considerably less important.

The Greek philosopher taught that there were two principles governing events in the life of the universe as in that of
the mind, and that these principles were eternally in conflict with each other. He called them *philia* (love) and
neikos (strife). Of these powers, which he really conceived
of as "natural forces working like instincts, and certainly not
intelligences with a conscious purpose,"[11] the one strives to
unite the atoms of these four elements into a single unity,
while the other seeks to dissolve these fusions and to separate
the atoms of the elements. Empedocles conceives of the world-
process as a continuous, never-ceasing alternation of periods
in which the one or the other of the two fundamental forces
triumphs, so that at one time love and, at another time, strife
fulfils its purpose and governs the universe, after which the
other, vanquished power asserts itself and in its turn prevails.

The two fundamental principles of Empedocles—*philia*
and *neikos*—are, both in name and in function, the same
as our two primal instincts, *Eros* and *Destructiveness*, the former of which strives to combine existing phenomena into ever
greater unities, while the latter seeks to dissolve these combinations and destroy the structures to which they have given
rise. But we shall not be surprised to find that this theory has
changed in certain respects on its re-emergence after two and
a half millennia. Apart from our being necessarily restricted to
the biopsychical field, we no longer take as our basic substance
the four elements of Empedocles; animate matter is now
sharply differentiated from inanimate and we no longer think
of the mingling and separation of particles of matter but of
the fusion and defusion of instinctual components. Moreover,
we now have a certain biological basis for the principle of

11 Capelle (1935), 186.

"strife," since we have traced back the destructive instinct to the death instinct, the urge of animate matter to return to an inanimate state. We are not denying by this that an analogous instinct already existed earlier; nor are we asserting, of course, that such an instinct only came into existence with the emergence of life. Nor can anyone foresee in what guise the nucleus of truth contained in the theory of Empedocles will present itself to the vision of a later day.

7

In 1927, Ferenczi read an instructive paper [published 1928] entitled "Das Problem der Beendigung der Analysen." He concluded it with the comforting assurance that "analysis is by no means an interminable process. On the contrary, if the analyst has a thorough knowledge of his business and a sufficient fund of patience the treatment can be carried to a natural conclusion." The paper as a whole, however, seems to me to convey a warning not to aim at the shortening but rather at the deepening of the analytic process. Ferenczi makes the further important point that success very largely depends upon the analyst's having profited by the lesson of his own "errors and mistakes," and got the better of "the weak points in his own personality." This is an important contribution to our problem. Amongst the factors which influence the prospects of an analysis and add to its difficulties in the same manner as the resistances, we must reckon not only the structure of the *patient's* ego but the personal characteristics of the *analyst*.

It cannot be disputed that analysts do not in their own personalities wholly come up to the standard of psychical normality which they set for their patients. Opponents of analysis often point this out derisively and use it as an argument to prove the uselessness of the analytic method. We might seek to refute the criticism by asserting that it makes an unjustifiable demand upon analysts, who are individuals trained in the practice of a certain art and are presumably ordinary human beings. Nobody surely maintains that a physician is incapable of treating internal diseases because his own internal organs happen to be unsound. On the contrary, it may be argued that there is a certain advantage when a man who is himself threatened with tuberculosis specializes in the treatment of that disease. But the cases are not on all fours. So long as he is capable of practising at all, a physician suffering from lung or heart trouble is not handicapped in diagnosing or treating internal disease. The analyst, on the other hand, because of the peculiar conditions of his work, is really impeded by his own defects in his task of discerning his patient's situation correctly and reacting to it in a manner conducive to cure. So there is some reason in the demand for a comparatively high degree of psychical normality and correct adjustment in the analyst as one of his qualifications for his work. And there is another point: he must be in a superior position in some sense if he is to serve as a model for his patient in certain analytic situations and, in others, to act as his teacher. Finally, we must not forget that the relationship between analyst and patient is based on a love of truth, that is, on the acknowledgment of reality, and that it precludes any kind of sham or deception.

Here let us pause for a moment to assure the analyst that he has our sincere sympathy in the very exacting requirements he is expected to fulfil. It almost looks as if analysis were the third of those "impossible" professions in which one can be quite sure of unsatisfying results. The other two, much older-established, are the bringing-up of children and the government of nations. Obviously we cannot demand that the prospective analyst should be a perfect human being before he takes up analysis, and that only persons of this rare and exalted perfection should enter the profession. But where and how is even the most inadequate of individuals to acquire the ideal qualifications for his work? The answer is: in his own analysis, with which he begins his preparation for his future activity. For practical reasons this analysis can be only short and incomplete: the main object of it is to enable the instructor to form an opinion whether the candidate should be accepted for further training. It has accomplished its purpose if it imparts to the learner a sincere conviction of the existence of the unconscious, enables him through the emergence of repressed material in his own mind to perceive in himself processes which otherwise he would have regarded as incredible and gives him a first sample of the technique which has proved to be the only correct method in conducting analyses. This in itself would not constitute adequate instruction, but we hope and believe that the stimuli received in the learner's own analysis will not cease to act upon him when that analysis ends, that the processes of ego-transformation will go on of their own accord and that he will bring his new insight to bear upon all his subsequent experience. This does indeed happen and, in so far as it happens, it qualifies the learner who has been analysed to become an analyst.

Unfortunately something else happens as well. One can only give one's impressions in describing this second result. Hostility on the one hand and partisanship on the other create an atmosphere unfavourable to objective investigation. It looks as if a number of analysts learn to make use of defensive mechanisms which enable them to evade the conclusions and requirements of analysis themselves, probably by applying them to others. They themselves remain as they are and escape the critical and corrective influence of analysis. This seems to confirm the dictum of a writer who warns us that it is hard for a mortal who acquires power not to misuse it.[12] Sometimes when we try to understand this attitude in analysts, we are irresistibly and disagreeably reminded of the effect of X-rays on those who use them without due precaution. It would scarcely be surprising if constant pre-occupation with all the repressed impulses which struggle for freedom in the human mind should sometimes cause all the instinctual demands which have hitherto been restrained to be violently awakened in the analyst himself. These are "dangers of analysis," threatening not the passive but the active partner in the analytic situation, and it is our duty to face them. There can be no doubt how they must be encountered. Every analyst ought periodically himself to enter analysis once more, at intervals of, say, five years, and without any

---

[12] Anatole France, *La révolte des anges*.

feeling of shame in so doing. So not only the patient's analysis but that of the analyst himself has ceased to be a terminable and become an interminable task.

At this point we must guard against a misconception. It is not my intention to assert that analysis in general is an endless business. Whatever our theoretical view may be, I believe that in practice analyses do come to an end. Every analyst of experience will be able to think of a number of cases in which he has taken permanent leave of the patient *rebus bene gestis*. There is a far smaller discrepancy between theory and practice in cases of so-called character-analysis. Here it is not easy to predict a natural end to the process, even if we do not look for impossibilities or ask too much of analysis. Our object will be not to rub off all the corners of the human character so as to produce "normality" according to schedule, nor yet to demand that the person who has been "thoroughly analysed" shall never again feel the stirrings of passions in himself or become involved in any internal conflict. The business of analysis is to secure the best possible psychological conditions for the functioning of the ego; when this has been done, analysis has accomplished its task.

8

Both in therapeutic and character-analyses we are struck by the prominence of two themes which give the analyst an extraordinary amount of trouble. It soon becomes clear that some general principle is at work here. These two themes are connected with the difference between the sexes: one is characteristic of men and the other equally characteristic of women. In spite of the difference in their content there is an obvious correspondence between the two. Some factor common to both sexes is forced, by the difference between them, to express itself differently in the one and in the other.

The two corresponding themes are, in women, envy for the penis—the striving after the possession of a male genital—and, in men, the struggle against their passive or feminine attitude towards other men. What is common to these two themes was singled out by early psychoanalytic nomenclature as an attitude to the castration complex. Subsequently Alfred Adler brought the term "masculine protest" into current use. It fits the case of men perfectly; but I think that, from the first, "repudiation of femininity" would have been the correct description of this remarkable feature in the psychical life of mankind.

Supposing that we now try to introduce this notion into the structure of psychoanalytical theory we shall find that, by its very nature, this factor cannot occupy the same place in the case of both sexes. In males the masculine striving is from the beginning and throughout entirely ego-syntonic; the passive attitude, since it implies an acceptance of castration, is energetically repressed, and often the only indications of its existence are exaggerated over-compensations. In females also the striving after masculinity is ego-syntonic at a certain period, namely, in the phallic phase, before development in the direction of femininity has set in. But later it succumbs to that momentous process of repression, the outcome of which (as has often been pointed out) determines the fortunes of the woman's femininity. A great deal depends upon whether a sufficient amount of her masculinity-complex escapes repression and exercises a lasting influence on her character. Normally, large portions of that complex undergo transformation and contribute to the development of femininity: the unsatisfied wish for a penis should be converted into a wish for a child and for a man, who possesses a penis. Very often indeed, however, we find that the wish for masculinity persists in the unconscious and, in its repressed state, exercises a disturbing influence.

As is plain from what has just been said, in both cases it is the attitude belonging to the sex opposite to the subject's own which succumbs to repression. I have stated elsewhere[13] that it was Wilhelm Fliess who called my attention to this point. Fliess was inclined to regard the difference between the sexes as the true cause and original motive of repression. I can only repeat that I do not accept this view: I do not think we are

13 " 'A Child Is Being Beaten' " (1919), *Sexuality and the Psychology of Love,* Collier Books edition BS 192V.

justified in sexualizing repression in this way—that is to say, in explaining it on a biological instead of a purely psychological basis.

The paramount importance of these two themes—the wish for a penis in women and, in men, the struggle against passivity—did not escape the notice of Ferenczi. In the paper that he read in 1927 he laid it down as a principle that in every successful analysis these two complexes must have been resolved.[14] From my own experience I would observe that in this I think Ferenczi was asking a very great deal. At no point in one's analytic work does one suffer more from the oppressive feeling that all one's efforts have been in vain and from the suspicion that one is "talking to the winds" than when one is trying to persuade a female patient to abandon her wish for a penis on the ground of its being unrealizable, or to convince a male patient that a passive attitude towards another man does not always signify castration and that in many relations in life it is indispensable. The rebellious over-compensation of the male produces one of the strongest transference-resistances. A man will not be subject to a father-substitute or owe him anything and he therefore refuses to accept his cure from the physician. There is no analogous form of transference which can arise from the feminine wish for a penis, but it is the source of attacks of acute depression, because women patients feel an inner conviction that the analysis will avail them nothing and that they will be none the better for it. We can only agree with them when we discover that their strongest motive in coming for treatment was the hope that they might somehow still obtain a male organ, the lack of which is so painful to them.

All this shows that the form of the resistance is immaterial: it does not matter whether it appears as a transference or not.

---

[14] ". . . in every male patient the sign that his castration-anxiety has been mastered must be forthcoming, and this sign is a sense of equality of rights with the analyst; and every female patient, if her cure is to rank as complete and permanent, must have finally conquered her masculinity-complex and become able to submit without bitterness to thinking in terms of her feminine role." (Ferenczi, 1928,8.)

The vital point is that it prevents any change from taking place—everything remains as it was. We often feel that, when we have reached the wish for a penis and the masculine protest, we have penetrated all the psychological strata and reached "bedrock" and that our task is accomplished. And this is probably correct, for in the psychical field the biological factor is really the rock-bottom. The repudiation of femininity must surely be a biological fact, part of the great riddle of sex.[15] Whether and when we have succeeded in mastering this factor in an analysis is hard to determine. We must console ourselves with the certainty that everything possible has been done to encourage the patient to examine and to change his attitude to the question.

[15] We must not be misled by the term "masculine protest" into supposing that what the man repudiates is the *attitude* of passivity, or, as we may say, the social aspect of femininity. Such a notion is speedily contradicted by the observation that the attitude such men display towards women is often masochistic or actually slavish. What they reject is not passivity in general but passivity in relation to *men*. That is to say, the "masculine protest" is in fact nothing other than fear of castration.

XX

Constructions in Analysis[1]
(1937)

1

It has always seemed to me to be greatly to the credit of a certain well-known man of science that he treated psychoanalysis fairly at a time when most other people felt themselves under no such obligation. On one occasion, nevertheless, he gave expression to an opinion upon analytic technique which was at once derogatory and unjust. He said that in giving interpretations to a patient we treat him upon the famous principle of "Heads I win, tails you lose." That is to say, if the patient agrees with us, then the interpretation is right; but if he contradicts us, that is only a sign of his resistance, which again shows that we are right. In this way we are always in the right against the poor helpless wretch whom we are analysing, no matter how he may respond to what we put forward. Now, since it is in fact true that a "No" from one

[1] ["Konstruktionen in der Analyse." First published *Int. Z. Psycho-Anal.*, 23 (1937), 459; reprinted *Ges. W.*, 16. Translation, reprinted from *Int. J. Psycho-Anal.*, 19 (1938), 377, by James Strachey.]

of our patients is not as a rule enough to make us abandon an interpretation as incorrect, a revelation such as this of the nature of our technique has been most welcome to the opponents of analysis. It is therefore worth while to give a detailed account of how we are accustomed to arrive at an assessment of the "Yes" or "No" of our patients during analytic treatment—of their expression of agreement or of denial. The practising analyst will naturally learn nothing in the course of this apologia that he does not already know.

It is familiar ground that the work of analysis aims at inducing the patient to give up the repressions (using the word in the widest sense) belonging to his early life and to replace them by reactions of a sort that would correspond better to a psychically mature condition. It is with this purpose in view that he must be got to recollect certain experiences and the emotions called up by them which he has at the moment forgotten. We know that his present symptoms and inhibitions are the consequences of repressions of this kind: that is, that they are a substitute for these things that he has forgotten. What sort of material does he put at our disposal which we can make use of to put him on the way to recovering the lost memories? All kinds of things. He gives us fragments of these memories in his dreams, invaluable in themselves but seriously distorted as a rule by all the factors concerned in the formation of dreams. Again, he produces ideas, if he gives himself up to "free association," in which we can discover allusions to the repressed experiences and derivatives of the suppressed emotions as well as of the reactions against them. And finally, there are hints of repetitions of the affects belonging to the repressed material to be found in actions performed by the patient, some important, some trivial, both inside and outside the analytic situation. Our experience has shown that the relation of transference, which becomes established towards the analyst, is particularly calculated to favour the reproduction of these emotional connections. It is out of such raw material—if we may so describe it—that we have to put together what we are in search of.

What we are in search of is a picture of the patient's forgotten years that shall be alike trustworthy and in all essential respects complete. But at this point we are reminded that the work of analysis consists of two quite different portions, that it is carried on in two separate localities, that it involves two people, to each of whom a distinct task is assigned. It may for a moment seem strange that such a fundamental fact should not have been pointed out long ago; but it will immediately be perceived that there was nothing being kept back in this, that it is a fact which is universally known and even self-evident and is merely being brought into relief here and separately examined for a particular purpose. We all know that the person who is being analysed has to be induced to remember something that has been experienced by him and repressed; and the dynamic determinants of this process are so interesting that the other portion of the work, the task performed by the analyst, has been pushed into the background. The analyst has neither experienced nor repressed any of the material under consideration; his task cannot be to remember anything. What then *is* his task? His task is to make out what has been forgotten from the traces which it has left behind or, more correctly, to *construct* it. The time and manner in which he conveys his constructions to the person who is being analysed, as well as the explanations with which he accompanies them, constitute the link between the two portions of the work of analysis, between his own part and that of the patient.

His work of construction, or, if it is preferred, of reconstruction, resembles to a great extent an archaeologist's excavation of some dwelling-place that has been destroyed and buried or of some ancient edifice. The two processes are in fact identical, except that the analyst works under better conditions and has more material at his command to assist him, since what he is dealing with is not something destroyed but something that is still alive—and perhaps for another reason as well. But just as the archaeologist builds up the walls of the building from the foundations that have remained standing, determines the number and position of the columns from depressions in the floor and reconstructs the mural decorations and paintings from the remains found in the débris, so does the analyst proceed when he draws his inferences from the fragments of memories, from the associations and from the behaviour of the subject of the analysis. Both of them have an undisputed right to reconstruct by means of supplementing and combining the surviving remains. Both of them, moreover, are subject to many of the same difficulties and sources of error. One of the most ticklish problems that confronts the archaeologist is notoriously the determination of the relative age of his finds; and if an object makes its appearance in some particular level, it often remains to be decided whether it belongs to that level or whether it was carried down to that level owing to some subsequent disturbance. It is easy to imagine the corresponding doubts that arise in the case of analytic constructions.

The analyst, as we have said, works under more favourable conditions than the archaeologist since he has at his disposal material which can have no counterpart in excavations, such as the repetitions of reactions dating from infancy and all that emerges in connection with these repetitions through the transference. But in addition to this it must be borne in mind that the excavator is dealing with destroyed objects of which large and important portions have quite certainly been lost, by mechanical violence, by fire and by plundering. No amount of effort can result in their discovery and lead to their being united with the surviving fragments. The one and only course left open is that of reconstruction, which for this very reason can often reach only a certain degree of probability. But it is different with the psychical object whose early history the analyst is seeking to recover. Here we are regularly met by a situation which in archaeology occurs only in such rare circumstances as those of Pompeii or of the tomb of Tutankhamen. All of the essentials are preserved, even things that seem completely forgotten are present somehow and somewhere, and have merely been buried and made inaccessible to the subject. Indeed, it may, as we know, be doubted whether any psychical structure can really be the victim of total destruction. It depends only upon analytic technique whether we shall succeed in bringing what is concealed completely to light. There are only two other facts that weigh against the extraordinary advantage which is thus enjoyed by the work of analysis: namely, that psychical objects are incomparably more complicated than the excavator's material ones and that we have insufficient knowledge of what we may expect to find, since their finer structure contains so much that is still mysterious. But our comparison between the two forms of work can go no further than this; for the main difference between them lies in the fact that for the archaeologist the reconstruction is the aim and end of his endeavours while for analysis the construction is only a preliminary labour.

2

It is not, however, a preliminary labour in the sense that the whole of it must be completed before the next piece of work can be begun, as, for instance, is the case with housebuilding, where all the walls must be erected and all the windows inserted before the internal decoration of the rooms can be taken in hand. Every analyst knows that things happen differently in an analytic treatment and that there both kinds of work are carried on side by side, the one kind being always a little ahead and the other following upon it. The analyst finishes a piece of construction and communicates it to the subject of the analysis so that it may work upon him; he then constructs a further piece out of the fresh material pouring in upon him, deals with it in the same way and proceeds in this alternating fashion until the end. If, in accounts of analytic technique, so little is said about "constructions," that is because "interpretations" and their effects are spoken of instead. But I think that "construction" is by far the more appropriate description. "Interpretation" applies to something that one does to some single element of the material, such as an association or a parapraxis. But it is a "construction" when one lays before the subject of the analysis a piece of his early history that he has forgotten, in some such way as this: "Up to your nth year you regarded yourself as the sole and unlimited possessor of your mother; then came another baby and brought you grave disillusionment. Your mother left you for some time, and even after her reappearance she was never again devoted to you exclusively. Your feelings towards your mother became ambivalent, your father gained a new importance for you,". . . and so on.

In the present paper our attention will be turned exclusively to this preliminary labour performed by constructions. And here, at the very start, the question arises of what guarantee we have while we are working on these constructions that we are not making mistakes and risking the success of the treatment by putting forward some construction that is incorrect. It may seem that no general reply can in any event be given to this question; but even before discussing it we may lend our ear to some comforting information that is afforded by analytic experience. For we learn from it that no damage is done if, for once in a way, we make a mistake and offer the patient a wrong construction as the probable historic truth. A waste of time is, of course, involved, and anyone who does nothing but present the patient with false combinations will neither create a very good impression on him nor carry the treatment very far; but a single mistake of the sort can do no harm. What in fact occurs in such an event is rather that the patient remains as though he were untouched by what has been said and reacts to it with neither a "Yes" nor a "No." This may possibly mean no more than that his reaction is postponed; but if nothing further develops we may conclude that we have made a mistake and we shall admit as much to the patient at some suitable opportunity without sacrificing any of our authority. Such an opportunity will arise when some new material has come to light which allows us to make a better construction and at the same time to correct our error. In this way the false construction drops out, as if it had never been made; and, indeed, we often get an impression as though, to borrow the words of Polonius, our bait of falsehood had taken a carp of truth. The danger of our leading a patient astray by suggestion, by persuading him to accept things which we ourselves believe but which he ought not to, has certainly been enormously exaggerated. An analyst would have had to behave very incorrectly before such a misfortune could overtake him; above all, he would have to blame himself with not allowing his patients to have their say. I can assert without boasting that such an abuse of "suggestion" has never occurred in my practice.

It already follows from what has been said that we are not at all inclined to neglect the indications that can be inferred from the patient's reaction when we have offered him one of our constructions. The point must be gone into in detail. It is true that we do not accept the "No" of a person under analysis at its face value; but neither do we allow his "Yes" to pass. There is no justification for accusing us of invariably twisting his remarks into an assent. In reality things are not so simple and we do not make it so easy for ourselves to come to a conclusion.

A plain "Yes" from a patient is by no means unambiguous. It can indeed signify that he recognizes the correctness of the construction that has been presented to him; but it can also be meaningless, or can even deserve to be described as "hypocritical," since it may be convenient for his resistance to make use of an assent in such circumstances in order to prolong the concealment of a truth that has not been discovered. The "Yes" has no value unless it is followed by indirect confirmations, unless the patient, immediately after his "Yes," produces new memories which complete and extend the construction. Only in such an event do we consider that the "Yes" has dealt completely with the subject under discussion.

A "No" from a person in analysis is no more unambiguous than a "Yes," and is indeed of even less value. In some rare cases it turns out to be the expression of a legitimate dissent. Far more frequently it expresses a resistance which may have been evoked by the subject-matter of the construction that has been put forward but which may just as easily have arisen from some other factor in the complex analytic situation. Thus, a patient's "No" is no evidence of the correctness of a construction, though it is perfectly compatible with it. Since every such construction is an incomplete one, since it covers only a small fragment of the forgotten events, we are free to suppose that the patient is not in fact disputing what has been said to him but is basing his contradiction upon the part that has not yet been discovered. As a rule he will not give his assent until he has learnt the whole truth—which often covers a very great deal of ground. So that the only safe interpretation of his "No" is that it points to incompleteness; there can be no doubt that the construction has not told him everything.

It appears, therefore, that the direct utterances of the patient after he has been offered a construction afford very little evidence upon the question whether we have been right or wrong. It is of all the greater interest that there are indirect forms of confirmation which are in every respect trustworthy. One of these is a form of words that is used (almost as though there were a conspiracy) with very little variation by the most different people: "I've never thought (or, I should never have thought) that (or, of that)." This can be translated without any hesitation into: "Yes, you're right this time—about my *unconscious*." Unfortunately this formula which is so welcome to the analyst, reaches his ears more often after single interpretations than after he has produced an extensive construction. An equally valuable confirmation is implied (expressed this time positively) when the patient answers with an association which contains something similar or analogous to the subject-matter of the construction. Instead of taking an example of this from an analysis (which would be easy to find but lengthy to describe) I prefer to give an account of a small extra-analytical experience which presents a similar situation so strikingly that it produces an almost comic effect. It concerned one of my colleagues who—it was long ago— had chosen me as a consultant in his medical practice. One day, however, he brought his young wife to see me, as she was causing him trouble. She refused on all sorts of pretexts to have sexual relations with him, and what he expected of me was evidently that I should lay before her the consequences of her ill-advised behaviour. I went into the matter and explained to her that her refusal would probably have unfortunate results for her husband's health or would lay him open to temptations that might lead to a breakup of their marriage. At this point he suddenly interrupted me with the remark: "The Englishman you diagnosed as suffering from a cerebral tumour has died too." At first the remark seemed incomprehensible; the "too" in his sentence was a mystery, for we had not been speaking of anyone else who had died. But a short time afterwards I understood. The man was evidently intending to confirm what I had been saying; he was meaning to say: "Yes, you're certainly quite right. Your diagnosis was confirmed in the case of the other patient too." It was an exact parallel to the indirect confirmations that we obtain in analysis from associations. I will not attempt to deny that there were other thoughts as well, put on one side by my colleague, which had a share in determining his remark.

Indirect confirmation from associations that fit in with the content of a construction—that give us a "too" like the one in my story—provide a valuable basis for judging whether the construction is likely to be confirmed in the course of the analysis. It is particularly striking when a confirmation of this kind slips into a direct denial by means of a parapraxis. I once published elsewhere a nice example of this.[2] The name "Jauner" (a familiar one in Vienna) came up repeatedly in one of my patient's dreams without a sufficient explanation appearing in his associations. I finally put forward the interpretation that when he said "Jauner" he probably meant "Gauner" [swindler], whereupon he promptly replied: "That seems to me too 'jewagt' [instead of 'gewagt' (far-fetched)]." Or there was the other instance, in which, when I suggested to a patient that he considered a particular fee too high, he meant to deny the suggestion with the words "Ten dollars mean nothing to me" but instead of dollars put in a coin of lower denomination and said "ten shillings."

If an analysis is dominated by powerful factors that impose a negative therapeutic reaction, such as a sense of guilt, a masochistic need for suffering or a striving against receiving help from the analyst, the patient's behaviour after he has been offered a construction often makes it very easy for us to arrive at the decision that we are in search of. If the construction is wrong, there is no change in the patient; but if

[2] [In Chapter V of *Zur Psychopathologie des Alltagslebens* (1904) (not included in the English translation of 1914).]

it is right or gives an approximation to the truth, he reacts to it with an unmistakable aggravation of his symptoms and of his general condition.

We may sum the matter up by asserting that there is no justification for the reproach that we neglect or underestimate the importance of the attitude taken up by those under analysis towards our constructions. We pay attention to them and often derive valuable information from them. But these reactions on the part of the patient are rarely unambiguous and give no opportunity for a final judgement. Only the further course of the analysis enables us to decide upon the correctness or uselessness of our constructions. We do not pretend that an individual construction is anything more than a conjecture which awaits examination, confirmation or rejection. We claim no authority for it, we require no direct agreement from the patient, nor do we argue with him if at first he denies it. In short, we conduct ourselves upon the model of a familiar figure in one of Nestroy's farces—the man-servant who has a single answer on his lips to every question or objection: "All will become clear in the course of future developments."

3

It is hardly worth while describing how this occurs in the process of the analysis—the way in which our conjecture is transformed into the patient's conviction. All of this is familiar to every analyst from his daily experience and is intelligible without difficulty. Only one point requires investigation and explanation. The path that starts from the analyst's construction ought to end in the patient's recollection; but it does not always lead so far. Quite often we do not succeed in bringing the patient to recollect what has been repressed. Instead of that, if the analysis is carried out correctly, we produce in him an assured conviction of the truth of the construction which achieves the same therapeutic result as a recaptured memory. The problem of what the circumstances are in which this occurs and of how it is possible that what appears to be an incomplete substitute should nevertheless produce a complete result—all of this is material for a later enquiry.

I shall conclude this brief paper with a few remarks which open up a wider perspective. I have been struck by the manner in which, in certain analyses, the communication of an obviously apt construction has evoked in the patients a surprising and at first incomprehensible phenomenon. They have had lively recollections called up in them—which they themselves have described as "unnaturally distinct"—but what they have recollected has not been the event that was the subject of the construction but details relating to that subject. For instance, they have recollected with abnormal sharpness the faces of the people involved in the construction or the rooms in which something of the sort might have happened, or, a step further away, the furniture in such rooms—on the subject of which the construction had naturally no possibility of any knowledge. This has occurred both in dreams immediately after the construction had been put forward and in waking states in the nature of a day-dream. These recollections have themselves led to nothing further and it has seemed plausible to regard them as the product of a compromise. The "upward drive" of the repressed, stirred into activity by the putting forward of the construction, has striven to carry the important memory-traces into consciousness; but a resistance has succeeded—not, it is true, in *stopping* that movement—but in *displacing* it on to adjacent objects of minor significance.

These recollections might have been described as hallucinations if a belief in their actual presence had been added to their clearness. The importance of this analogy seemed greater when I noticed that true hallucinations occasionally occurred in the case of other patients who were certainly not psychotic. My line of thought proceeded as follows. Perhaps it may be a general characteristic of hallucinations to which sufficient attention has not hitherto been paid that in them something that has been experienced in infancy and then forgotten re-emerges—something that the child has seen or heard at a time when he could still hardly speak and that now forces its way into consciousness, probably distorted and displaced owing to the operation of forces that are opposed to this re-emergence. And, in view of the close relation between hallucinations and particular forms of psychosis, our line of thought may be carried still further. It may be that the delusions into which these hallucinations are so constantly incorporated may themselves be less independent of the upward drive of the unconscious and the return of the repressed than we usually assume. In the mechanism of a delusion we stress as a rule only two factors: the turning away from the real world and its forces on the one hand and the influence exercised by wish-fulfilment upon the subject-matter of the delusion on the other. But may it not be that the dynamic process is rather that the turning away from reality is exploited by the upward drive of the repressed in order to force its subject-matter into consciousness, while the resistances stirred up by this process and the impulse to wish-fulfilment share the responsibility for the distortion and displacement of what is recollected? This is after all the familiar mechanism of dreams, which intuition has equated with madness from time immemorial.

This view of delusions is not, I think, entirely new, but it nevertheless emphasizes a point of view which is not usually brought into the foreground. The essence of it is that there is not only *method* in madness, as the poet has already perceived, but also a fragment of historic truth; and it is plausible to suppose that the compulsive belief attaching to delusions derives its strength precisely from infantile sources of this kind. All that I can produce to-day in support of this theory are reminiscences, not fresh impressions. It would probably be worth while to make an attempt to study cases of the disorder in question on the basis of the hypotheses that have been here put forward and also to carry out their treatment upon the same lines. The vain effort would be abandoned of convincing the patient of the error of his delusion and of its contradiction of reality; and, on the contrary, the recognition of its kernel of truth would afford common ground upon which the therapeutic process could develop. That process would consist in liberating the fragment of historic truth from its distortions and its attachments to the actual present day and in leading it back to the point in the past to which it belongs. The transposing of material from a forgotten past on to the present or on to an expectation of the future is indeed a habitual occurrence in neurotics no less than in psychotics. Often enough, when a neurotic is led by an anxiety-state to expect the occurrence of some terrible event, he is in fact merely under the influence of a repressed memory (which is seeking to enter consciousness but cannot become conscious) that something which was at that time terrifying did really happen. I believe that we should gain a great deal of valuable knowledge from work of this kind upon psychotics even if it led to no therapeutic success.

I am aware that it is of small service to handle so important a subject in the cursory fashion that I have here employed. But none the less I have not been able to resist the seduction of an analogy. The delusions of patients appear to me to be the equivalents of the constructions which we build up in the course of an analytic treatment—attempts at explanations and cure, though it is true that these, under the conditions of a psychosis, can do no more than replace the fragment of reality that is being repudiated in the present by another fragment that had already been repudiated in the remote past. It will be the task of each individual investigation to reveal the intimate connections between the material of the present repudiation and that of the original repression. Just as our construction is only effective because it recovers a fragment of lost experience, so the delusion owes its convincing power to the element of historic truth which it inserts in the place of rejected reality. In this way a proposition which I originally asserted only of hysteria would apply also to delusions—namely, that those who are subject to them are suffering from their own recollections. I never intended by this short formula to dispute the complexity of the causation of the illness or to exclude the operation of many other factors.

If we consider mankind as a whole and substitute it for the single human individual, we discover that it too has developed delusions which are inaccessible to logical criticism and which contradict reality. If, in spite of this, they are able to exert an extraordinary power over men, investigation leads us to the same explanation as in the case of the single individual. They owe their power to the element of historic truth which they have brought up from the repression of the forgotten and primaeval past.